Development Education in Policy and Practice

Development Education in Policy and Practice

Edited by
Stephen McCloskey
Director, Centre for Global Education

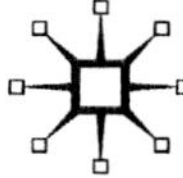

First published 2014 by
PALGRAVE MACMILLAN

Palgrave Macmillan in the UK is an imprint of Macmillan Publishers Limited, registered in England, company number 785998, of Houndmills, Basingstoke, Hampshire RG21 6XS.

Palgrave Macmillan in the US is a division of St Martin's Press LLC, 175 Fifth Avenue, New York, NY 10010.

Palgrave Macmillan is the global academic imprint of the above companies and has companies and representatives throughout the world.

Palgrave® and Macmillan® are registered trademarks in the United States, the United Kingdom, Europe and other countries

ISBN: 978-1-137-32465-8

This book is printed on paper suitable for recycling and made from fully managed and sustained forest sources. Logging, pulping and manufacturing processes are expected to conform to the environmental regulations of the country of origin.

A catalogue record for this book is available from the British Library.

A catalog record for this book is available from the Library of Congress.

Contents

List of Tables and Figures

Tables

Figures

Foreword
Global Learning in Europe – Looking Back and Moving Forward

Helmuth Hartmeyer

The 'European Congress on Global Education to 2015' held in Maastricht, The Netherlands, in 2002 brought together for the first time stakeholders from governments, parliaments, local authorities and civil society across the European continent to take stock of Development and Global Education at the turn of the century. The document which came out of the convention (The Maastricht Declaration) became a significant policy framework, which formed the strategic basis for the work of international organisations and networks active in the field of Development and Global Education. It drew attention to the political necessity of institutional and financial support to this area of work; it pointed to the need for national reviews and strategies; and it especially emphasised the importance of quality education and cooperation within academia in the future conceptual development of Global Education.

Global Education had come from a variety of educational practices, among them Development Education, Human Rights Education, Intercultural and Inter-religious Education and Global Environmental Education. There was an emerging consensus that citizens living in a globalising world needed competencies to meet the challenges posed by it. The German educationalist Annette Scheunpflug phrased it thus: 'Global Education/Global Learning is the attempt to react in a pedagogically adequate way to the challenges of globalisation and to the increasing complexity in our world'.

Ten years later, in 2012, The Global Education Network Europe (GENE) at The Hague International Symposium reflected on the progress made since Maastricht in advancing Global Education. This progress includes strengthened European policy frameworks, growing cooperation at international level (GENE for example has grown to a network of over 40 ministries and agencies in 25 countries with responsibility for Development and Global Education), and a greater geographic spread and growth in national strategies. It also includes a greater emphasis on evaluation, a growing interest in research and moves towards greater conceptual quality. In a series of debates that have accompanied each move toward growth in Global Education policy its pedagogical roots and diverse areas of practice have assumed increasing importance. The term 'Global Learning' has become a synonym for this emerging educational understanding. It is reflected in the extent to which Global Education is moving to the centre of mainstream practice rather than being an 'add-on' at the margins.

In a new book published by GENE in 2013 titled *Global Education in Europe*, a number of pan-European perspectives are outlined: the need to build on existing review and evaluation models in order to further improve the quality of the work; to strengthen mechanisms for international cooperation and coordination through shared policy learning; to include voices from outside Europe (especially from the global South); and to go beyond the North-South paradigm to include a more global perspective.

However despite its many advances, several key challenges remain for Development/Global Education to consolidate the progress made over the last decade. They include the current crises in the fields of international relations, global economics and finances, the ecological system, and human security – all of which pose a challenge to education. These developmental challenges are global and complex, and therefore place great demands on Global Education and the mainstream development sector. Another related developmental challenge concerns the competencies of citizens in Global Education which need to be informed by a Global Learning perspective. Global Learning has a crucial role to play in all national education systems to elicit improvement in the teaching of development but also the strengthening of educational landscapes. And the debates around Global Learning go beyond the formal education sector to encompass non-formal and informal learning which have been addressed within this book.

This text also considers the importance of research in strengthening Global Learning in higher education and advancing innovation and experimentation in Global Education practice. A crucial component of this debate is the need to ensure adequacy of funding to support research that is rigorous, critical, innovative and informed by contemporary policy and practice. Much of the good practice in Development/Global Education practice in research, and formal and informal sectors has been developed and implemented in the field by civil society organisations in the global North and South. Their creativity, flexibility, competence and commitment will remain crucial to the development of the Global Education sector particularly in today's parlous economic climate.

Another ongoing challenge for the sector is the importance of quality monitoring procedures including appropriate quantitative and qualitative evaluation processes. There is greater scrutiny today of how projects are implemented and how they are impacting on stakeholders which places a greater premium on quality evaluation. It will be decisive to achieve greater coherence between the fields of development and education through common bilateral as well as plurilateral policy learning and networking. Finally, Global Learning is inspired by dialogue and participation, and a strong commitment to participative learning and active citizenship. A lot remains to be done until all people in Europe have access to quality Global Learning that will create the critical mass necessary to effect positive policy change in the key development issues that will persist in the post-2015 Millennium Development Goals era. The challenge for Global Education is to maintain the momentum that has carried us from The Maastricht Declaration in 2002 to a robust GENE network that reflects increased governmental support for Global Education across Europe some ten years later.

This important text reflects the growth of Global/Development Education over the past few decades, particularly in Europe where the number of practitioners and civil society organisations delivering quality Global Education has increased considerably. This book reflects on the achievements of Development/Global Education in supporting educational delivery across a range of formal and informal sectors. It takes stock of Development Education policy and poses important questions about the future of the sector in the context of the 2008 international financial crisis. It also very successfully celebrates the diversity, flexibility and depth of quality Development Education while never losing sight of its underlying mission to supporting critical consciousness, understanding, reflection and action toward social justice. It reconnects the sector with its Freirean origins and repeatedly exhorts learners to use education as a means toward self-development and the development of their community. It connects the local to the global and reminds us that Development Education is an essential component of a learner's development in an increasingly globalised world.

References

Forghani-Arani, N, Hartmeyer, H, O'Loughlin, E and Wegimont, L (eds) (2013) *Global Education in Europe: Policy, Practice and Theoretical Challenges*, Münster/New York/Munich/Berlin: Waxmann.

Scheunpflug, A and Hirsch, K (eds) (2000) *Globalisierung als Herausforderung für die Pädagogik*, Frankfurt am Main: IKO.

Helmuth Hartmeyer is Chair of GENE (Global Education Network Europe) and Director of the Civil Society Department at Austrian Development Agency (ADA). He is also Senior Lecturer at Vienna University in the Institute for International Development.

Notes on Authors

Paul Adams is a professionally qualified (JNC) Youth and Community worker and holds an MA in Social Justice and Education. He has been working in the youth work and education sectors for over 26 years. As national youth programme manager at the Development Education Association he was responsible for supporting the development of 'global youth work' and for six years was a trustee of Y-Care International (a youth focused INGO). Paul is currently a senior lecturer and programme leader for the MA Youth and Community work at the Cass School of Education and Communities at the University of East London (UEL).

Douglas Bourn is Director of the Development Education Research Centre at the Institute of Education, University of London and editor of the *International Journal of Development Education and Global Learning*. He is author of numerous articles and books on development education and related areas such as global citizenship, education for sustainable development and global perspectives in education. His main publications in recent years have included an edited volume on *Development Education: Debates and Dialogues* (2008), a chapter on development education in *The Routledge Companion to Education* (2012) and a series of research reports on development education and global learning within schools published by his Research Centre at www.ioe.ac.uk/derc. Prior to being Director of the Research Centre, Dr. Bourn was Director of the Development Education Association (now renamed as Think Global). Contact: d.bourn@ioe.ac.uk

Audrey Bryan holds a PhD in Comparative Education and Sociology from Columbia University, New York. She teaches courses in Sociology across the range of offerings on the Humanities and Education programmes at St. Patrick's College, Drumcondra and is a Visiting Faculty member of the Paris School of International Affairs (PSIA) at SciencesPo University and at University College Dublin. She has published nationally and internationally in the areas of Development Studies and Citizenship Education. She is the co-author (with Meliosa Bracken) of *Learning to Read the World? Teaching and Learning about Global Citizenship and International Development in Post-Primary Schools.*

Vanessa de Oliveira Andreotti is a professor of global education at the University of Oulu in Finland. She has extensive experience working across sectors internationally in areas of education related to international development, global citizenship, indigeneity and social accountability. Her work combines poststructuralist and postcolonial concerns in examining educational discourses and designing viable pedagogical pathways to address problematic patterns of international engagements, flows and representations of inequality and difference in education.

Dorothy Grace Guerrero is coordinator of the Climate and Environmental Justice Programme of Focus on the Global South. She joined Focus' Bangkok office in 2005 and worked as coordinator of the organisation's China Programme until 2012. She has an MA in Development Studies from the International Institute of Social Studies, University of Rotterdam. Originally from the Philippines, Dorothy is an educator, writer, researcher and organiser. She can be contacted via email at d.guerrero@focusweb.org or Dorothy.Guerrero@gmail.com

Fumiyo Kagawa is Research Director of Sustainability Frontiers, a not-for-profit international organisation with offices in Canada and the United Kingdom <http://www.sustainabilityfrontiers.org/>. Her expertise includes holistic and transformative theory and practice in global education, emergency education, disaster risk reduction education, climate change education and sustainability-related education. She was engaged in a number of pedagogical and educational change research and innovation initiatives in different cultural contexts including within Canada, the United Kingdom, Ireland, South Africa, Vanuatu and the Central and Southeast Asian countries. As co-consultant, Fumiyo has been involved in projects with UNESCO, UNICEF, Save the Children and Plan International. Published outcomes of recent consultancy work with David Selby have included: *Disaster Risk Reduction in School Curricula: Case Studies from Thirty Countries* (2012), *Climate Change in the Classroom: UNESCO Course for Secondary Teachers on Climate Change Education for Sustainable Development* (2013) and *Towards a Learning Culture of Safety and Resilience: Technical Guidance for Integrating Disaster Risk Reduction in the School Curriculum* (2013).

Su-ming Khoo is a Lecturer in the School of Political Science and Sociology and Vice-Dean for Internationalisation (College of Arts) at the National University of Ireland, Galway. Her recent research, teaching and publications focus on human rights and development, particularly Right to Food, Right to Health and Right to Education, higher education policy, public goods, capability theory, consumer activism, development education and public scholarship. From 2005–2009, she was joint project leader (with Dr Diarmuid O'Donovan) of the Development Education and Research Network at NUI Galway, a programme funded by Irish Aid to promote the mainstreaming of development education through professional education pathways. She is an active member of the Development Studies Association.

Dip Kapoor is Professor, International Education in the Department of Educational Policy Studies at the University of Alberta and volunteer Research Associate, Center for Research and Development Solidarity (CRDS), a Dalit-Adivasi rural people's organisation in Orissa, India. His research interests include critical studies in international development, globalisation and education. His latest edited collections are: *NGOization: Complicity, Contradictions and Prospects* (2013) and *Globalization, Culture and Education: Critical Perspectives* (2012).

Peadar Kirby is Professor Emeritus of International Politics and Public Policy at the University of Limerick, Ireland. He has written several books on the Irish economy including *Celtic Tiger in Collapse: Explaining the Weaknesses of the Irish Model* (2010) and *Towards a Second Republic: Irish Politics after the Celtic Tiger* (with Mary P. Murphy, 2011). His latest book, co-edited with Barry Cannon, is entitled *Civil Society and the State in Left-led Latin America* (2012). He held the UNESCO South-North Chair in the University of Valencia, Spain, in the autumn of 2012.

Gerard McCann is senior lecturer in European Studies at St. Mary's University College, Belfast. He has lectured at universities in Memphis, Cork, Seattle, Lusaka, Kosice and Paderborn. He was academic manager of the Department for International Development (2005–2008) and the Trócaire (2008–2010) funded 'Global Dimension in Education Project'. He is the coordinator of a partnership programme with the University of Zambia and a member of the University Association for Contemporary European Studies (UACES). He specialises in the European Union's economic and development policies, EU policy in Ireland and development education.

Stephen McCloskey is Director of the Centre for Global Education, a development non-governmental organisation based in Belfast. He is editor of *Policy and Practice: A Development Education Review*, a peer reviewed, open access journal. He combines education and activism on development issues and publishes regularly on development education and international development. His publications include: *From the*

Local to the Global: Key Issues in Development Studies (2009) co-edited with Gerard McCann and *The East Timor Question: The Struggle for Independence from Indonesia* (2000) co-edited with Paul Hainsworth.

Ronaldo Munck is Head of Civic Engagement at Dublin City University and visiting Professor of Latin American Studies at the University of Liverpool. He has written widely on development, migration and development issues and is author of the recent *Contemporary Latin America* (Palgrave, 2012). He is chair of the Development Studies Association of Ireland (www.dsaireland.org) and editor of the journal *Latin American Perspectives* (http://lap.sagepub.com/).

David Selby is Founding Director of Sustainability Frontiers, a not-for-profit international organisation with offices in Canada and the United Kingdom. He works principally in the fields of climate change education, disaster risk reduction education and education for sustainability. He co-edited, with Fumiyo Kagawa, *Education and Climate Change: Living and Learning in Interesting Times* (2010), the first comprehensive academic treatment of climate change education. His upcoming book, again edited with Fumiyo Kagawa, is *Sustainability Frontiers: Transformative Voices from the Borderlands of Sustainability Education* (2013). Published outcomes of recent consultancy work with Fumiyo Kagawa have included: *Disaster Risk Reduction in School Curricula: Case Studies from Thirty Countries* (2012) and *Climate Change in the Classroom: UNESCO Course for Secondary Teachers on Climate Change Education for Sustainable Development* (2013). David is the co-author of the highly influential handbooks on global education, *Earthrights: Education as if the Planet Really Mattered* (1987), *Global Teacher, Global Learner* (1988), *Greenprints for Changing Schools* (1989), and *In the Global Classroom Book One* and *Book Two* (1999, 2000). With Fumiyo Kagawa and two other colleagues he was awarded the Canadian Peace Education Prize in 2003 for the post-9/11 secondary level manual used in schools across Canada, *Cultivating Peace in the 21st Century*. His other published works include: *Weaving Connections: Educating for Peace, Social and Environmental Justice* (2000) and *Green Frontiers: Environmental Educators Dancing Away from Mechanism* (2008). For Sustainability Frontiers go to: http://www.sustainabilityfrontiers.org/

Glenn Strachan has taught at all levels of formal education in the UK. His posts have included Head of Geography in a secondary school, Advisory Teacher for Political and International Understanding, Deputy Head of Community Education and Training in an FE College, Co-Director of the Education for Sustainability MSc at London South Bank

University and Senior Research Fellow at the International Research Institute for Sustainability at the University of Gloucestershire. Glenn is currently a tutor on the Education for Sustainability MSc at LSBU and an independent consultant in the fields of education and sustainability.

Roland Tormey is coordinator of the Teaching Support Centre at the École polytechnique fédérale de Lausanne, Switzerland. He previously worked at the University of Limerick where, among other roles, he was Head of the Department of Education and Professional Studies. He also worked with the Irish National Council for Curriculum and Assessment where he developed curriculum materials on social and political education and on intercultural education. An author of half a dozen books, tens of chapters and more than 20 journal articles, he has worked in development education since the 1990s and has represented Ireland on a number of United Nations bodies on education for sustainable development.

Mwangi Waituru is a policy research and advocacy officer at the Seed Institute, a community organisation in Kenya whose mission is to inform, inspire and mobilise community members to take action against poverty. He is also National Coordinator of the Global Campaign Against Poverty (GCAP) in Kenya and co-chair of the Beyond 2015 steering committee. He is the International co-Chair of Beyond 2015, a network of over 800 actors in over 70 countries, working towards a strong and legitimate MDGs successor framework. At a national level, Mwangi is a member of the facilitation team for the UN-led National Dialogue process in Kenya. He is also pursuing a doctorate thesis at Kenyatta University.

Fionnuala Waldron is Dean of Education in St Patrick's College, Drumcondra, where she specialises in the teaching of history, human rights and citizenship education. She is also Chair of the Centre for Human Rights and Citizenship Education, which engages in research, resource creation and programme development. Most recently, Fionnuala has been heavily engaged in the redesigning of initial teacher education programmes as part of the current process of reform in the system. Her most recent publications include two co-edited collections, *Human Rights Education: Reflections on Theory and Practice* (2010) and *Re-imagining Initial Teacher Education: Perspectives on Transformation* (2012).

Acknowledgements

I could not have completed this book without the support of my employer, the Centre for Global Education, which not only delivers education services on development issues but provides a learning environment for its staff. One of my roles in the Centre is editing a development education journal, *Policy and Practice: A Development Education Review* (www.developmenteducationreview.com), which informed the development and structure of the book and has consistently demonstrated the burgeoning interest in local and global development issues.

The proposal for the book came originally from my good friend and colleague Gerard McCann who not only contributed a chapter but also read proofs. The artwork for the cover came from Sean McCrystal at S-Design. At Palgrave Macmillan, my thanks are owed to Christina Brian and Ambra Finotello who contributed many welcome suggestions for improving the book and very patiently responded to queries. An editor is always dependent on contributors keeping to deadlines and delivering quality manuscripts, and I was very fortunate to have authors who delivered in both respects. I am indebted to all of the contributors to this text and, as editor, take full and ultimate responsibility for the content of this publication.

My parents, brothers and sisters have always offered me support when needed. I have to thank ten nieces and nephews for keeping me on my toes: Aidan, Aoife, Eimear, Maria, Matthew, Meabh, Michael, Naoise, Niamh and Ribh. I hope that development education can contribute to a better future for their generation.

List of Abbreviations

ACODEV	Fédération des ONG de coopération au développement
ADB	Asian Development Bank
AU	Africa Union
BME	black and minority ethnic
BRICS	Brazil, Russia, India, China and South Africa (new emerging economies)
CDA	critical discourse analysis
CEO	Chief Executive Officer
CEPAL	Comisión Económica para América Latina y el Caribe/the United Nations Economic Commission for Latin America and the Caribbean
CIDA	Canadian International Development Agency
CONCORD	The European NGO Confederation for Relief and Development
CPD	Continuing Professional Development
CRDS	Center for Research and Development Solidarity
CSO	civil society organisation
CSPE	Civic, Social and Political Education
CYEC	Commonwealth Youth Exchange Council
DARE	Development Awareness Raising and Education
DDP	development-displaced-peoples
DA	development awareness
DE	development education
DEA	Development Education Association
DEAR	development education and awareness raising
DEC	development education centre
DEEEP	Developing Europeans' Engagement for the Eradication of Global Poverty
DFID	Department for International Development (UK)
DICE	Development and Intercultural Education
DNGO	development no-governmental organisation
EDD	European Development Days
ESD	education for sustainable development
EU	European Union
FSA	Financial Services Authority
FTA	free trade agreement

G/CE	Global/Citizenship Education
GE	Global Education
G20	bloc of 20 developing countries
G8	Group of Eight – a forum for 8 of the world's largest economies
GCAP	Global Campaign Against Poverty
GDP	Gross Domestic Product
GENE	Global Education Network in Europe
GHG	Greenhouse Gas
GNI	Gross National Income
GNP	Gross National Product
GYA	Global Youth Action
GYWPEM	Global Youth Work Partnership East Midlands
HEI	Higher Education Institution
HLP	High Level Panel
ICT	Information and Communication Technology
IDEA	Irish Development Education Association
IEA	International Energy Agency
IFAD	International Fund for Agricultural Development
IFI	international financial institution
IIA	International Investment Agreement
IMF	International Monetary Fund
INGO	International Non-Governmental Organisation
INSET	In-service Training
IPAD	Portuguese Development Agency
IPCC	Inter-governmental Panel on Climate Change
IT	information technology
ITE	initial teacher education
JNC	Joint Negotiating Committee
LAM	Lok Adhikar Manch
LSE	London School of Economics
LSIS	Learning Skills and Improvement Service
MDG	Millennium Development Goal
MFF	Multiannual Financial Framework
MPH	Make Poverty History
MST	Movimento dos Trabalhadores Rurais Sêm Terra/Landless Workers Movement
NAO	National Audit Office
NASA	National Aeronautics and Space Administration
NBA	*Niyamgiri Bachao Andolan*
NCCA	National Council for Curriculum and Assessment

NGDO	non-governmental development organisation
NGO	non-governmental organisation
NOS	National Occupational Standards
NSM	New Social Movement
NYA	National Youth Agency
OBC	Other Backward Castes
ODA	Official Development Assistance
ODA	overseas development assistance
OECD	Organisation for Economic Co-operation and Development
OSDE	Open Spaces for Dialogue and Enquiry
PAR	participatory action research
PRE-SET	Pre-service Training
QAA	Quality Assurance Agency
RE	Religious Education
SD	sustainable development
SDG	Sustainable Development Goal
SEZ	special economic zones
SSHRC	Social Sciences and Humanities Research Council
SSM	Subaltern Social Movement
STEM	Science, Technology, Engineering and Mathematics
TNCs	transnational corporations
TUC	Trades Union Congress
UK	United Kingdom
UKCCMC	UK Climate Change Migration Coalition
UN	United Nations
UNEP	United Nations Environment Programme
UNESCO	United Nations Educational, Scientific and Cultural Organisation
UNFCCC	UN Framework Convention on Climate Change
US	United States
WCED	World Commission on Environment and Development
WEF	World Economic Forum
WSIC	White Savior Industrial Complex
WSSD	World Summit on Sustainable Development
WTO	World Trade Organisation

1
Introduction: Transformative Learning in the Age of Neoliberalism

Stephen McCloskey

Development education has been occupying an increasingly important and enlarged space within formal and informal education over the past 50 years as a radical pedagogy rooted in the global South with the capacity for self- and communal transformation. It represents the enduring capacity of education to raise the learner beyond his or her physical environment, extend their imagination to new horizons, attain new forms of cultural expression, overcome societal inequalities and embrace humanisation above the 'otherness' of materialism. This concept of education as a means of empowerment and justice is largely drawn from the work of the radical educator, philosopher, activist and writer Paulo Freire and was moulded in literacy programmes with poor *campesinos* in his native Brazil in the 1960s. He succeeded in relating the individual's process of conscientisation through problem posing education and critical thinking to that of wider society's struggle for social justice. Thus, just as the learner could become liberated by an awakening of critical consciousness so could society become liberated from the shackles of oppression. This was a truly revolutionary vision of education that resonated throughout Latin America and directly informed the practice of educators in the global North.

This radical approach to learning has operated under various labels but development education is perhaps the most apposite as it explores the intrinsic link between education and development and addresses the fundamental causes of inequality and injustice. It is distinguished from orthodox education policy and practice by suggesting that education is political, ideological and demands an ethical position: 'washing one's hands of the conflict between the powerful and the powerless means to side with the powerful, not to be neutral' (www.freire.org). This radical pedagogy was always likely to struggle for recognition and acceptance within states driven by neoliberal economies that allowed markets to shape the structure and content of education delivery rather than societal wellbeing. Indeed, the ebbs and flows of development education over the past 50 years have to a large extent reflected the political landscape in which it has been delivered. The resilience of the sector has resulted from increasing professionalism and steadfast dedication within its ranks, the flexibility of its delivery in terms of sectors and target groups, and the acceleration of globalisation from the 1980s onward which has renewed the sector's relevance in the context of persistent poverty.

A key question for development education, and this book, is how the sector has mediated the ideas of Freire in its practice within an increasingly marketised education system. To what extent, as Selby and Kagawa put it in Chapter 9, has there been a 'compromising of values and trimming of original vision in the light of the economic growth agenda and global marketplace?' Has the sector struck a 'Faustian bargain' ... 'for knowledge or power or influence, closing one's eyes to the consequences?' A theme that permeates the book is how development education can demystify social, economic and cultural relations within the neoliberal system that perpetuates inequality and contribute to the debate on alternative, transformative paradigms that are sustainable, equitable and just. This chapter will begin with an overview of key aspects of development education practice including core components of Freirean pedagogy. It will then consider how policy changes have impacted on development education drawing upon the author's experiences of the sector in Britain and Ireland before outlining the aims of the book and introducing the contributions that follow.

Development education in practice

In describing an area of practice it is customary to serve up standard definitions to guide the reader as to the main parameters, methods, aims and target groups that will help distil its purpose. This is particularly difficult in the area of development education given its flexibility and breadth as a learning process. For example, does the definition focus on: its active learning and participative methodology; the social and economic justice issues that it seeks to address; the skills, values and attitudes that it imparts; the education sectors in which it operates (adult, community, tertiary, youth, schools etc); the social relations it addresses (class, racial, global South v global North etc); the outcomes it seeks (social and economic justice); or the tools it employs (teaching resources, social media, information technology)? The task is complicated further by the various labels applied to development education by practitioners and policy-makers, including the contributors to this book. Some of the labels used include: global citizenship education; global education; global dimension; sustainable development (suggesting links with environment education); development awareness; and development education and awareness raising (DEAR) often used in a European Union (EU) context. Those who frown upon the use of definitions suggest that they anchor development education in a specific point in history when it is a fluid process operating within a shifting economic, social and political context. They also suggest that definitions sometimes push development education into sectoral silos (formal, non-formal, tertiary) or seek to modify, perhaps dilute, its methodology and goals.

On the positive side, definitions can usefully summarise the distinctive qualities of development education, while suggesting how it complements related sectors like human rights education, global citizenship, environment education and education for sustainable development. So, while being mindful of the limitations of definitions, here are a few that point to its purpose. The first is one of the earliest and most enduring definitions from the United Nations which states that development education seeks:

> to enable people to participate in the development of their community, their nation and the world as a whole. Such participation implies a critical awareness of local, national and international situations based on an understanding of social, economic and political processes (Osler, 1994: 51).

The UN definition then goes on to explore some aspects of development education content as being:

> concerned with issues of human rights, dignity, self-reliance and social justice in both development and developing countries. It is concerned with the causes of underdevelopment and the promotion of what is involved in development, of how different countries go about undertaking development, and of the reasons for and ways of achieving a new international economic and social order (Ibid.: 51).

This definition is not short of ambition – 'a new international economic and social order' – coming from a multilateral institution such as the UN. However, it is rather scant on the methodology and as to how this is to be achieved. The Irish Development Education Association (IDEA) is more forthcoming on the 'how' of development education, defining it as:

> An educational process aimed at increasing awareness and understanding of the rapidly changing, interdependent and unequal world in which we live. It seeks to engage people in analysis, reflection and action for local and global citizenship and participation. It is about supporting people in understanding, and in acting to transform the social, cultural, political and economic structures which affect their lives and others at personal, community, national and international levels (www.ideaonline.ie).

The IDEA approach to development education as a process of awareness raising, analysis and action is shared by the Development Awareness Raising and Education (DARE) Forum, which comprises representatives from national development education platforms across Europe. In 2004, the DARE Forum agreed a definition which states that:

> Development education is an active learning process, founded on values of solidarity, equality, inclusion and co-operation. It enables people to move from basic awareness of international development priorities and sustainable human development, through understanding of the causes and effects of global issues to personal involvement and informed actions (DARE, 2004).

In summary then, the themes that permeate most definitions of development education are as follows:

- the need to encourage action as an outcome of the educational process;
- the local-global axis of education, involving both an understanding of development issues and our interdependence with other societies;
- the development of new skills, values, attitudes, knowledge and understanding that will inform individual action;
- the use of participative, active-learning methodologies;
- education as a visioning exercise toward social transformation;

- social justice, inclusion and equality;
- the need to inform practice with a developing world perspective (McCloskey, 2009: 240–241).

The challenges for the sector in realising the vision outlined in these definitions are, of course, manifold. They include: integrating development issues into national schools curricula; securing sustainable funding lines that do not limit the sector's independence; monitoring and evaluating the impact of practice on learners; strengthening the sector's foothold in tertiary education through quality research; operating within shifting and sometimes hostile policy environments; and delivering practice that is informed by the needs of countries in the global South. What is remarkable is the sector's capacity to sustain its growth and break new ground despite these challenges. For example, a Europe-wide survey of development education in national schools curricula commissioned by DEEEP (Developing Europeans' Engagement for the Eradication of Global Poverty) in 2010 details 'the expanding range and currency of what are perceived as "global" issues influencing school curricula and linked to subject teaching in the classroom' (DEEEP/CONCORD, 2010: 6). While the survey does not address the qualitative aspects of delivery and learning, it points to increased exposure to development issues in schools across Europe.

At a policy level, the European Parliament voted in favour of an official declaration on development education and active global citizenship in July 2012 which reflects the strengthening policy environment for development education in Brussels. As Gerard McCann suggests in Chapter 15: 'The assertiveness of the declaration left all agencies involved in the sector with no doubt as to the seriousness of the institutional base of the EU in its intentions towards DE'. The sector therefore continues to gather a considerable foothold at policy and practice levels but one persistent challenge that the sector has yet to adequately address is that of the action outcome which I turn to next.

Action toward social change

One of the dimensions of the vision for development education shared by both governments and non-governmental organisations is the concept of education toward action and social change. For example, the Irish government, which has a longstanding record of support for the sector, suggests that development education 'aims to deepen understanding, and encourage people towards taking action for a more just and sustainable world. It provides a unique opportunity for people in Ireland to reflect on their roles and responsibilities as global citizens' (Irish Aid, 2013: 35). What has yet to be properly elucidated either by the non-governmental development sector, statutory development bodies or national governments is what kind of process or steps they propose to take to achieve 'a more just and sustainable world'. If pressed, these bodies are likely to suggest transactional forms of development involving consumerist 'actions' such as purchasing fair-trade commodities or, perhaps, engaging in 'clicktivism' whereby learners sign petitions or endorse campaigns from their computer terminals.

In research commissioned by Oxfam called *Finding Frames* (Darnton and Kirk, 2011), it is argued that this more ephemeral engagement with the public, rooted in consumerist values, does not result in the kind of transformative outcomes sought by development education. The report uses the example of the Make Poverty History campaign in 2005 which succeeded as a mass mobilisation but its transformative potential was 'drowned out by the noise of celebrities, white wristbands and pop concerts' (Darnton and Kirk, 2011: 6). Make Poverty History's public mobilisation was therefore not sustained as it was largely informed by a transactional frame 'in which support for tackling poverty is understood simply as making donations to charities' (p. 7). The authors of *Finding Frames* accept that their research does not as yet provide answers, but they do suggest that: 'Ultimately, we see change as a process of reflective practice, pursued through deliberation and debate' (p. 9). The term 'reflective practice' is one of the central elements of Freirean practice suggesting that more development education is likely to result in the kind of sustainable public engagement with global issues that NGOs and governments seek to achieve. Part of this process involves moving toward action outcomes that are less facile, transient and transactional to become more political, ideological and deep-rooted. The next section briefly considers some key aspects of Freirean practice including 'reflective action'.

Freirean pedagogy

Paulo Freire's key work is *Pedagogy of the Oppressed* (1970) in which he argued that the poor were maintained in a state of ignorance and poverty through economic, social and political domination. By 'submerging' the poor in a 'culture of silence', a powerful economic and political elite maintained unjust and exploitative social relations that were based, at least in part, on an education system designed to maintain a rigid conformity. Freire sought to end this 'culture of silence' through reflective action – a union of theory and practice. This process involves: critical awareness of the social relations and power structures within society like the media and government; contemplative dialogue within the dominated class as a means of analysis; and reflective action informed by dialogue and analysis. For Freire, reflection without an action outcome is mere 'verbalism' and action without reflection is pure 'activism' (action for action's sake). He suggests that a 'revolution is achieved with neither verbalism nor activism, but rather with praxis, that is, with *reflection* and *action* directed at the structures to be transformed' (emphasis in original text, 1970: 107).

In reflecting on how the learner can achieve the critical awareness necessary to intervene in the world, Freire rejected authoritarian teacher-pupil models that assume 'the teacher knows everything and the students know nothing' (p. 54). Freire described this model as the 'banking concept of education' in which knowledge is deposited by the teacher as 'narrator' into students as 'receptacles' or 'containers' (pp. 52–53). 'Education thus becomes an act of depositing, in which the students are the depositories and the teacher is the depositor' (p. 53). The antithesis of this approach is, according to Freire, teacher and student becoming co-investigators in problem-posing education in which knowledge is shared in acts of cognition rather than acts of transferral. 'The teacher is no longer merely the one-who-teaches, but one who is himself (sic) taught in dialogue with the students, who in turn while being taught also teach' (p. 61).

The Marxist concept of the dialectic informs Freirean praxis whereby conflicting ideas and propositions enable us to become critically aware through the 'emergence of consciousness' which in turn facilitates a 'critical intervention in reality' (p. 62). Just as Marx believed that Hegel rendered philosophy too abstractly – 'Philosophers have only interpreted the world in various ways; the point is to change it' (1845: 173) – Freire believed that education should become a form of intervention in the world. He suggested that:

> I cannot be a teacher if I do not perceive with ever greater clarity that my practice demands of me a definition of where I stand. A break with what is not right ethically. I must choose between one thing and another thing. I can not be in favour merely of people, humanity, vague phrases far from the concrete nature of educative practice. Mass hunger and unemployment, side by side with

> opulence, are not the result of destiny, as certain reactionary circles would have us believe, claiming that people suffer because they can do nothing about the situation (quoted in Regan et al., 2006: 113).

One of the main challenges for educators in the age of neoliberalism is securing a foothold in mainstream education provision to make the kind of radical interventions advocated by Freire. A consequence of this struggle can be the dilution of Freire's radical vision to obtain a level of purchase within neoliberal policies and institutions. For example, educators may adopt the active learning, participative methodology in Freirean pedagogy but divorce it from its wider social, economic and political transformative goals. As Donaldo Macedo suggests:

> the mechanization of Freire's revolutionary pedagogical proposals not only leads to the depolitization of his radically democratic work but also creates spaces for even those liberals who embrace Freire's proposals to confuse 'the term he employs to summarize his approach to education, pedagogy' [which] is often interpreted as a 'teaching method' rather than a philosophy or a social theory (Donaldo Macedo, 2005: 24).

The next section examines the ebbs and flows of development education policy and practice over the past 50 years by primarily drawing upon developments within the British and Irish sectors.

Development education: From marginalisation to the mainstream

Hugh Starkey traces the beginnings of the development education movement in the UK to 1966 when Oxfam established an education programme on development issues that were impacting on countries in the global South. In this period of decolonisation in many parts of the South, aid agencies were shifting their focus to 'conditions in the newly independent countries of what was starting to be referred to as the "Third World"' (1994: 13). However, development education as a concept began to seriously take shape within the world of education in the early 1970s spurred on by the publication of Freire's *Pedagogy of the Oppressed* (1970) and returned missionaries and development workers from the global South who recognised the importance of public awareness and political change at home as well as development assistance overseas. As Regan et al. suggest: 'Central to this shift of emphasis among some agencies was the recognition that awareness raising and education around development issues was pivotal to the realisation of their overall objective – human development with justice' (2006: 108). The rationale behind this support for development education was the need to enhance public awareness of development issues in the global North to effect action for positive social change in the global South, particularly as many key policy decisions impacting on developing countries are made by multilateral agencies and governments in the North.

The role of development education *vis-a-vis* public engagement has been a contested one however with some statutory agencies regarding it as a means to strengthen support for aid delivery rather than engage in political advocacy. This situation has been partly borne out of most governments supporting development education from overseas aid budget lines rather than from domestic education budgets. For example, the overseas aid arms of the British and Irish governments, the Department for International Development (DFID) and Irish Aid, fund development education rather than the Department of Education in each country. This in turn means that the policy agenda for development education is more closely aligned with overseas development assistance than the domestic national curricula, which could make greater statutory provision for the teaching of development issues in schools. The funding and policy context for development education has therefore regularly presented problems to practitioners in trying to integrate development issues into national curricula and seek statutory support and recognition for their work in schools.

From the early 1970s the development education sector was largely funded by development agencies who, in Britain and Ireland, established with limited statutory support a network of development education centres (DECs) located mostly in urban centres with the role of providing training and resources on development issues in both formal and informal education sectors. DECs mostly operated on the basis of grant support from agencies and represented a hub for development education activity in their regions. For example, the Belfast-based organisation, Centre for Global Education, was established in 1986 by eight development agencies to challenge myths and stereotypes often applied to developing countries in the global North. It was founded in the aftermath of the Band Aid initiative of 1984 which was an international fundraising appeal, concert and single supported by international rock artists to raise funds for victims of famine in Ethiopia. Band

Aid's portrayal of Africans as wretched victims without agency in need of support from the global North and its framing of development as a problem resolved by public donations appeared to accentuate dominant myths about developing countries, particularly in Africa.

DECs were the mainstay of development education for over two decades, funded mostly by development agencies but increasingly by the European Union which introduced financial support for DEAR projects by 'non-state actors and local authorities' (Europeaid, 2013). The lack of state support for development education in the UK to the late 1990s was acknowledged by former Secretary of State for International Development Clare Short when she said:

> For much of the last 20 years, the UK government has attached little importance to development education work in the UK, leaving others, particularly the network of Development Education Centres and others in the voluntary sector, to take the lead in promoting greater awareness and understanding (DFID, 1999).

The election of a New Labour government in 1997 in Britain saw a more demand-side approach to development education with 'increased government commitments and greater policy engagement' (Khoo, 2011: 1). Between 1997 and 2006 the British government published three White Papers on international development, the first of which stated that: 'Every child should be educated about development issues, so that they can understand the key global considerations which will shape their lives' (DFID, 1997). This was closely mirrored by an Irish government *White Paper on International Development* (2006) which stated that: 'Every person in Ireland will have access to educational opportunities to be aware of and understand their rights and responsibilities as global citizens and their potential to effect change for a more just and equal world'. The White Papers were supported by the introduction of development education strategic plans and new funding strands while the formation of a European Union development education network, DEEEP, strengthened co-ordination, advocacy and networking within the EU.

The development education sector was therefore becoming integrated into official development policy having previously languished in the 1970s and 1980s on the margins of education policy and practice. As late as 1996, Ann McCollum suggested in a development education conference in Dublin that the sector 'was largely talking to itself and failing to engage at a strategic level with key stakeholders in formal and non-formal education' (McCollum, 1996). The more interventionist approach of the government regrettably resulted in reduced support for development education from within the non-governmental development sector which prioritised other areas of activity such as campaigns, fundraising and overseas aid. The attitudinal and behavioural change sought by development education demands sustained engagement with learners in terms of both time and resources, and many NGOs reduced or withdrew their support of the sector on the back of a more pro-active position from the government. This left the sector more dependent on government resources and vulnerable to changes in policy.

Some practitioners began to question whether this dependence was resulting in a 'deradicalisation' and 'declawing' of the sector in an era of neoliberal shaped globalisation (Bryan, 2011; McCloskey, 2011; Selby and Kagawa, 2011). Bryan, for example, questioned 'why the development education sector endorses, tacitly or otherwise, the very ideologies and political-economic arrangements that are responsible for producing or exacerbating conditions of poverty and injustice, while simultaneously encouraging people to take action against this poverty and injustice?' (2011: 1). But as the implications of the sector's dependence on government were debated by practitioners the development education sector began to feel the effects of the global recession. Overseas aid from OECD (Organisation for Economic Co-operation and Development) members, through which development education work is resourced in most industrialised countries, was cut by 4 percent in 2012 – the largest drop since 1997 – and 2 percent in 2011 (*Guardian*, 3 April 2013). While the aid budget was ring-fenced by the newly elected British government in May 2010, its development education work was severely curtailed as some projects 'risked the credibility of international aid by not showing a clear link between funding and poverty reduction' (DFID, 2 July 2010). The new mantra from government was 'value for money' and 'demonstrating impact' as the sector 'moved from an expansionary to a contractionary or survivalist mode' (Khoo, 2011: 1).

As the sector navigates its way through an entrenched recession, it is seeking more sustainable and independent forms of financial support and, at the same time, debating how it should respond to the financial crisis. A recent seminar in Dublin argued that the sector could 'foster community resilience and enable citizens to advocate for change' suggesting a connection or reconnection with the first principles of Freirean pedagogy (DEEEP/Dochas/IDEA, 2013).

Development education in policy and practice

For a sector with an international profile within civil society, national governments and multilateral institutions like the EU and UN, development education has a markedly limited literature. This is partly explained by the sector's roots in the global North within the non-governmental sector which mostly focused its resources on teaching materials for schools and informal education audiences rather than resourcing development education practice in the higher education sector. It is also a consequence of the sector's relatively weak profile in the tertiary sector which in turn has limited the output of quality published research on development education (Bourn, 2007). The strong NGO base in development education has also resulted in research focusing mostly on aspects of practice rather than reflecting on the theoretical underpinnings of the sector or locating it within broader education debate. This situation has started to change over the past decade with the establishment of a Development Education Research Centre in 2006 in the Institute of Education at the University of London with the aim of embedding development education 'within mainstream education policy and research' and acting as 'the hub for generating issues and areas for knowledge generation, new thinking and quality output on development education' (DERC, 2013).

There are also new journals on development education theory and practice including: *Critical Literacy: Theories and Practices; the International Journal of Development Education and Global Learning;* and *Policy and Practice: A Development Education Review*. These publications reflect a higher level of development education activity in the tertiary sector focused on strengthening the sector's profile in initial teacher education (ITE), degree courses, post-graduate education and doctorate research. However, the sector continues to lack a single over-arching volume that comprehensively introduces development education both in terms of its practical application in different sectors of education and its policy context. The aim of this book is to provide the reader with a text that captures the breadth of development education in terms of its relationship with related sectors, support of learning at all levels of education, and capacity to challenge the dominant neoliberal paradigm that frames current development and education practice. The book is informed by Freire's concept of theory and practice which suggests that they need to radically interact to result in transformative action. Freire argued that words – or theory – without action result in 'idle chatter' and action without reflection lacks transformative agency. Thus:

> We must not negate practice for the sake of theory. To do so would reduce theory to a pure verbalism or intellectualism. By the same token, to negate theory for the sake of practice, as in the use of dialogue as conversation, is to run the risk of losing oneself in the disconnectedness of practice. It is for this reason that I never advocate either a theoretic elitism or a practice ungrounded in theory, but the unity between theory and practice. In order to achieve this unity, one must have an epistemological curiosity – a curiosity that is often missing in dialogue as conversation (Freire, 2005: 19).

The Centre for Global Education commenced publication of *Policy and Practice: A Development Education* in 2005 to stimulate the need for positive policy change for development education at local and international levels, reinforce the radical theoretical underpinnings of the sector and to never lose sight of the need for action outcomes rooted in good practice. Over its 16 issues the journal has become something of a weather vane in the sector and contributed to the framing of the discourse in this book and its structure. Part I is titled 'Soft versus Critical Development Education' and considers the extent to which development education is equipping learners with the critical thinking skills needed to make meaningful interventions in the social and political relations that underpin poverty and injustice. In Chapter 2, Vanessa de Oliveira Andreotti reviews the idea of critical literacy in the context of development education offering examples from her own academic and pedagogical practice in this area. She then goes on to expand on the idea of soft and critical approaches to global citizenship and development education 'by presenting a new conceptual cartography with four different "root" narratives as a critical literacy stimulus for dialogue and analyses that may open new possibilities of thinking and practice'.

In Chapter 3, Audrey Bryan draws upon recently published research which considers the strengths, possibilities and limits in existing pedagogical and curricular approaches to development education. She presents some of the key findings from her study on how citizenship and international development issues are taught in post-primary schools. In Chapter 4, Douglas Bourn argues for a constructivist approach to development education whereby social and economic interventions are tailored to the particular pedagogical needs being addressed. He suggests that there has perhaps 'been too much emphasis on rhetoric for social change but too little on looking at pedagogical challenges and opportunities and recognising the limits to progress'. Roland Tormey's starting point in Chapter 5 is that the term 'critical thinking' tends to be assumed in development education rather than made explicit, and he goes on to present two contrasting perspectives on 'critique' that are found in the sector. In the second half of his chapter he argues that development education has tended to rely heavily on social and political philosophical perspectives which have resulted in the neglect of psychological perspectives on critical thinking.

Part II of the book looks at how development education is practiced in three different sectors: youth, initial teacher education and higher education. In Chapter 6 Paul Adams identifies some of the perceived differences between global youth work and school-based development education in regard to aims and methodology, in particular youth work's principle of 'voluntarism' and a desire to be 'action focused' involving the active participation of young people in curriculum design and delivery. Fionnuala Waldron in Chapter 7 confronts the challenges in trying to 'construct a practice that negotiates the spaces between the familiar discourses of initial teacher education in mainstream programmes and the disruptive possibilities of development education'. She suggests 'how teacher educators might forge a holistic approach to development education within initial teacher education without sacrificing its critical and counterhegemonic stance'. Chapter 8 explores the relationship between research and development education in the higher education sector. Su-ming Khoo suggests 'a number of ways in which research enhances development education capacity, but argues that "research" and the academic contribution need to be re-imagined to address problematic divides'.

Part III has two chapters exploring the relationship between development education and sustainable development. Chapter 9 by David Selby and Fumiyo Kagawa examines the interrelated fields of development education and education for sustainable development in the context of the dominant neoliberal economic growth agenda. The authors share their 'concern that two fields of status quo critical and transformative purpose are, through omission or commission, and with eyes wide shut, sailing too close to the twin agendas of economic growth and globalisation and are, like Faustus, in proximate danger of selling their souls'. Chapter 10 by Glenn Strachan considers the impact of climate change, particularly on countries in the global South before considering how development education can contribute to public understanding of the need to adapt now and in the future to meet the challenge posed by the warming of the earth's atmosphere given the anthropogenic nature of the problem.

Part IV considers the global context in which development education is presently being delivered and draws upon specific models of paradigm change in the global South that could influence the work of practitioners in the global North. In Chapter 11, Peadar Kirby draws attention to some of the deeper and less exposed features of the global financial crisis and, at the same time, focuses on 'the nature of the paradigm change to which this crisis challenges us'. He considers the adequacy of our forms of education 'for the transition to a new paradigm of society' and goes on to assess the process of paradigm change in Latin America, particularly highlighting the role played by education. In Chapter 12, Ronaldo Munck offers a critical Latin American perspective on the extent to which the continent offers a 'new paradigm for social transformation' and assesses 'how the region's experiences and conceptual paradigms are received and reworked in the global North'. In Chapter 13, Dip Kapoor considers what development educators can learn from subaltern social movements in rural India, particularly their critique of New Social Movements (NSMs) in the global North and development education's engagement with political society. What might development educators learn from Subaltern Social Movements that could inform their engagements in formal (including civil) spaces within modernity? Chapter 14 by Dorothy Guerrero argues that resistance to neoliberal globalisation has pointed to the limits and downside of globalisation. She offers an alternative to neoliberalism championed by her organisation, Focus on the Global South, called deglobalisation, and discusses the role that development education can play in the realisation of its vision.

Part V debates the shifting policy landscape of development education and its impact on practice. In Chapter 15, Gerard McCann charts the emergence of a DEAR strategy within the European Union and surveys the manner in which development education has consolidated its position within EU education and development policy. He goes on to assess how development education as a discipline will need 'to reconfigure itself in order to capitalise on its potential within an institution broadly sympathetic to its principles'. In Chapter 16, Mwangi Waituru draws upon leading positions within civil society organisations in the global South to offer an assessment of the kind of global development policy framework needed beyond 2015, the end point for the Millennium Development Goals. Taking into account current global trends and realities, this chapter suggests the role that development education can play in monitoring and evaluating the contribution of the post-2015 framework against its stated goals. Chapter 17 considers the future of the development education sector in the context of a resilient neoliberal economic paradigm, shifting national and international policy landscapes, reduced aid commitments, and the persistent challenge of penetrating mainstream education delivery. It argues that Freirean pedagogy compels the sector to reconnect with its natural constituency among those most deeply impacted by neoliberalism, both at home and in the global South.

The book's contributors comprise some of the foremost practitioners in the field of development education. They combine extensive publishing experience with a profound knowledge of development education practice in formal and informal education. The book also offers a useful mix of contributors from a range of educational backgrounds, which enriches the learning shared by the book. It offers the prospect of strengthening the practice of those already active in the sector but also represents an invitation to those new to the sector to become engaged in a radical and truly transformative educational process.

References

Bourn, D (2007) 'Building academic support for development education', *Policy and Practice: A Development Education Review*, Vol. 5, Autumn 2007, pp. 31–42, available: http://www.developmenteducationreview.com/issue5-focus3 (accessed 20 June 2013).

Bryan, A (2011) 'Another cog in the anti-politics machine? The "de-clawing" of development education', *Policy and Practice: A Development Education Review*, Vol. 12, Spring 2011, pp. 1–14, available: http://www.developmenteducationreview.com/issue12-editorial (accessed 12 June 2013).

Critical Literacy: Theories and Practices, available: http://www.criticalliteracyjournal.org/ (accessed 20 June 2013).

DARE Forum (2004) 'Definition of development education', available: http://www.deeep.org/dear-definitions.html (accessed 14 June 2013).

Darnton, A and Kirk, M (2011) *Finding Frames: New Ways to Engage the UK Public in Global Poverty*, Oxford: Oxfam, available: http://www.findingframes.org/Finding%20Frames%20Bond%20Report%202011%20Executive%20Summary%20DRAFT.pdf (accessed 14 June 2013).

DEEEP/CONCORD (2010) *Development Education and the School Curriculum in the European Union: A Report on the Status and Impact of Development Education in the Formal Education Sector and School Curriculum in Member States of the European Union*, available: http://www.deeep.org/schoolcurricula.html (accessed 14 June 2013).

DEEEP/Dochas/IDEA (2013) 'Development education: Responding to the global crisis?', a one day seminar held in Dublin on 17 May 2013, available: http://www.deeep.org/component/content/article/362.html (accessed 20 June 2013).

Development Education Research Centre (DERC) (2013), available: http://www.ioe.ac.uk/research/150.html (accessed 20 June 2013).

DFID (1997) *Eliminating World Poverty: A Challenge for the 21st Century, a White Paper on International Development*, London: Department for International Development.

DFID (1999) 'Education and Our Global Future', a speech by Clare Short, Secretary of State for International Development at the Annual Conference of the Secondary Heads Association, Brighton, 24 April, DFID, London.

DFID (2010) 'Cost saving measures to boost help for world's poor', Press Release, DFID, 2 July 2010, available: https://www.gov.uk/government/news/cost-saving-measures-to-boost-help-for-worlds-poor (accessed 12 June 2013).

Europeaid (2013) 'Development and co-operation', available: http://ec.europa.eu/europeaid/how/finance/dci/non_state_actors_en.htm (accessed 12 June 2013).

European Parliament (5 July 2012) 'Declaration on development education and active global citizenship', Strasbourg (C 316 E/149), available: http://eurlex.europa.eu/LexUriServ/LexUriServ.do?uri=OJ:C:2012:316E:0149:0182:EN:PDF (accessed 14 June 2013).

Freire, P (1970) *Pedagogy of the Oppressed*, London: Penguin.

Freire, P (2005) *Pedagogy of the Oppressed* (30th anniversary edition), New York/London: Continuum, available: http://www.users.humboldt.edu/jwpowell/edreformFriere_pedagogy.pdf (accessed 13 June 2013).

Freire Institute: this site reflects the continuing influence of Freirean pedagogy around the world. See: http://www.freire.org

Guardian, 'Aid from rich countries falls for second year in a row says OECD', 3 April 2013, available: http://www.guardian.co.uk/global-development/2013/apr/03/aid-rich-countries-falls-oecd (accessed 12 June 2013).

International Journal of Development Education and Global Learning, available: http://www.ioe.ac.uk/research/4502.html#Journal (accessed 20 June 2013).

Irish Aid (2006) *White Paper on International Development*, Dublin: Government of Ireland.

Irish Aid (2013) *One World, One Future: Ireland's Policy for International Development*, Dublin: Government of Ireland, May 2013.

Irish Development Education Association (IDEA): its definition of development education is available at: http://www.ideaonline.ie/content/about-development-education (accessed 14 June 2013).

Khoo, S (2011) 'The shifting policy landscape of development education', *Policy and Practice: A Development Education Review*, Vol. 13, Autumn 2011, pp. 1–10, available: http://www.developmenteducationreview.com/issue13-editorial (accessed 12 June 2013).

Macedo, D (2005) 'Introduction to the anniversary edition' in P Freire (2005) *Pedagogy of the Oppressed* (30th anniversary edition), New York/London: Continuum, pp. 11–29.

Marx, K (1845) 'Theses on Feuerbach', quoted in D McLellan, *Karl Marx: Selected Writings*, Oxford: Oxford University Press, 2000, p. 173.

McCloskey, S (2009) 'Development education as an agent of social change: The theory and practice' in G McCann and S McCloskey, *From the Local to the Global: Key Issues in Development Studies*, London: Pluto Press.

McCloskey, S (2011) 'Rising to the challenge: Development education, NGOs and the urgent need for social change', *Policy & Practice: A Development*

Education Review, Vol. 12, Spring 2011, pp. 32–46, available: http://www.developmenteducationreview.com/issue12-focus4 (accessed 12 June 2013).

McCollum, A (1996) 'Bridging the Gap between Theory and Practice', a paper presented to the Network of Development Education Centres and Groups (NODE) conference, *Development Education in Ireland Today*, 26 May 1996.

Osler, A (1994) *Development Education: Global Perspectives in the Curriculum*, London: Cassell.

Policy and Practice: A Development Education Review (2005) a peer-reviewed, online development education journal published by the Centre for Global Education, Belfast, available: http://www.developmenteducationreview.com

Regan, C et al. (ed.) (2006) *80:20 Development in an Unequal World (5th edition)*, Bray, Ireland: 80:20.

Selby, D and Kagawa, F (2011) 'Development education and education for sustainable development: Are they striking a Faustian bargain?', *Policy & Practice: A Development Education Review*, Vol. 12, Spring 2011, pp. 15–31, available: http://www.developmenteducationreview.com/issue12-focus3 (accessed 12 June 2013).

Starkey, H (1994) 'Development education and human rights' in A Osler (ed.) *Development Education: Global Perspectives in the Curriculum*, London and New York: Cassell.

Part I

Soft versus Critical Development Education

2
Soft versus Critical Global Citizenship Education

Vanessa de Oliveira Andreotti

Introduction

At the end of a 'Make Poverty History' (MPH) training session for activists, as an inspiration for a group of about 30 young people to write their action plans, a facilitator conducts the following visualisation (reproduced from my notes):

> Imagine a huge ball-room. It is full of people wearing black-tie. They are all celebrities. You also see a red carpet leading to a stage on the other side. On the stage there is Nelson Mandela. He is holding a prize. It is the activist of the year prize. He calls your name. You walk down that corridor. Everyone is looking at you. What are you wearing? How are you feeling? Think about how you got there: the number of people that have signed your petitions, the number of white bands on the wrists of your friends, the number of people you have taken to Edinburgh. You shake Mandela's hands. How does that feel? He gives you the microphone. Everyone is quiet waiting for you to speak. They respect you. They know what you have done. Think about the difference you have made to this campaign! Think about all the people you have helped in Africa...

Listening to this as a Southern person was disturbing, but what was even more worrying was to observe that, when the young people opened their eyes and I asked around if they thought the visualisation was problematic, the answer was overwhelmingly 'no'. They confirmed that their primary motivation for 'training as an activist' was related to self-improvement, the development of leadership skills or simply having fun, enhanced, of course, by the moral supremacy and vanguardist feeling of being responsible for changing or saving the world 'out there'. This actually echoed one of the sayings in a poster of the organisation that was running the course 'do what you love doing, but save the world while you do it'.

Part of the reason why I felt so uncomfortable was that the group seemed to be unaware that the thought patterns and effects of 'what they love doing' could be directly related to the causes of the problems they were trying to tackle in the first place. This points to a central issue in global citizenship education: whether and how to address the economic and cultural roots of the inequalities in power and wealth/labour distribution in a global complex and uncertain system. In order to understand global issues, a complex web of cultural and material local/global processes and contexts needs to be examined and unpacked. My argument is that if we fail to do that in global citizenship education, we may end up promoting a new 'civilising mission' as the slogan for a generation who take up the 'burden' of saving/educating/civilising the world. This generation, encouraged and motivated to 'make a difference', will then project their beliefs and myths as universal and reproduce power relations and violence similar to those in colonial times. How can we design educational processes that move learners away from this tendency?

This chapter aims to introduce the argument for *critical* global citizenship education. It is divided into three parts. In the first part I present Andrew Dobson's arguments in relation to the grounds for global citizenship and his critique of the notions of the 'global citizen' and 'interdependence'. In the second part, I present Gayatri Spivak's analysis of some cultural effects of colonialism in the relationship/assumptions of North and South. In the last part I compare and contrast soft and critical citizenship education in general terms based on Dobson's and Spivak's analyses and briefly explore the notion of critical literacy as a significant dimension of critical global citizenship education. I argue that, for educators, a careful analysis of the context of work is paramount for informed decisions in terms of what focus to choose, but that it is imperative to know the risks and implications of the options available in order to make responsible pedagogical choices.

Common humanity or justice: The material dimension of citizenship education

Andrew Dobson is a British political author and Professor at the Open University, specialising in environmental politics. His most famous work is entitled *Green Political Thought*. He addresses the grounds for global citizenship and the notions of a 'global citizen' and 'interdependence'. He starts his analysis with what he perceives as a common question in the 'Northern' context:

> How can severe poverty of half of humankind continue despite enormous economic and technological progress and despite the enlightened moral norms and values of our heavily dominant Western civilisation? (Pogge, 2002: 3 cited in Dobson, 2006: 170).

He states that, for many in the political sciences today, it is precisely the assumptions of progress and values/morality of the West that are at the root of the problem. He poses another question: 'what should (then) be the basis for our concern for those whom we have never met and are never likely to meet?' He proposes that the answer should be framed around political obligation for doing justice and the source of this obligation should be a recognition of complicity or 'causal responsibility' in transnational harm (Dobson, 2006).

Dobson argues that the globalisation of trade creates ties based on 'chains of cause and effect that prompt obligations of justice, rather than sympathy, pity or beneficence' (p. 178). He offers the ecological footprints as an illustration of how this operates 'as a network of effects that prompts reflection on the nature of the impacts they comprise' (p. 177). He also mentions unjust practices imposed by the North as a global institutional order that reproduce poverty and impoverish people (Ibid.). Two of the central pleas of the MPH campaign point in the same direction. The calls for trade justice and debt relief suggested that the North had something to do with the poverty created elsewhere. However, this acknowledgement of complicity did not translate into the campaigning strategies. The use of images, figures and slogans emphasised the need to be charitable, compassionate and 'active' locally (in order to change institutions), based on a moral obligation to a common humanity, rather than on a political responsibility for the causes of poverty.

Dobson argues that acts grounded on this moral basis are easily withdrawn and end up reproducing unequal (paternalistic) power relations and increasing the vulnerability of the recipient (Dobson, 2006). For him, justice is a better ground for thinking as it is political and prompts fairer and more equal relations. He makes a distinction between being human and being a citizen: being human raises issues of morality; being a citizen raises political issues (Dobson, 2005). Unlike what was suggested in the 'Make Poverty History' campaign, Dobson emphasises individual – rather than institutional – responsibility. He quotes Pogge to stress this point:

> We are familiar, through charity appeals, with the assertion that it lies in our hands to save the lives of many or, by doing nothing, to let these people die. We are less familiar with the assertion examined here of a weightier responsibility: that most of us not merely let people starve but also participate in starving them (Pogge, 2002: 214 cited in Dobson, 2006: 182).

Dobson also challenges the concepts of a 'global citizen', interdependence and world-wide interconnectedness that often accompany unexamined notions of a common humanity in global citizenship education. He asserts that they do not take sufficient account of unequal power relations between the North and the South, as Vandana Shiva states:

> The 'global' in the dominant discourse is the political space in which a particular dominant local seeks global control, and frees itself of local, national and international restraints. The global does not represent the universal human interest; it represents a particular local and parochial interest which has been globalised through the scope of its reach. The seven most powerful countries, the G7, dictate global affairs, but the interests that guide them remain narrow, local and parochial (Shiva, 1998: 231 cited in Dobson, 2005: 261).

Shiva and Dobson argue that only certain countries have globalising powers – others are globalised. In this sense, the North has a global reach while the South only exists locally:

> Globalisation is, on this reading, an asymmetrical process in which not only its fruits are divided up unequally, but also in which the very possibility of 'being global' is unbalanced (Dobson, 2005: 262).

Having the choice to traverse from the local to the global space is the determining factor for whether or not you can be a global citizen. If you are not 'global', 'the walls built of immigration controls, of residence laws and of "clean streets" and "zero tolerance" grow taller' (Bauman, 1998: 2 cited in Dobson, 2005: 263) to try to contain the diffusion of ideas, goods, information and peoples in order to protect specific local spaces from unwanted 'contamination'. Thus, we end up with a one way transfusion (in its legal form at least) rather than a diffusion. As the capacity to act globally is limited, Dobson concludes that those who can and do act globally are in effect often projecting their local (assumptions and desires) as everyone else's global (Dobson, 2005: 264). This is well illustrated in one of MPH's campaign slogans: 'Make History' (Whose history? Who is making this history? In whose name? For whose benefit?).

Dobson's analyses raise important questions for global citizenship education: who is this global citizen? What should be the basis of this project? Whose interests are represented here? Is this an elitist project? Are we empowering the dominant group to remain in power? Are we doing enough to examine the local/global dimensions of our assumptions? However, Dobson's account also seems to oversimplify North-South relations by presenting the South as only a site for Western forceful dominance or some 'grassroots' resistance. In analysing the cultural aspects of the historical construction of this relationship, other critics present a more complex picture, taking into account the 'complicity' of the South itself in maintaining Northern dominance.

Sanctioned ignorance: The cultural dimension

A cultural analysis raises complementary questions for global citizenship education. The emphasis here is on the implications of the projection of Northern/Western values and interests as global and universal which naturalises the myth of Western supremacy in the rest of the world. Gayatri Spivak, a professor at Columbia University in the United States who has had a great impact on the theoretical development in the areas of cultural studies, critical theory and colonial discourse analysis, calls this process 'worlding of the West as world' (Spivak, 1990). Spivak argues that this naturalisation occurs by a disavowal of the history of imperialism and the unequal balance of power between the 'First' and 'Third' Worlds in the global capitalist system. The outcome of this naturalisation is a discourse of modernisation in which colonialism is either ignored or placed securely in the past, so that we think it is over and does not affect – and has not affected – the construction of the present situation.

The result is a sanctioned ignorance (constitutive disavowal) of the role of colonialism in the creation of the wealth of what is called the 'First World' today, as well as the role of the international division of labour and exploitation of the 'Third World' in the maintenance of this wealth. Within this naturalised logic, the beginning of the Third World is post-WWII 'with "First" World growth patterns serving as history's guide and goal' (Kapoor, 2004: 669). This ideology produces the discourse of 'development' and policies of structural adjustment and free trade which prompt Third World countries to buy (culturally, ideologically, socially and structurally) from the 'First' a 'self-contained version of the West', ignoring both its complicity with and production by the 'imperialist project' (Spivak, 1988). Also within this framework, poverty is constructed as a lack of resources, services and markets, and of education (as the right subjectivity to participate in the global market), rather than a lack of control over the production of resources (Biccum, 2005: 1017) or enforced disempowerment. This sanctioned ignorance, which disguises the worlding of the world, places the responsibility for poverty upon the poor themselves and justifies the project of development of the Other as a 'civilising mission'.

For Spivak the epistemic violence of colonialism (where colonialism affects the coloniser's capacity to know their situation of real exploitation) makes this sanctioned ignorance work both ways with complementary results: the First World believes in its supremacy and the Third World forgets about the worlding and '*wants*' to be civilised/catch up with the West. In line with Said, Bhabha and Fanon, Spivak affirms that the colonial power changes the subaltern's perception of self and reality and legitimises its cultural supremacy in the (epistemic) violence of creating an 'inferior' other and naturalising these constructs. Spivak illustrates that in the 'First World' it reinforces Eurocentrism and triumphalism as people are encouraged to think that they live in the centre of the world, that they have a responsibility to 'help the rest' and that 'people from other parts of the world are not fully global' (Spivak, 2003: 622). This is echoed in policies related to the 'global dimension' in England in the notion that different cultures only have 'traditions, beliefs and values' while the West has (universal) knowledge (and even constructs knowledge *about* these cultures). The idea of a 'common history', which only acknowledges the contribution of other cultures to science and mathematics also reinforces this perception, which projects the values, beliefs and traditions of the West as global and universal, while foreclosing the historical processes that led to this universalisation.

This has significant implications for the notion of 'global citizenship'. However, in terms of the reproduction of this ideology, for Spivak the class culture is more important than geographic positioning: she refers to an elite global professional class (consisting of people in or coming from the First and the Third Worlds) marked by access to the internet and a culture of managerialism and of international non-governmental organisations involved in development and human rights. She maintains that this global elite is prone to project and reproduce these ethnocentric and developmentalist mythologies onto the Third World 'subalterns' they are ready to help to 'develop'. She also states that in order to change this tendency educational interventions should emphasise 'unlearning' and 'learning to learn from below' (Spivak, 2004).

The analyses of Dobson and Spivak are not isolated examples in their disciplines. Several academics and practitioners have questioned the ideologies behind development and global citizenship education in recent years and a few pedagogical initiatives have been developed based on these analyses. However, in general terms, the articulations between new thinking and new practices have been weak.

Soft versus critical citizenship education and the notion of critical literacy

From the analyses of Dobson and Spivak it is possible to contrast soft and critical frameworks in terms of basic assumptions and implications for citizenship education. Table 2.1 illustrates this comparison in *very general* terms, in order to prompt discussion.

The notions of power, voice and difference are central for critical citizenship education. Thus, for the creation of an ethical relationship with learners (and with the South), the development of critical literacy becomes necessary. I conceptualise critical literacy as a level of reading the word and the world that involves the development of skills, critical engagement and reflexivity: the analysis and critique of the relationships among perspectives, language, power, social groups and social practices *by the learners*. Criticality, in this context, does not refer to the dominant notion that something is right or wrong, biased or unbiased, true or false. It is an attempt to understand origins of assumptions and implications. In this sense, critical literacy is not about 'unveiling' the 'truth' for the learners, but about providing the space for them to reflect on their context and their own and others' epistemological and ontological assumptions: how we came to think/be/feel/act the way we do and the implications of our systems of belief in local/global terms in relation to power, social relationships and the distribution of labour and resources.

Table 2.1 Soft versus critical citizenship education

	Soft Global Citizenship Education	Critical Global Citizenship Education
Problem	Poverty, helplessness	Inequality, injustice
Nature of the problem	Lack of 'development', education, resources, skills, culture, technology, etc.	Complex structures, systems, assumptions, power relations and attitudes that create and maintain exploitation and enforced disempowerment and tend to eliminate difference.
Justification for positions of privilege (in the North and in the South)	'Development', 'history', education, harder work, better organisation, better use of resources, technology.	Benefit from and control over unjust and violent systems and structures.
Basis for caring	Common humanity/being good/sharing and caring. Responsibility *FOR* the other (or *to teach* the other).	Justice/complicity in harm. Responsibility *TOWARDS* the other (or to *learn with* the other) – accountability.
Grounds for acting	Humanitarian/moral (based on normative principles for thought and action).	Political/ethical (based on normative principles for relationships).
Understanding of interdependence	We are all equally interconnected, we all want the same thing, we can all do the same thing.	Asymmetrical globalisation, unequal power relations, Northern and Southern elites imposing own assumptions as universal.
What needs to change	Structures, institutions and individuals that are a barrier to development.	Structures, (belief) systems, institutions, assumptions, cultures, individuals, relationships.
What for	So that everyone achieves development, harmony, tolerance and equality.	So that injustices are addressed, more equal grounds for dialogue are created, and people can have more autonomy to define their own development.
Role of 'ordinary' individuals	Some individuals are part of the problem, but ordinary people are part of the solution as they can create pressure to change structures.	We are all part of the problem and part of the solution.

Table 2.1 Soft versus critical citizenship education – *continued*

	Soft Global Citizenship Education	Critical Global Citizenship Education
What individuals can do	Support campaigns to change structures, donate time, expertise and resources.	Analyse own position/context and participate in changing structures, assumptions, identities, attitudes and power relations in their contexts.
How does change happen	From the outside to the inside (imposed change).	From the inside to the outside.
Basic principle for change	Universalism (non-negotiable vision of how everyone should live, what everyone should want or should be).	Reflexivity, dialogue, contingency and an ethical relation to difference (radical alterity).
Goal of global citizenship education	Empower individuals to act (or become active citizens) according to what has been defined for them as a good life or ideal world.	Empower individuals to reflect critically on the legacies and processes of their cultures, to imagine different futures and to take responsibility for decisions and actions.
Strategies for global citizenship education	Raising awareness of global issues and promoting campaigns.	Promoting engagement with global issues and perspectives and an ethical relationship to difference, addressing complexity and power relations.
Potential benefits of global citizenship education	Greater awareness of some of the problems, support for campaigns, greater motivation to help/do something, feel good factor.	Independent/critical thinking and more informed, responsible and ethical action.
Potential problems	Feeling of self-importance and self-righteousness and/or cultural supremacy, reinforcement of colonial assumptions and relations, reinforcement of privilege, partial alienation, uncritical action.	Guilt, internal conflict and paralysis, critical disengagement, feeling of helplessness.

Critical literacy is based on the strategic assumption that all knowledge is partial and incomplete, constructed in our contexts, cultures and experiences. Therefore, we lack the knowledge constructed in other contexts, cultures and experiences. So we need to engage with our own and other perspectives to learn and transform our views, identities and relationships – to think otherwise. Action is always a choice of the individual after a careful analysis of the context of intervention, of different views, of power relations (especially the position of who is intervening) and of short- and long-term (positive and negative) implications of goals and strategies.

In contrast with soft global citizenship education, this approach tries to promote change without telling learners what they should think or do, by creating spaces where they are safe to analyse and experiment with other forms of seeing/thinking and being/relating to one another. The focus is on the historical/cultural production of knowledge and power in order to empower learners to make better informed choices – but the choices of action and meaning (what 'we' are or 'should be') are never imposed, as the 'right to signify' is recognised and respected (as an ethical relationship 'commands').

However, as there is no universal recipe or approach that will serve all contexts, it is important to recognise that 'soft' global citizenship education is appropriate to certain contexts – and can already represent a major step. But it cannot stop there or the situation illustrated at the beginning of this paper will become the norm. If educators are not 'critically literate' to engage with assumptions and implications/limitations of their approaches, they run the risk of (indirectly and unintentionally) reproducing the systems of belief and practices that harm those they want to support. The question of how far educators working with global citizenship education are prepared to do that in the present context in the North is open to debate.

Note

* This article was first published as Andreotti, V (2006) 'Soft versus critical global citizenship education', *Policy & Practice: A Development Education Review*, Vol. 3, Autumn, pp. 40–51. A forthcoming article 'Critical Literacy: Theories and Practices in Development Education' reflects on and extends further the ideas presented here. The article will be available from *Policy & Practice: A Development Education Review* in 2014 at www.developmenteducationreview.com

References

Bauman, Z (1998) *Globalization: The Human Consequences*, New York: Columbia University Press.

Bhabha, H (1994) *The Location of Culture*, London: Routledge.

Biccum, A (2005) 'Development and the "new" imperialism: A reinvention of colonial discourse in DFID promotional literature', *Third World Quarterly*, Vol. 26, pp. 1005–1020.

Dobson, A (2005) 'Globalisation, cosmopolitanism and the environment', *International Relations*, Vol. 19, pp. 259–273.

Dobson, A (2006) 'Thick cosmopolitanism', *Political Studies*, Vol. 54, pp. 165–184.

Kapoor, I (2004) 'Hyper-self-reflexive development? Spivak on representing the third world "Other"', *Third World Quarterly*, Vol. 4, pp. 627–647.

Pogge, T (2002) *World Poverty and Human Rights*, Cambridge: Polity Press.

Shiva, V (1998) 'The greening of global reach' in G Thuatail, S Dalby and P Routledge (eds) *The Geopolitics Reader*, New York: Routledge, pp. 231–236.

Spivak, G (1988) 'Can the subaltern speak?' in C Nelson and L Grossberg (eds) *Marxism and the Interpretation of Culture*, Chicago: University of Illinois Press, pp. 271–313.

Spivak, G (1990) *The Post-colonial Critic: Interviews, Strategies, Dialogues*, New York and London: Routledge.

Spivak, G (2003) 'A conversation with Gayatri Chakravorty Spivak: Politics and the imagination', interview by J Sharpe, *Signs: Journal of Women in Culture and Society*, Vol. 28, pp. 609–624.

Spivak, G (2004) 'Righting wrongs', *The South Atlantic Quarterly*, Vol. 103, pp. 523–581.

3

Learning to Read the World? Educating for 'Active (Global) Citizenship' in the Formal Curriculum

Audrey Bryan

Introduction

Some years ago – while flicking through a citizenship education textbook designed for use with Irish 12–15 year olds – I came across a story about Craig Kielburger, the Canadian-born anti-child labour activist, who, at the age of 12, founded the International Non-Governmental Organisation *Free the Children*. The rationale for inclusion of a young, white, middle class Canadian activist's story in a textbook designed for Irish students is presumably to motivate students as young as 12 to feel empowered to take action against injustice, just as Kielburger was inspired to establish an organisation to end child labour, having read a newspaper article about the young Pakistani bonded labourer – Iqbal Masih – who was active in the *Bonded Labour Liberation Front* before his murder at the age of 12. In addition to learning about Kielburger's efforts 'on behalf of working poor, and marginalised young people' Irish schoolchildren learn that he is a 'much in demand speaker', and about the 'international recognition' and the 'many awards' that Craig has received for his work and his 'critically acclaimed' book, *Free the Children* (Cassidy and Kingston, 2004: 51).

In other words, central to the narrative about this model active citizen is the idea that meeting one's global responsibilities also implies personal reward or dividends for the agent, such that 'doing good' is portrayed as an individualistic endeavour through which one can simultaneously advance and empower oneself (Kearns, 1992; Kennelly, 2011; Chouliaraki, 2013). Kielburger who has been influential in shaping the content of citizenship education in his native Canada (see

Kennelly, 2011) – advocates voluntaristic, charitable, consumerist and individualised actions as the primary means of 'taking action' and 'making a difference' in the world. Kielburger's story – particularly the way in which what it means to be an active global citizenship is constructed within it – was the catalyst for a research study exploring representations of international development and social justice in post-primary schools in the Republic of Ireland (see Bryan and Bracken, 2011).[1]

This chapter presents some of the key findings from this larger study of teaching and learning about global citizenship and international development in post-primary schools. It particularly emphasises how young people in formal educational settings are encouraged to 'perform' solidarity with distant Others (Chouliaraki, 2013). While the larger study examined representations of global citizenship across nine academic subjects, the focus here is on how active global citizenship is imagined more narrowly in two academic subjects, Citizenship Education (or Civic, Social and Political Education [CSPE])[2] and Religious Education (RE), because these are the two subjects which most explicitly 'call young people to action' by suggesting, either explicitly or tacitly, specific responses to a range of local and global injustices and by showcasing model 'active citizens' through which young people learn what it means to be a 'good citizen'.

Setting the context: Active global citizenship in an era of neoliberalism

Analytically, the research is informed by the distinction within the global citizenship education literature between 'soft' and more 'critical' versions of global citizenship education, discussed elsewhere in this volume (see de Oliveira Andreotti, Chapter 2 and Tormey, Chapter 5). As Andreotti (2011) explains, there is a tendency for mainstream development education interventions to promote 'soft', 'un-complicated' or 'easy' solutions to global problems that do not require systemic change. As outlined in more detail below, formal educative efforts to educate for democratic citizenship in the Republic of Ireland are undergirded by a 'soft' approach to global citizenship which encourages young people to take action in response to crises and trends as significant as global warming, global poverty, and the unjust policies and practices of international institutions and transnational corporations (Pattie et al., 2003) primarily through individualised, voluntaristic, and typically 'light-touch' and 'feel-good' actions that tend to involve no more than minimal effort on the part of the actor (Chouliaraki, 2013).

The research takes further inspiration from the citizenship education literature concerned with the 'politics of educating for democracy' (Westheimer and Kahne, 2004: 237). Westheimer and Kahne (2004) suggest that educational initiatives can be underpinned by competing visions of citizenship reflecting differing political and ideological interests which shape how these programmes and curricula are designed and enacted (Westheimer and Kahne, 2004: 237). They identify three different visions of the 'good citizen' evident in programmes designed to advance the democratic purposes of education, each reflecting a relatively distinct set of theoretical and curricular goals: the *personally responsible citizen*, the *participatory citizen* and the *justice-oriented citizen.* Programmes premised upon the *personally responsible citizen* are undergirded by an individualistic vision of good citizenship, as opposed to an emphasis on collective social action and a more radical pursuit of social justice. The *personally responsible citizen* acts responsibly in his/her community by, for example, making charitable donations, picking up litter, giving blood, recycling and obeying laws. Curricula designed to develop the *participatory citizen* focus on how government and other institutions work (e.g., community-based organisations, churches etc.) and on the importance of planning and participating in organised efforts to care for those in need. The *social justice* orientation towards citizenship, according to Westheimer and Kahne, is the model least commonly pursued. It calls explicit attention to matters of injustice and to the importance of pursuing social justice goals. Justice-oriented citizens critically assess social, political, and economic structures, consider collective strategies for change that challenge injustice and are concerned with addressing the root causes of social and global problems (Westheimer and Kahne, 2004: 240).

While many advocates of development education are optimistic about the potential of state-sanctioned efforts to educate for global citizenship to redress social and global inequities, a more cynical perspective is that the advancement of 'soft' or 'personally responsible' versions of the citizenship in the formal curriculum is designed to support and sustain – not to challenge – existing political-economic structures (Banks, 2008). Kearns (1992) explains how the concept of 'active citizenship' was first deployed as part of a wider strategy within the Thatcher administration to replace central and local government's direct provision of services, by encouraging individual citizens to share their talents and skills in the management of public and welfare services (Biesta, 2011). From this more cynical vantage point, far from empowering citizens to engage in socially transformative practices, active citizenship functions as a conscience-salving discourse for acquisitive individuals who are encouraged to pursue 'guilt-free' profit through performing charitable and voluntaristic acts on behalf of those 'less fortunate than themselves'. The chapter seeks to illuminate some of the broader ethical consequences and ideological effects of dominant discourses about what it means to be a 'responsible' active global citizen and the 'light touch' activism which often accompanies it, in an effort to promote more complex understandings of what it means to 'take action' in response to global problems and to engage with the suffering of 'distant Others'.

Methodology

The research sought to provide a representative critique of textbooks designed for use with post-primary students in the Republic of Ireland which explicitly address development themes and issues. Critical discourse analysis (CDA) techniques of selected texts were employed to interrogate key ideas and realms of development knowledge. Discourse refers to 'a group of statements which provide a language for talking about – a way of representing the knowledge about – a particular topic at a particular historical moment' (Hall, 1992: 291; cited in Hall, 1997). Discourse – as a system of representation – governs the way that a topic can be meaningfully discussed and understood and shapes and informs how ideas are put into practice. As Hall (1997: 44) explains, 'just as discourse "rules in" certain ways of talking about a topic, defining an acceptable and intelligible way to talk, write, or conduct oneself, so also, by definition, it "rules out", limits and restricts other ways of talking, of conducting ourselves in relation to the topic or constructing knowledge about it'. CDA involves a multilayered process of reading, writing, interpreting, rereading, rewriting and reinterpreting each of the texts to derive recurring patterns and themes. As such, it involves examining various degrees of presence or absence in the texts, such as foreground information (those ideas that are present and emphasised), background information (those ideas that are explicitly mentioned but de-emphasised), presupposed information (that information which is present at the level of implied or suggested meaning) and absent information (Fairclough, 2003). Focusing on what is not said, as much as on what is openly stated in textbooks which explicitly address a range of development themes, the intention was to examine which understandings of development are privileged and which kinds of development practice and activism endorsed, to the exclusion of alternative forms of development knowledge, practice and activism. Using the framework and techniques of CDA, the research sought to examine how particular development 'problems' get constructed as well as how certain forms of development intervention and activism are enabled while others are precluded by the discourse (Doty, 1993).

Key findings

The personally responsible citizen

As outlined above, social justice or critically-oriented approaches to citizenship education emphasise the root causes of social and global problems, offer a critical assessment of social, political, and economic structures, and focuses on collective strategies for change (Westheimer and Kahne, 2004; Andreotti, 2006). The analysis revealed minimal evidence of a social justice orientation towards citizenship education within CSPE or RE texts, but ample evidence of personally responsible and 'soft' versions of global citizenship. 'Soft' global citizenship encourages young people to 'perform' solidarity through individualised, voluntaristic, and typically 'low-cost' actions that tend to involve no more than minimal effort on the part of the actor who engages in them as the primary responses to crises and trends as substantive as global warming, global poverty, and the unjust policies and practices of international institutions and transnational corporations (Pattie et al., 2003).

Global good guys

In those instances where a more collective orientation to social justice activism is presented, it frequently takes the form of narratives about the generosity of the Irish people in the face of humanitarian disasters or through accounts of popular spectacles, such as Live 8, which was spearheaded by Irish-born celebrity humanitarian, Bob Geldof. The national 'we' is thus defined as compassionate, concerned and caring, and development becomes 'knowable' and 'intelligible' to young people primarily in terms of on 'our' collective 'capacity to care' (Razack, 2007).

> ... there are few nations that have contributed more than Ireland, even in times which were difficult for this country, to the cause of peace and human rights around the world (cited in Murphy and Ryan, 2006: 7.34).

> [The Tsunami Disaster] brought out the best in people and Irish people can be proud of the efforts they made in helping people such as the Sri Lankan fishermen to get back to work. The money raised made a huge difference and will go a long way towards developing the economy of Sri Lanka (Murphy and Ryan, 2006: 6.23).

Through such discursive practices, other people's suffering becomes a source of pleasure as 'we' are reminded and encouraged to contemplate our own humanity (Razack, 2007). Geldof and fellow Irish-born musician, celebrity and humanitarian Bono, feature prominently in CSPE and RE texts, often to present Irish people as compassionate global citizens driven by a humanitarian impulse to 'help' less fortunate others. For example, in *We are the World*, we learn that 'Goal Director John O'Shea believes Bono will achieve more in ten days than the international community has in ten years' (Cassidy and Kingston, 2004: 233). In some instances, these celebrity humanitarians act as *the* symbol of development, with *Stand Up, Speak Up!* (Holmes and O'Dwyer, 2010: 5) choosing to introduce the very concept of development itself at the outset of the textbook with a photograph of Bob Geldof and a caption about how he has 'worked tirelessly to bring food and medical aid to people in Africa affected by drought and famine' and speaks of his desire 'to help the developing world'.

While ostensibly *about* the lives of those whom they seek to uplift and save, discourses of high-profile Western benevolence, concern and compassion, actively position 'our guys' as *the* stars of the development show, while the objects of national (and Northern) benevolence merely function as the backdrop to a story which is *really* about 'us'. In other words, the experiences and suffering of the distant Other are rendered subordinate to stories about 'us' and our national or Northern capacity to care (Chouliaraki, 2013). While affording 'us' a way of knowing and defining ourselves as 'global good guys' (Heron, 2007: 87), these narratives of global humanitarianism do little, if anything, to counter stereotypical assumptions about the dependency of those in the global South on 'us' in the global North. Moreover, by presenting citizens of the global South as objects of pity and benevolence, these narratives have the effect of obscuring global power relations and preventing individuals seeing how they themselves are implicated in sustaining these relations through their participation in, and the benefits they derive from, harmful global economic institutions and practices (Jefferess, 2008; Esquith, 2010; Jefferess, 2012).

The power of one?

A number of RE and CSPE textbooks implicitly or explicitly make the point that individualised responses, no matter how small, can have a positive effect on other individuals in need. This is perhaps best encapsulated by *The Starfish Story*, which is recounted both in the CSPE text *Make a Difference!* (Harrison and Wilson, 2007) and in the RE text *Community of Faith* (Quigley, 2002). The story tells the tale of a young man who comes across 'a frail old woman' 'on a deserted beach' who is saving stranded starfish from dying by returning them one at a time back into the water (p. 277). The story ends with the old woman explaining how she, acting in isolation, made a difference to the life of a single starfish, the implication being that our individual actions, no matter how small or seemingly insignificant, matter:

> But there must be thousands of starfish on this beach alone explained the young lad. 'How can you make a difference?' The old woman looked at the small starfish in her hand and as she threw it to the safety of the sea, she said 'I made a difference to that one, didn't I?' (Harrison and Wilson, 2007: 277).

This individualised approach to 'making a difference' arguably serves as the broader ideological motif for the text as a whole, as the front cover contains an image of a lone starfish washed up on a sandy beach. The version of this story recounted in a junior cycle Religious Education textbook *Community of Faith*, is almost identical, but is entitled 'Small Ripples' (Quigley, 2002: 140).

Evoked to provide students with concrete and constructive ideas about how they can 'make a difference' in the world, rather than feeling powerless about the world's problems, the focus of active global citizenship within CSPE and RE textbooks generally remains squarely upon the self as a benevolent actor, and on *the individual's* experiences of 'taking action', rather than the systems and structures of oppression which are ultimately responsible for the problems the active citizen, or those who are subjected to these systemic problems, seeks to address.

While it is understandable that textbooks and teachers might seek to protect young students from feeling paralysed or overwhelmed by the scale of global poverty and social injustice, offering bite-sized activism as both a coping mechanism and a solution to the world's ills downplays the importance of a cohesive and synchronised commitment to social justice and equality. This one-to-one social justice approach is invariably underpinned by assumptions that 'you can't save everybody' and encourages students to see themselves as isolated individuals in an indifferent world who must perform 'ethical and psychological triage, deciding which victims of human suffering [to] help, which [to] ignore' (Ostrom, 1992) – surely an approach that is equally liable to paralyse and overwhelm. Moreover, the promotion of individualised activism forecloses any consideration of the need to alter or dismantle existing institutions and structures that lie beneath the injustices they seek to inform students about; in other words, they narrow possibilities for understanding citizenship and activism within alternative paradigms and frameworks while offering assurance, absolution and resolution to complex realities which would require radically different responses if they were actually to be meaningfully addressed.

For example, while entire chapters of CSPE textbooks are devoted to stewardship and to documenting the detrimental effects of climate change, such as, water scarcity, the spread of tropical diseases, rising sea levels, the extinction of endangered species, etc., young people are encouraged to focus their political energies on individual strategies for environmental protection, such as recycling, switching off lights to save energy, taking public transportation or walking, or not throwing litter. Equally problematic is the way in which narratives which are critical of multinational or transnational corporations (TNCs) typically gravitate towards (and are 'resolved' by) encouraging students to buy fair or ethical trade products. While ethical consumerism has obvious advantages over other purchasing practices, the presentation of fair trade as *the* 'solution' to the exploitative and unjust practices of multinational corporations forecloses critical analysis of global economic and social relationships and occludes alternative practices and actions that seek to reform or indeed transform these structures of inequality and injustice.

The three Fs – Fundraising, fasting and having fun

The curriculum analysis revealed the pervasiveness of a 'three Fs' approach to citizenship education – comprising *fundraising, fasting and having fun in aid of specific causes* – in both the formal and informal curriculum (Bryan, 2012). The promotion of fundraising as a legitimate response to problems as intractable as global poverty and HIV/AIDS was a very common feature of state-sanctioned curriculum materials.

One particularly salient illustration of the three Fs approach to global citizenship appears in a senior cycle RE text *The Inner Place* (Gunning, 2006: 299) which recounts a young Irish school girl's feelings of moral obligation in response to a famine appeal taking place in 'some Third

World country' that 'really affected' her. Finding no relief from saying a prayer 'for those people', Mary recounts how she felt 'God wanted [her] to do something'. Deciding to shave her hair off to raise money, she talks about the response she received – the 'thrilled' charity who sent her sponsorship forms, the people who 'thought she was mad', the newspaper reporters who came to the hotel where she had her hair shaved and 'everyone at school' who wanted to rub her head afterwards 'like a pet'. Watching the television a few nights later, the same ad appeared and Mary reports: 'I felt good watching it'. The narrative is accompanied by 'before and after' photographs of Mary and a reproduction of the newspaper coverage her fundraising event received. Notable only by their absence are the experiences and voices of 'those poor people' whom Mary was endeavouring to help. Strikingly, it is not *their* story that is being told here, nor is it about Mary's desire to help, although that information is assumed. Instead, Mary's experience of the attention she receives takes centre stage – the newspaper coverage, the attention at school and the gratitude of the charity.

In critiquing the three Fs approach to active citizenship, my point is not to deny the importance of fostering a sense of agency and efficacy in students, or to negate the capacity for fundraising initiatives to meet immediate needs. However, the perceived need to produce tangible outcomes and to provide meaningful reassurances to students that they can indeed 'make a difference' may, paradoxically, mean that a more symptomatic approach will win out over other less tangible educative efforts to promote radical, long-term societal change. As Matt Baillie Smith argues, fundraising as a form of active global citizenship, actually frustrates the learning goals of citizenship education by reinforcing – rather than challenging – learners' stereotypes about the recipients' dependency on a benevolent donor and perpetuates a particular understanding of international development as being primarily about charity from the global North to the global South (Smith, 2004). Moreover, while charitable giving may be a means of 'helping', it does little to transform the situation that produces the conditions of poverty and human suffering in the first place (cited in Jefferess, 2008). In other words, the range of imagined possibilities for responding to global injustices as complex and intractable as the HIV/AIDS pandemic, resource extraction and climate change are restricted to 'feel good' and 'do-good' responses such as fundraising, fair-trade consumption and having fun in aid of specific development causes – practices which support and sustain, but do not challenge existing political-economic structures.

Conclusion

The foregoing analysis has highlighted the predominance of 'personally responsible' and 'soft' versions of global citizenship in the CSPE and RE curricula in post-primary schools in the Republic of Ireland. This particular discursive construction of the active global citizen is informed by a vision of solidarity that privileges personal empowerment, self-enhancement and the opportunity to salve one's social conscience through 'light touch' actions which typically require no more than minimal effort or sacrifice on the part of the agent but which promise instant gratification in return. As Westheimer and Kahne (2004) argue, the privileging of the personally responsible citizen in citizenship education curricula is not arbitrary, but rather reflects a specific set of political choices with ideological and material effects (Westheimer and Kahne, 2004).

I contend that the implementation of 'personally responsible' citizenship education curricula reflects the encroachment of neoliberalisation in all spheres of life – including education – and is part of a wider effort of helping individuals to resolve the disabling tensions that inevitably occur when trying to develop or retain a moral sense of self against the backdrop of a structurally unjust global capitalist system. Between 1981 and 2008, there has only been a modest drop in the number of people living below $2 per day – the average poverty line for developing countries – from 2.59 to 2.47 billion. In 2008, there were 1.18 billion people living on $1.25 to $2 per day, and it is estimated that about one billion people will still live in extreme poverty in 2015 (World Bank, 2013). Illuminating the injustices of this market-led system, from which some benefit, while others are forced to live in abject poverty, Steven Klees (2009: 305) remarks: 'The fact that the market pays someone $1.50 for a day of backbreaking labour while others get millions of dollars for their white collar labour is akin to a form of slavery for which no one takes responsibility and which is disguised by the rhetoric of freedom'. Citizenship education programmes undergirded by a personally responsible citizen framework do little, if anything to engage learners with uncomfortable truths about their participation in a political economic system that is akin to slavery, which benefits a minority of the world's inhabitants, at the expense of a majority, who are located mainly (although not exclusively) in the global South.

These school-based efforts to promote 'personally responsible' citizens are reflective of a wider socio-political shift in the expression of solidarity which is evident in celebrity-dominated media and among international development agencies themselves (Jefferess, 2012; Chouliaraki, 2013). Chouliaraki (2013) argues that traditional humanitarian campaigns – which were centred on the plight of the Other – have been replaced by 'post-humanitarian' politics, at the heart of which is a self-oriented morality which is deeply embedded in a public culture of consumption and an ethos of mutual benefit with minimal effort' (p. 178). As Chouliaraki explains, the ethic of solidarity characteristic of the present historical moment represents 'a shift from the idea that doing good to others without expecting a response is both desirable and possible to the idea that doing good to others is desirable when there is something to gain from the act' (p. 179). In other words, citizenship education has become premised upon a form of solidarity that is expressed through one's lifestyle or consumerist habits, and justified in terms of its capacity to enhance our social conscience or to advance us personally, as opposed to a 'solidarity of conviction' (p. 185) wherein taking action does not need to be justified or authenticated in terms of something external to ourselves (Chouliaraki, 2013). Within this context, self-interest or personal empowerment, as opposed to a belief in a better world, thus becomes recognised as *the* legitimate basis for social action, while distant Others remain 'shadow figures in someone else's story' (Chouliaraki, 2013: 187).

As Kennelly (2011) observes, the conflation of good or responsible citizenship with a narrowly conceived version of activism modelled by individuals like Craig Kiehlburger and legitimised through citizenship education curricula has a range of problematic effects, including the regulation and curtailment of activism and the undermining of an alternative set of activist practices, particularly those which pose a challenge to state legitimacy. Somewhat ironically, therefore, academic subjects such as CSPE and RE, while ostensibly concerned with enabling young people to come to a deeper understanding of social and global injustice, and to 'make a difference' by 'taking action' against these injustices in effect work to constrain young people's imagination about what is possible, and how they might engage in the struggle for a more egalitarian world. Speaking specifically about environmental problems, Michael Maniates (2001: 33) captures the implications of the individualisation of politics succinctly:

> When responsibility for environmental problems is individualised, there is little room to ponder institutions, the nature and exercise of political power and influence in society – in other words, to 'think

institutionally'. Instead, the serious work of confronting the threatening socio-environmental processes...falls to individuals, acting alone, usually as consumers.

In other words, when political issues become individualised, our capacity to think about the nature and exercise of political power, to challenge the actors and agencies who wield so much influence over people's lives, or to imagine alternatives to existing political-economic arrangements and institutions which promote unjust global relations and practices, is curtailed (Dowie, 1996; Maniates, 2001). Rather than seeking to produce 'obedient' or 'compliant' activists who engage in individualised 'feel good' responses to complex global problems which would demand ongoing, complex and collective action if they were to be meaningfully addressed (Bryan and Bracken, 2011; Kennelly and Llewellyn, 2011), citizenship education should strive to equip young people with a range of conceptual and analytical tools through which they can imagine and pursue a variety of productive responses to global injustices, from individual action to community organisation to whole-scale institutional change (Dowie, 1996).

Pedagogically, this implies the need to promote reflexive engagement with the political dimensions of human suffering and to engage learners with fundamental questions about power, injustice, oppression and the meanings of solidarity (Chouliaraki, 2013). Chouliaraki (2013: 205), for example, advocates an 'agonistic engagement' with questions of global justice and Otherness (p. 205), one that involves raising questions about justification (why is this important?), antagonism (what is right and wrong?), complexity (is donating enough?), and Otherness and historicity (what makes people who they are?). Similarly, the critical development education framework proposed by Andreotti (2006) demands that we confront our own historical and contemporary responsibility and implicatedness in the suffering of Others, and engage critically and reflexively with a range of questions such as: What informs my assumptions about development? How do my life experiences filter my understandings of it? How/why might someone else's perspectives differ from mine? Undergirding such alternative, social justice oriented approaches to global citizenship is a question of how to promote more radical imaginings of solidarity, such as those which reclaim justice as the new imperative of action on human suffering (Chouliaraki, 2013). While these alternatives to soft and personally responsible models of citizenship are by no means a panacea to the increasing disparities and injustices throughout the globe, being able to learn about – and imagine the development apparatus and development education differently – may be a small, yet essential part of what Britzman (1998: 119) refers to as the 'interminable work of social justice and ethical understanding'.

Notes

1 The terms 'development education' and 'global citizenship education' are used interchangeably throughout this chapter.
2 CSPE was introduced as a mandatory examination subject at Junior Certificate (lower secondary) level in 1997 to respond to a growing concern about 'young people'[s]...disaffection with and alienation from formal politics and institutions' (National Council for Curriculum and Assessment and Irish Aid, 2006: 12). CSPE seeks to promote 'active exploration and study of citizenship at all levels (personal, local, national, global) in the context of contemporary social and political issues' (DES, 2006: 7).

References

Andreotti, V (2006) 'Soft versus critical global citizenship education', *Policy and Practice: A Development Education Review*, Vol. 3, pp. 83–98.

Andreotti, V (2011) *Actionable Postcolonial Theory in Education*, New York: Palgrave Macmillan.

Banks, J (2008) 'Diversity, group identity, and citizenship education in a global age', *Educational Researcher*, 37(3), pp. 129–139.

Biesta, G (2011) *Learning Democracy in School and Society: Education, Lifelong Learning and the Politics of Citizenship*, Rotterdam: Sense.

Britzman, D (1998) *Lost Subjects, Contested Objects: Toward a Psychoanalytic Inquiry of Learning*, Albany, NY: State University of New York Press.

Bryan, A (2012) 'Band-aid pedagogy, celebrity humanitarianism, and cosmopolitan provincialism: A critical analysis of global citizenship education' in C Wankel and S Malleck (eds) *Ethical Models and Applications of Globalization: Cultural, Socio-Political and Economic Perspectives*, Hershey, PA: IGI Global.

Bryan, A and Bracken, M (2011) *Learning to Read The World? Teaching and Learning about Global Citizenship and International Development in Post-Primary Schools*, Dublin: Irish Aid.

Cassidy, C and Kingston, P (2004) *We are the World: Civic, Social and Political Education*, Dublin: Mentor.

Chouliaraki, L (2013) *The Ironic Spectator: Solidarity in the Age of Post-Humanitarianism*, Cambridge: Polity Press.

Department of Education and Skills (2006) *Junior Certificate Civic Social and Political Education Syllabus*, Dublin: DES.

Doty, R (1993) 'Foreign policy as social construction: A post-positivist analysis of US counterinsurgency policy in the Philippines', *International Studies Quarterly*, 37(2), pp. 297–320.

Dowie, M (1996) *Losing Ground: American Environmentalism at the Close of the Twentieth Century*, Cambridge, Ma: MIT Press.

Esquith, S (2010) *The Political Responsibilities of Everyday Bystanders*, PA: Penn State Press.

Fairclough, N (2003) *Analysing Discourse: Textual Analysis for Social Research*, London: Routledge.

Gunning, T (2006) *The Inner Place: Senior Cycle Religious Education*, Dublin: Veritas.

Hall, S (1997) 'The work of representation' in S Hall (ed.) *Representation: Cultural Representations and Signifying Practices*, London: Open University Press.

Harrison, C and Wilson, M (2007) *Make a Difference! 2nd Edition. Junior Certificate Civic, Social and Political Education*, Dublin: Folens.

Heron, B (2007) *Desire for Development: Whiteness, Gender and the Helping Imperative*, Ontario: Wilfrid Laurier University Press.

Holmes, H and O'Dwyer, G (2010) *Stand up, Speak Up! CSPE for Junior Certificate*, Dublin: Mentor.

Jefferess, D (2008) 'Global citizenship and the cultural politics of benevolence', *Critical Literacy: Theories and Practices*, 2(1), pp. 27–36.

Jefferess, D (2012) 'The "Me to We" social enterprise: Global education as lifestyle brand', *Critical Literacy: Theories and Practices*, 6(1), pp. 18–30.

Kearns, A (1992) 'Active citizenship and urban governance', *Transactions of the Institute of British Geographers*, 17(1), pp. 20–34.

Kennelly, J (2011) *Citizen Youth: Culture, Activism and Agency in a Neoliberal Era*, New York: Palgrave Macmillan.

Kennelly, J and Llewellyn, K R (2011) 'Educating for active compliance: Discursive constructions in citizenship education', *Citizenship Studies*, 15(6–7), pp. 897–914.

Klees, S (2008) 'Reflections on theory, method, and practice in comparative and international education', *Comparative Education Review*, 52(3), pp. 301–328.

Maniates, M (2001) 'Individualization: Plant a tree, buy a bike, save the world?' *Global Environmental Politics*, 3(1), pp. 31–52.

Murphy, D and Ryan, J (2006) *One World: Studies in Civic Social Political Education for Junior Certificate*, Dublin: EDCO.

National Council for Curriculum and Assessment and Irish Aid (2006) *A Study of Opportunities for Development Education at Senior Cycle*, Dublin: NCCA.

Ostrom, C (1992) 'Our struggle with our hearts: "Haves" chafe in sorting out responsibility to help world's pitiful people', *The Seattle Times*, available: http://community.seattletimes.nwsource.com/archive/?date=19920810&slug=1506707 (accessed 22 November 2010).

Pattie, C, Seyd, P and Whitleley, P (2003) 'Citizenship and civic engagement attitudes and behaviour in Britain', *Political Studies*, Vol. 51, pp. 443–468.

Quigley, L (2002) *Community of Faith*, Dublin: Veritas.

Razack, S (2007) 'Stealing the pain of others: Reflections on Canadian humanitarian responses', *Review of Education, Pedagogy, and Cultural Studies*, 29(4), pp. 375–394.

Smith, M (2004) 'Mediating the world: Development, education and global citizenship', *Globalization, Societies and Education*, 2(1), pp. 67–81.

Westheimer, J and Kahne, J (2004) 'What kind of citizen? The politics of educating for democracy', *American Educational Research Journal*, 41(2), pp. 237–269.

World Bank (2013) Global Monitoring Report 2012, Washington, DC: World Bank.

Acknowledgements

I would like to thank Meliosa Bracken who co-authored the original report upon which this chapter is based. I would also like to thank Greg Bowe for his assistance in preparing this chapter for publication.

4

Typologies of Development Education: From Learning About Development to Critical Global Pedagogy

Douglas Bourn

Introduction

In January 2013, the Department for International Development (DFID) announced a new five year programme for development education in England. This programme whilst having a strong element of learning about development within its key components demonstrated that the discourses and practices around this term are still alive and well. The launch of the programme above all demonstrated the need for continued dialogue and debate as to what the concept means and how it is being interpreted within different educational locations. To some commentators on development education this could be perceived as further tailing to government agendas (Cameron and Fairbrass, 2004; Selby and Kagawa, 2011) and to others as an opportunity which creates spaces for schools and teachers to promote understanding about development and global themes from their own perspective.

This chapter suggests that a more constructive approach would be to reflect on the different interpretations of development education, and relate these to examples of practice from schools and further education. It proposes that what is needed is to identify the particular pedagogical perspectives being addressed and then relate these to forms of social and educational interventions. It also suggests that perhaps there has been too much emphasis on rhetoric for social change but too little on looking at pedagogical challenges and opportunities and recognising the limits to progress.

What do we mean by development education?

Development education has been a feature of educational practice in most industrialised countries for the past 25 to 30 years. Central to much of that practice, where it has been led by non-governmental organisations (NGOs), has been the goal of educational and social transformation. Inspired by the ideas of Paulo Freire, development education has been seen by both its supporters and opponents as an approach towards learning that not only challenged dominant ideas in society but also offered an alternative perspective and methodology (McCollum, 1996; Bourn, 2008). Selby and Kagawa (2011) imply that development education needs to be much more critical of dominant economic discourses. Whilst this author would agree that a perceived weakness of practices of NGOs in the UK has been their failure to address economic agendas such as corporate power (Egan, 2011), there has been a tendency to criticise without analysing why this is the case or reflecting on the skills and expertise within the development education communities of practice.

It is suggested in this chapter that before critiques are made as to the failings or shortcomings of development education practice, there needs to be a debate that recognises both the history and range of traditions and perspectives behind it and also to recognise the opportunities and constraints that funding can provide. Whilst development education as an educational approach has had links with broader issue-based movements such as global and human rights education, its practices have tended to have a number of distinctive features which are likely to pose tensions and complex relationships with dominant social and political ideas.

Firstly, development education practice in most industrialised countries emerged in response to the decolonisation process (McCollum, 1996; Harrison, 2008). Secondly the vast majority of practice that has been promoted as development education has operated within the discourses, policies and funding of international development, whether from governments or international NGOs. Yet there has been little debate amongst development education practitioners about what is meant by development, the relevance of its different interpretations and relationship to global social change. Some commentators on this area (Seitz, quoted in Hartmeyer, 2008) have questioned the continued relevance of the term. Bodies such as the Global Education Network Europe (O'Loughlin, 2006) and NGOs in Canada (Mundy, 2007) argue that you cannot divorce talking about development from talking about globalisation, human rights or sustainable development; and that the term global education is a more appropriate one for bringing together all of these issue-based or adjectival educations.

Yet amongst many NGOs in Europe and certain countries (notably Spain, Ireland and Norway) the use of the concept development education remains the dominant framework for engaging in debates, policies and practices around learning about development and global themes within education. An example of this is the 'European Consensus Document on Development', first agreed in 2005, which has support from a range of stakeholders across Europe and refers to development education as follows:

> The aim of development education and awareness raising is to enable every person in Europe to have life-long access to opportunities to be aware of and understand global development concerns and the local and personal relevance of those concerns, and to enact their rights and responsibilities as inhabitants of an interdependent and changing world by effecting change for a just and sustainable world (European Consensus on Development, 2005: 5).

Whilst variations of this term can be seen in strategies and practices across Europe, the term does reflect some common underlying principles that reflect how many academics and policy-makers would summarise what is perceived to be 'good development education'. They are as follows:

- understanding the globalised world including links between our own lives and those of people throughout the world;
- ethical foundations and goals including social justice, human rights and respect for others;
- participatory and transformative learning processes with the emphasis on dialogue and experience;
- developing competencies of critical self-reflection;
- supportive active engagement;
- active global citizenship (Rajacic et al., 2010: 121).

Although this summary produced for the European Commission accurately reflects these common principles, it does mask some major divisions as to how development education is interpreted and put into practice. What is suggested in this chapter is the need for a more critical and deeper analysis as to how development education is interpreted. It is this lack of analysis and critical reflection that can easily lead to simple conclusions such as accommodation to dominant discourses or being too political.

Typologies of development education

Recent reviews of development education for the European Commission (Rajacic et al., 2010) suggests that a great deal of its practice is related to promoting or supporting aims of the government, NGOs or an emphasis on action and campaigning, with minimal attention given to deepening learning and understanding. These observations are not new. Arnold (1987) in his critique of development education in the 1980s noted different pedagogies around information-critical skills and mobilisation with three visions: charity, interdependence and empowerment. Krause (2010) whilst noting that aspects of these past approaches still exist, has suggested that a key change has been the recognition of global interdependence. He proposed the following typologies:

- development education as public relations for development aid;
- development education as awareness raising – public dissemination of information;
- development education as global education – focussing on local-global interdependence;
- development education as enhancement of life skills – focussing on learning processes and critical thinking.

Manuela Mesa Peinado, a leading Spanish academic in development education noted that there is no single and exclusive definition of development education. The variations depend on the sense given to the words development and education, and the context and time in which they are framed. Therefore, development education is a dynamic process, which generates reflection, analysis and critical thought regarding development and North-South relations; it is centred on a teaching process that combines cognitive capacities with the acquisition of values and attitudes, aimed at the construction of a fairer world, in which everybody can share access to power and resources (Mesa Peinado, 2011a).

Mesa Peinado in her review of the evolution of development education in Spain refers to five generations:

- The charitable and assistance-based approach;

- The development approach and the emergence of development education;
- A critical and solidarity-based development education;
- Human and sustainable development education;
- Global citizenship education (2011b).

Whilst there is value in these typologies, it is suggested here that a much more complex picture exists if one looks at development education in a global context and relates the approaches more to their aims and specific context. For example, the term is used in differing ways in South Africa (Hoppers, 2008) and India (Kumar, 2008) that relate more directly to broader educational goals in those contexts. Also there are clear distinctions between those organisations which emphasise broader universal goals around global citizenship or even human development and those which focus on critical pedagogy, and voices for the dispossessed and excluded.

Therefore the following typology is suggested as a basis for further dialogue and discussion:

- Development education as development awareness – based around building support for development, and increased understanding and support for aid as exemplified by most governments who fund development education (DFID, 1998);
- Learning about development – that essentially sees development education as knowledge and concepts around development including the Millennium Development Goals, as perceived by the Coalition government in the UK, and some international NGOs (CIO, 2011);
- Human development as education – a view that has resonance particularly beyond Europe and is influenced by the thinking of Amartya Sen (2009), Martha Nussbaum (2011) and sees a linkage with aspirations of development education organisations with goals such as Education for All;
- Using the term global education to include development education but extending it to make connections with themes such as intercultural education and human rights, as for example in Finland or the Netherlands;
- Learning in a global society – this perspective which is sometimes called global learning sees development education as linked to debates around globalisation, e.g. Think Global (2011);

- Development education as public engagement for global justice – this is the approach taken by larger NGOs in Europe who promote the term global citizenship, e.g. Oxfam, CAFOD;
- Development education as critical pedagogy – an approach that can be most clearly seen in some Development Education Centres in the UK and by academics who have been directly influenced by the thinking of Freire and Henry Giroux.

These different interpretations and typologies should not be seen in terms of right or wrong ways but in terms of understanding the roots of their approach, their goals and ways of working. So for example a government funded programme on development education is very unlikely to see development education as about critical pedagogy. Also if it is focussed on influencing the public in the global North it is going to be less interested in seeing human development as education in a global context. Some grassroots NGOs however, whose *raison d'etre* is about trying to change society, to question and challenge inequality in the world, are unlikely to accept an approach that is simply focussed on learning about the Millennium Development Goals for example. This however does not mean that an organisation engaged in development education practice merely responds to the funder agenda or the specific policy focus; what it means is that there is a need to debate and clarify how an organisation sees its contribution to broader policy goals and objectives.

McCollum (1996), Andreotti (2006) and Marshall (2007) have suggested the need for development education to give greater consideration to theory. This does not mean ignoring funding priorities or goals. Andreotti (with De Souza, 2008) for example, who has perhaps been one of the most influential writers on development education, developed a radical series of resources that have a strong postcolonial and Freirean background, with funding from the UK government (Open Spaces for Dialogue and Enquiry (OSDE); Through Other Eyes). The questions any NGO needs to consider in looking at the opportunity for taking forward their ideas through publicly funded programmes are:

- does the funding enable the organisation to explore and develop its ideas and practices?
- are there spaces for creativity and innovation?
- to what extent is there an opportunity for learning that might question or challenge dominant viewpoints and ideas?

What is summarised below are some examples from recent research by the Development Education Research Centre at the Institute of Education in London, all funded directly or indirectly by the UK government, which aim to demonstrate the different ways in which the principles and practices behind development education are being interpreted. What is behind these research examples is an approach that aims to interpret data and evidence on how learning and understanding about development issues and themes is interpreted and where they relate to broader traditions, theories and practice.

Engagement with schools

In most industrialised countries where development education has some status, it is because of its influence within schools. It would not be difficult to find examples of development education in a school in the UK, Ireland, the Netherlands, Austria or Finland. This could take a variety of forms, as the following research by the Institute of Education has identified. For example, Hunt's study on global learning in primary schools shows that where learning about global and development issues is more embedded within the school, there is greater awareness of socio-economic differences within the global South as well as between the North and South. What was evident in a number of schools where there was engagement with these themes was the emphasis on values such as rights, diversity, fairness and justice (Hunt, 2012: 76). Her study also showed less emphasis in primary schools on 'critical engagement with global learning and the teaching of controversial or "difficult issues"' (Ibid.).

This, as she suggests, is not surprising and it could be argued that 'softer approaches' provide the 'building blocks through which pupils can engage with more complex global issues as they grow older' (Ibid.). Similar evidence can be seen in research undertaken with secondary schools.

These examples by themselves tell us only about activities. As Edge et al. (2008) note in their research on secondary schools, the term global dimension, used in most English schools to promote the principles behind development education, has been interpreted in a variety of ways:

- awareness of and exposure to other and different cultures and the world context, and a sense of global social responsibility;

Table 4.1 Global dimension engagement and activities across schools (Bourn and Hunt, 2011: 28)

	Whole school approach	Curriculum	Extra curriculum	Professional development
Mission statements and strategies	International strategy	International baccalaureate		
Staff member responsible for global dimension	Advisor for international work and sustainable development	Curriculum advisor	Global Awareness Club	
School assemblies	Speakers or talks on global poverty, climate change			
International partnerships	Long standing link with a particular school, promoted via whole school projects	Using a link for specific curriculum projects, e.g. water, climate change	Involving local community and parents in raising money for partnerships	Teacher visits. Attending training workshops on developing international links
Work with local community groups		Local people from refugee communities giving talks in English, Geography or History	Cultural festivals	
Award programmes	Fairtrade School. International School Award Eco-School Award. UNICEF rights and responsibilities	International School Award. UNICEF rights and responsibilities	Eco-School Award	International School Award. UNICEF rights and responsibilities

Table 4.1 Global dimension engagement and activities across schools (Bourn and Hunt, 2011: 28) – *continued*

	Whole school approach	Curriculum	Extra curriculum	Professional development
Working with NGDOs or DECs or other similar bodies	Red Nose Day	Working with organisations such as Red Cross on curricular projects. Running sessions in classroom e.g. Red Cross, Plan UK, Practical Action. Teachers within a school help a Development NGO or Development Education Centre to produce curriculum resources.	Action Aid's Send My Friend to School programme	Using local Development Education Centres for training sessions
Pupil-based initiatives	School Councils acting as focus for discussions and debates		Supporting external campaigns on themes such as fair trade and climate change	

- helping students to understand that they are citizens of the world and to demonstrate the interconnectedness of the world we live in;
- teaching about global issues and understanding the impact of our actions;
- promoting and sustaining international links;
- understanding the bigger picture and their place in it;
- helping students to link their complex and different identities and their place in the world.

Behind these different interpretations are the motivations of teachers that relate closely to perceptions of development education. The following observations from teachers from secondary schools in England demonstrate first, a more charitable and developmental perspective; second, a more intercultural perspective; and third, a more critical approach:

> We've also got a link with a school/orphanage in Madagascar. That has really kind of opened people's eyes as well, like when we've set up pen pal contacts. If our pupils haven't received a letter recently and been complaining, we've told them there's civil unrest there at the moment, all the ports are closed, there's no import of food or fuel, not even any baby milk for the orphans (Bourn and Hunt, 2011: 32–33).

> Because we want our pupils to understand that other people do have their different ways of looking at life, they have their own cultures, religions, lifestyles, etc. And we're helping them to be able to communicate with people from different cultures and backgrounds, and helping them to respect others that is not something they would automatically do, but to understand, to respect and be able to communicate with those people (Ibid.: 18–19).

> I am very concerned that the Global Dimension agenda is currently driven by NGOs, not teachers and their agendas have not been acknowledged. Rather than giving children a better picture of the world and their place in it, I'm worried we are confirming the perception that the Global South is a place of powerlessness and poverty. I'm also worried we are giving children the impression that they are more powerful than they are by over-emphasising campaigning (Ibid.: 24).

These viewpoints demonstrate that the issue is not about encouraging development education principles in the classroom, but rather about debating what it means and the extent to which the practices are questioning and challenging dominant educational thinking. These examples demonstrate that there is still a prevalent view that seeks to locate learning about global themes within a context of aid and charitable support. This approach is still very prevalent not only in the UK but in many other industrialised countries (see Bryan and Bracken, 2011). But there is also evidence of more intercultural and cosmopolitan notions that bear some linkages to debates on global and cosmopolitan citizenship. Finally there is evidence of a more critical pedagogical and postcolonial perspective.

A potential challenge for many organisations that would like to take a more critical and radical approach to development education is therefore in noting and understanding the different starting points for teachers and educators; what opportunities and resources are available to them for posing different interpretations and encouraging critical reflection and dialogue. This would mean including learning activities that move beyond a traditional view of seeing the global South as 'just about poor people' who are helpless and need aid and charity. Positive examples would include learning that challenges assumptions and stereotypes, and locates poverty within an understanding of the causes of inequality and what people are doing to address them.

Global skills and further education

Further education is an area that has been tackled by few development education practitioners. Selby and Kagawa (2011) have criticised this author's work in this area, most notably his report on *Global Skills* (Bourn, 2008) for its failure to critique or address neoliberal agendas and economic growth models. Whilst there is some validity in their comments, any engagement in the debates in this area needs to start from a recognition of where further education programmes are located in the UK and probably in most other European countries, in relation to equipping learners with the skills for employment. The question to pose for development educationalists is in what ways could one intervene in these areas of educational practice, and with what aims in mind? Some of these issues have been addressed in the Development Education Research Centre's report for Learning Skills and Improvement Service (LSIS) (Bentall et al., 2010). The aim of this section is to address how colleges and other further education providers are interpreting a concept such as global skills and where they relate to the typologies on development education outlined earlier.

The starting point has to be the usage of the term 'global skills'. A large number of small training providers are increasingly using the term, partly as a way of marketing themselves but also because there is increasing recognition that new forms of skills are being required by companies. An example of this in the UK is The Global Skills College in London. This institution runs training workshops on areas such as teamwork, information technology (IT), conflict resolution and problem solving skills (The Global Skills Project). An example of the kind of skills needed in the private sector is outlined below by KPMG, the international audit company which states:

> So what exactly are we looking for when we recruit new people? Naturally, we want you to have good technical skills, problem-solving abilities and commercial focus. We're also looking for people with a lot of integrity – good team workers who can build effective relationships, learn from experience and bring out the best in others (KPMG, 2008).

A second approach to the usage of the term within further education is one that sees global skills as about intercultural understanding and developing a more global outlook, often related to international experience. Whilst elements of this can be seen in some of the comments made from companies above, they have a distinct tradition and approach that is based on a broader humanistic approach towards education, linked to cross-cultural education and cosmopolitanism. This tradition is rooted in discourses around intercultural education which is based on preparing learners to 'act as interpreters and mediators between different cultures on mutual bases' (Lasonen, 2009). In the context of further education, for example, this can be interpreted as adopting a 'co-operative and team-working approach as mediators, interpreters and active agents between different cultures' (Lasonen, 2009: 196).

One of the main manifestations of this approach within further education is international partnerships between colleges. For example, a former principal of Grimsby College has stated, 'part of our education in life is to absorb new cultures and embrace diversity. Our relationship with education establishments across the world will continue and we can become a real centre for international growth and cultural exchange'. The value of these international initiatives and exchanges have however been critiqued in relation to school education (Martin, 2007; Leonard, 2008). They question the extent to which this form of learning can merely reinforce existing dominant ideological perceptions of the partner country and culture. Rizvi and Lingard (2010) have noted in regard to higher education that there is little evidence that student exchanges and overseas visits challenge dominant orthodoxies between the rich and the poor in the world. They state that despite much talk about global interconnectivity and interdependence, 'international contact remains within globally differentiated cultural communities – the west versus the rest' (Ibid.: 175).

A third approach and usage of the term within further education is one that sees it as a way of promoting global perspectives and critical thinking. Here global skills can be seen as an approach that recognises complexity and critical thinking, and is linked closely to a values-based approach around social justice. Building on the work of Paulo Freire (1976) and Giroux (2005) this approach is based on recognition of an approach towards learning that is open and participatory but also deeply political, including recognition of power. Giroux (2005) talks about critical pedagogy starting, not with test scores, but with questions. He states that it is also about recognising competing views and vocabularies and the opening up of new forms of knowledge and creative spaces. This approach to global skills involves the following:

- recognising the value of learning about different perspectives and approaches;
- equipping the learner with the skills to question and develop the ability to enquire about and reflect critically upon a range of social, economic and cultural influences;
- emphasising the importance of positive social engagement and of seeking solutions;
- recognising the impact of globalisation on people's lives and the need to equip them with the ability to make sense of a rapidly changing world;
- making reference to the forces that shape societal and economic change.

It includes recognition of concepts and approaches using the first and second lenses outlined in this chapter, but takes this to a new level in terms of critical thinking, understanding of and valuing different perspectives; and above all recognising the impact of globalisation on relations between people and communities around the world. It also acknowledges the consequential differentials in terms of power and access to resources and learning opportunities. Two examples of these influences can be seen in the work of the Lancashire Global Education Centre and the Development Education Association (DEA)'s 'Global Learning in Further Education' initiative.

The Lancashire Global Education Centre in England developed a three year programme for tutors in their local college linked to language skills, most notably for migrant communities where English is a second language. They did this through the production of resources and training materials that related the skills deficits of learners to their own experiences and global issues. Themes covered include Fairtrade, the Millennium Development Goals, What You Can Do and the Global Drugs Trade (Lancashire Global Education Centre, 2008). Newell-Jones (2007) for the Development Education Association suggested also:

> That education and training for a global society should lead to the acquisition of skills is not in question. However unless this includes essential skills in critical engagement and also leads to the adoption of impact-orientated behaviours, learning will be ineffectual (Ibid.: 5).

The inclusion of linkages to understanding of global issues and questions of critical engagement bring the global skills concept back to the impact of globalisation on a person's life and how they make sense of the rapidly changing world around them – and have the confidence, knowledge and values-base to make a positive contribution to both the economy and society more widely. These elements could be summarised as:

- understanding what globalisation means, particularly in relation to the individual, their community and their employment;
- ability to understand and engage with global issues, such as climate change and poverty, in order to become a more informed and engaged citizen;
- development of skills to understand and respect a range of cultures and values, and to be able to reflect critically upon one's own values base.

This approach towards critical skills builds on the work of Andreotti and De Souza (2008) in posing the need to move from fixed content and skills that conform to a predetermined idea of society, towards concepts and strategies that address complexity, difference and uncertainty. It also means moving from an approach to learning that accepts given knowledge, to one that questions and moves positions and views. Finally this approach means moving from a universalist and ordered view of the world to one that recognises complex, multifaceted and different means of interpretation (Bourn and Neal, 2008). There are therefore opportunities within the spectrum and forms of intervention in further education, but they pose questions around the extent to which you operate within the dominant discourses on globalisation and global skills, or seek a more radical and transformatory approach. Organisations engaged in development education practice could engage in further education, reflecting these different approaches. Their input would in part depend on the perspective of the organisation, but also on what opportunities, openings and above all spaces that exist for more creative and transformatory approaches.

Conclusion

The two areas of schools and further education addressed in this article have shown that for organisations and individuals who are influenced and perhaps inspired by principles and practice from development education there are a range of opportunities and openings. However these 'spaces' will be determined by the goals and aims of the educational programme within which they are located. They will also be influenced above all by the sense in which there is recognition of broader educational goals in terms of participatory approaches towards learning, critical reflection and respect for different voices and perspectives.

In light of these points, it is suggested here that rather than starting from a position of criticising development education practitioners, there should be an understanding and analysis of the ways in which openings exist for approaches that encourage learning about the wider world that move beyond merely learning about development. It may be that the openings are minimal but that, despite this, some valuable knowledge could be made available about key concepts around development. On the other hand there may well be opportunities for more radical and transformatory approaches.

Above all, what organisations engaged in development education need to consider is their particular contribution to learning about global issues and questions. It is not about identifying one universal approach but about clarifying what is feasible and possible, and above all ensuring that the organisation has some clarity about its own approach and theoretical basis. There are many interpretations of development education. What is needed is to debate and encourage organisations to clarify what they see as their distinctive approach and to relate this to what is feasible to progress within a specific educational arena. Development education should not be seen as one particular approach or just a form of practice from a number of organisations but as a pedagogy and approach to learning. This pedagogy could have and should have a number of interpretations but central to it is that it opens minds to question their own assumptions, to promote and encourage reflection. Above all development education should encourage learning about different viewpoints about the wider world and to give the skills to the learner to effectively critique them.

References

Andreotti, V (2006) 'Soft versus critical global citizenship education', *Policy and Practice: A Development Education Review*, Vol. 3, Autumn 2006, pp. 40–51, available: http://www.developmenteducationreview.com/issue3-focus4

Andreotti, V and de Souza, L M (2008) 'Translating theory into practice and walking minefields: Lessons from the project "Through Other Eyes"', *International Journal of Development Education and Global Learning*, 1(1), pp. 23–36.

Arnold, S (1987) *Constrained Crusaders: NGOs and Development Education in the UK*, Occasional Paper, London, Institute of Education, University of London.

Bentall, C, Blum, N and Bourn, D (2010) *Learning and Skills in a Global Society: The Contribution of Further Education and Training Providers*, London: LSIS.

Bourn, D (2008) *Global Skills*, London: Centre for Excellence in Leadership.

Bourn, D and Hunt, F (2011) *The Global Dimension in Secondary Schools*, DERC Research Report No. 1, London: Institute of Education.

Bourn, D and Neal, I (2008) *The Global Engineer: Incorporating Global Skills within UK Higher Education of Engineers*, London, Engineers Against Poverty/ Development Education Research Centre, Institute of Education, University of London.

Bryan, A and Bracken, M (2011) *Learning to Read the World? Teaching and Learning about Global Citizenship and International Development in Post-Primary Schools*, Dublin: Irish Aid.

Cameron, J and Fairbrass, S (2004) 'From development awareness to enabling effective support: The changing profile of development education in England', *Journal of International Development*, Vol. 16.

Central Information Office (CIO) (2011) *Review of Using Aid Funds in the UK to Promote Awareness of Global Poverty – Review for DFID*, London: DFID.

Department for International Development (DFID) (1998) *Building Support for Development*, London: DFID.

Edge, K, Khamsi, K and Bourn, D (2008) *Exploring the Global Dimension in Secondary Schools*, research report for DCSF, London: DCSF.

Egan, A (2011) *Development Education and Corporate Power*, Unpublished MA dissertation, Institute of Education, University of London.

European Consensus on Development (2005), Brussels: European Commission, available: http://ec.europa.eu/development/icenter/repository/european_consensus_2005_en.pdf (accessed 14 February 2013).

Freire, P (1976) *Pedagogy of the Oppressed*, London: Penguin.

Giroux, H (2005) *Border Crossings*, New York: Routledge.

Harrison, D (2008) 'Antipoverty: England's first development education organisation (1971–1974)', *International Journal of Development Education and Global Learning*, 1(1), pp. 49–58.

Hartmeyer, H (2008) *Experiencing the World: Global Learning in Austria: Developing, Reaching Out, Crossing Borders*, Munster: Waxmann.

Hoppers, C (2008) *South African Research Chair in Development Education – Framework and Strategy*, Pretoria, South Africa: University of South Africa.

Hunt, F (2012) *Global Learning in Primary Schools*, DERC Research Paper no. 9, London: IOE.

KPMG (2008) 'The Global Skills Convergence', available: http://www.kpmg.com/Global/en/IssuesAndInsights/ArticlesPublications/Documents/The-global-skills-convergence.pdf (accessed 19 February 2010).

Krause, J (2010) *European Development Education Monitoring Report: Development Education Watch*, Brussels: European Multi-Stakeholder Forum.

Kumar, A (2008) 'Development education and dialogic learning in the 21st century', *International Journal of Development Education and Global Learning*, 1(1), pp. 37–48.

Lancashire Global Education Centre (2008) *Global Skills: Understanding the World Through English*, Preston: LGEC.

Lasonen, J (2009) 'Intercultural education: Promoting sustainability in education and training' in J Fien, R Maclean and M-G Park (eds) *Work, Learning and Sustainable Development*, Bonn: Springer.

Leonard, A (2008) 'Global school relationships: School linking and modern challenges' in D Bourn (ed.) *Development Education: Debates and Dialogues*, London: Bedford Way Papers.

Marshall, H (2007) 'Global education in perspective: Fostering a global dimension in an English secondary school', *Cambridge Journal of Education*, 37(3), pp. 355–374.

Martin, F (2007) 'School linking: A controversial issue' in H Claire and C Holden (eds) *The Challenge of Teaching Controversial Issues*, London: Trentham Books.

McCollum, A (1996) *On the Margins? An Analysis of the Theory and Practice of Development Education in the 1900s*, PhD thesis, Open University.

Mesa Peinado, M (2011a) 'Reflections on the five generations model of development in education', *Education Global Research*, Issue Zerio, available: http://educacionglobalresearch.net/wp-content/uploads/09-Comentario-Manuela-Mesa.pdf (accessed 18 January 2013).

Mesa Peinado, M. (2011b) 'Education and future challenges', *Education Global Research*, Issue Zerio available: http://educacionglobalresearch.net/manuelamesa1issuezero/ (accessed 18 January 2013).

Mundy, K (2007) *Charting Global Education in Canada's Elementary Schools*, Toronto: Ontario Institute for Studies in Education (OISE)/UNICEF.

Newell-Jones, K (2007) *Global Skills and Lifelong Learning*, London: DEA.

Nussbaum, M (2011) *Creating Capabilities: The Human Development Approach*, Cambridge, MA: Harvard UP.
O'Loughlin, E (ed.) (2006) *Global Education in Austria*, Lisbon: North-South Centre.
Open Spaces for Dialogue and Enquiry (OSDE), http://www.osdemethodology.org.uk/ (accessed 14 February 2013).
Rajacic, A, Surian, A, Fricke, H-J, Krause, J and Davis, P (2010) *Study on the Experience and Actions of the Main European Actors Active in the Field of Development Education and Awareness Raising: Interim Report*, Brussels: European Commission.
Rizvi, F and Lingard, B (2010) *Globalizing Education Policy*, Abingdon: Routledge.
Selby, D and Kagawa, F (2011) 'Development education and education for sustainable development: Are they striking a Faustian bargain?' *Policy & Practice: A Development Education Review*, Vol. 12, Spring 2011, pp. 15–31, available: http://www.developmenteducationreview.com/issue12-focus3.
Sen, A (2009) *The Idea of Justice*, Cambridge, Massachusetts: Belknap Press of Harvard.
Think Global (2011) 'The global skills gap', London: Think Global, available: http://clients.squareeye.net/uploads/dea/documents/BusinessPoll_online_TG.pdf (accessed 21 February 2013).
The Global Skills Project, http://www.lpi-global-skills.org.uk/workshop_schedule.php (accessed 19 February 2013).
Through Other Eyes, www.throughothereyes.org.uk (accessed 14 February 2013).

5
Critical Thinking and Development Education: How Do We Develop Meta-Cognitive Capacities?

Roland Tormey

Introduction

Half a century ago, W B Gallie (1955–1956) proposed that there were ideas for which it is fundamentally impossible to agree a definition because, while the term might be widely used, it is used by different people and groups in ways that are completely embedded in different sets of assumptions or beliefs (today we would probably say 'discourses'). In such a context there are multiple possible outcomes. One is what O'Sullivan (1999) has referred to as a 'phony consensus', in which different people and groups continue to use the same term as if they meant the same thing, even though they do not. O'Sullivan has referred to this as part of a process of *pastiche*-making, in which different ideas are merged or mixed together in a way which ignores or hides the possible for dynamic contestation between different positions (2005: 319). A second possibility is that the different perspectives on the contested term are made explicit and juxtaposed, enabling each perspective to provide what Gallie called 'a permanent potential critical value' (1955–1956: 193) to every other perspective. The goal of this chapter is to make explicit a number of different meanings of the term 'critical' as it is used in development education. The goal is not to identify 'the correct' or 'the best' meaning of the term, but rather to avoid *pastiche*-making and to allow the different perspectives to illuminate the strengths and weaknesses of each other. In other words, the goal is a kind of critical analysis of critical thinking.

The starting point for this chapter is that the term 'critical thinking' is widely used in development education, however, its meaning tends to be assumed rather than made explicit. In the first half of this chapter I will identify two related but distinct positions on 'critique' which are found in development education and which imply two different philosophical positions. In doing so, it will be possible to allow each position to offer a 'potential critical value' to the other. In the second half of this chapter I will argue that, in fact, development education has tended to rely heavily on social and political philosophical perspectives and has tended to neglect psychological perspectives on critical thinking. This is perhaps strange, given the wealth of literature and research on critical thinking in psychology. I therefore present some of the perspectives and findings from the psychological literature. Again, the aim is not to suggest that this perspective presents a correct or best meaning of critical thinking, but rather to allow it to offer different insights to those previously available. Some of those insights may be quite challenging for current development education practice. Before doing this, however, I will briefly explore the idea that critical thinking is a key idea in development education.

Critical thinking and development education

It is arguable that one of the key features of development education is that it claims to include a focus on developing critical thinking or 'critical consciousness'. In 2003 I reviewed a series of definitions of development education (including those offered by the Joint United Nations Information Committee in 1975, the Irish National Committee for Development Education in 1996 and the Development Education Commission in 1999) and concluded that they tend to have a number of common characteristics:

> All identify an action component to development education (they use phrases such as 'participate in the development of their community'; 'effective and long-term responses', '"writing" the world and the dynamics of change') and most contain the term 'critical', either as part of the term 'critical thinking' or in 'critical consciousness/critical awareness' (Tormey, 2003: 215).

A review of more recent publications does not change the picture in any way: Krausse (2010, cited in Doggett and Phelan, 2012) refers to the goal of developing a society which is 'critically aware of, knowledgeable about and responsive to the issues of global interdependence'; Hinchion and Hennessy (2009) refer to a process of developing critical literacy, (the same phrase is used by Egan [2012] and many others). Mahadeo (2009) describes the goal of development education as aiming 'to put into effect solidarity, critical analysis, societal transformation and the encouragement of active citizenship'. Repeatedly, the ideas of critical thinking and acting are found in descriptions of development education.

Some have argued, however, that not all development education is inherently 'critical'. In the last few years, the distinction offered by Andreotti (2006) between 'soft' and 'critical' approaches to development education has become influential and has been cited by influential writers like Bourn, Bryan, Khoo, McCloskey, Pashby and others (while Andreotti actually refers to 'global citizenship education', I am treating that term as being synonymous with development education – I have discussed this in a bit more detail in Tormey and Gleeson [2012]). Drawing on the work of Spivak (1988), Andreotti (2006) argues that it makes sense to differentiate between a 'soft' approach to global citizenship education (which emphasises poverty and helplessness, a lack of development, a need for humanitarian or moral responses, and has the goal of achieving development, harmony, tolerance and equality), and a 'critical' approach to global citizenship. This critical approach emphasises: global inequality and injustice; complex systems and power relations; colonial history; a need for justice and accountability for our own roles in social systems; and has the goal of addressing injustices, creating grounds for dialogue and enabling autonomy for people to define their own development. For the former ('soft') approach, the role of education is described as being to raise awareness of problems, support campaigns and increase motivation to help. For the more 'critical' approach the goal is seen to be independent/critical thinking and more informed, responsible and ethical action. For Andreotti, a 'soft' approach to development education may be appropriate in some circumstances, but 'it cannot stop there' (2006: 49). If it is generally clear that development educators do or should aim for 'critical thinking', this begs the question as to what is meant by 'critical'. I will now turn to address this question.

What is meant by the term 'critical' in development education?

The idea that there are different meanings to the word 'critical' is probably readily evident: for example when, in everyday speech, a person is described as 'a critic' or 'being critical' it generally denotes a sense of negative judgement, that is to say, the expression of adverse or disapproving comments. Indeed, this is the first definition for the term 'critical' which appears in the Oxford English Dictionary. However, in everyday use, the term also has another meaning, which is to say, a sense of analysing or weighing up in a balanced way the merits and flaws of an argument, or of a work of art. In fact, this second sense of the term is deeply engrained in the word 'critical', which originally derives from the Greek word 'krites', meaning 'judge'. When social and human scientists use the term 'critical' they typically draw on meanings which are close to these, but which are different in that they are embedded in different implicit belief systems (or discourses). In this section I will explore some different meanings associated with the term 'critical' in social and human sciences. Drawing on ideas which I previously explored in 2003 and 2011, I will distinguish between two different potential goals of 'critical thinking' in development education as informed by social and political philosophy. I will then move on to a third – more psychological – approach which has arguably been less influential in development education and which focuses, not on the goal of critical thinking, but instead on the process.

Social and political philosophical notions of 'critical'

One meaning of the term 'critical' in social sciences (and in development education) is represented in the Marxist tradition. For Marx, social systems and social structures were organised in such a way as to give rise to inequality. This was, he argued, the objective reality of modern societies. Yet some of those who suffered within such systems did not see the systems as being problematic or unfair because of a subjective 'veil' which hid their reality from them. For Marx this veil included nationalist ideas (which told them that the workers and the bosses were all on the same side as they all owed allegiance to the same nation) and religious ideas (which told them to accept their suffering today with the promise of a better afterlife). Other writers focused on how the contemporary social order was made to seem natural, productive ('survival of the fittest') or inevitable ('there is no alternative'). Later writers in this 'critical theory' tradition focused on how social and human sciences (Economics, Development Studies, Sociology, Anthropology, Psychology etc.) have been 'complicitous in special ways with the ills of the present age' (McCarthy, 1990: 439). Within this tradition, the purpose of being 'critical' was to clarify that these (widely held and unquestioned) ideas and beliefs were not the objective reality but were in fact hiding the reality of the exploitative nature of modern societies. As Carr and Kemmis have written:

> Critical theory is not 'critical' in the sense of voicing disapproval of contemporary social arrangements, but in the sense that it attempts to distil the historical processes which have caused subjective meanings to become systematically distorted... [It] is particularly focused on the ways of thinking which support such subjugation...[such as] in the dominance of a way of thinking which makes such oppression seem unproblematic, inevitable, incidental or even justified (Carr and Kemmis, 1986: 138).

According to this perspective, the role of being critical is to uncover for people the 'truth' about exploitation, about the social structures which give rise to exploitation and about the ways of thinking which support the continued operation of these social structures. The role of development education is to develop this critical thinking capacity. Paulo Freire highlighted this idea when he quoted a former factory worker who said: 'When I began this course I was *naïve*, and when I found out how naïve I was, I started to get *critical*' (emphasis in original, 1970: 15). There are traces of the same idea in Andreotti's work when she argues that critical global citizenship education sees the nature of the problem to be addressed by education as being 'structures, systems, assumptions, power relations and attitudes that create and maintain exploitation and enforced disempowerment' (2006: 46). It is worth being clear here that I am not suggesting that the work of Freire or Andreotti follows a Marxist orthodoxy. Rather, as Andreotti has argued (2007, 2010), her work borrows some analytical tools from Marxism (and, as I will explore below, others from poststructuralism).

As Steward Clegg (1989) has pointed out, one of the problems with this version of 'critical' is that it starts from the assumption that the 'critical thinker' (the sociologist, the political economist, the development educator etc.) has a better understanding of the objective nature of a person's reality than the person themselves. There is, as Clegg notes, a persistent problem with people who view themselves as radicals claiming 'both theoretical and, more seriously, practical primacy in determining what real interests should be, despite what people maintain their interests to be. The historical tragedies arising from such claims to omniscience are too well known to recount here' (1989: 95). Indeed, this problem has been recognised by radical educators. Paulo Freire has argued that there are those who see themselves as progressive educators and who, at the same time, display a tendency towards authoritarianism:

> To criticise the arrogance, the authoritarianism of intellectuals of Left and Right, who are both basically reactionary in an identical way – who judge themselves the proprietors of knowledge, the former, of revolutionary knowledge, the latter, of conservative knowledge... – this I have always done (1999: 79).

This brings us to a second meaning of the term 'critical' as it is used in social sciences and social philosophy, a sense which draws its inspiration from the work of the French writer Michel Foucault and, through him, from the German philosopher, Frederick Nietzsche. As with other writers, Foucault was interested in the way in which ideas were tied to power and subjugation, and was particularly focused on the role of human sciences in such subjugation (McCarthy, 1990). In this respect, an analysis from this perspective could look a lot like that offered from a critical theory perspective. For Foucault, however, any claim that something is 'true' is always made from within some perspective or discourse and making the claim is always an articulation of power. Therefore, he argues that we should not draw a distinction between the 'ideological' perspectives that serve the interests of 'the powerful' and the 'liberating' perspectives that serve the interests of 'the powerless'. For him, every claim that some perspective is true or liberating is tied to power – in the words of Paul Rabinow: 'For Foucault, there is no external position of certainty, no universal understanding that is beyond history and society' (1991: 4).

When faced with questions concerning supposedly universal ideas that are seen as emancipatory, like 'justice', Foucault disagrees that we should simply accept such ideas as an appropriate basis for our actions: 'it seems to me that the idea of justice in itself is an idea which in effect has been invented and put to work in different types of societies as an instrument of a certain political and economic power or as a weapon against that power' (quoted in Rabinow, 1991: 6). As such, for Foucault, it is not just the ideas which are associated with the imperialist project, colonialism, Eurocentrism and triumphalism that need to be challenged. For him, the anti-imperialist and anti-colonial ideas and projects must also be subject to the same process of cutting to their roots to put them in historical and social context so that they become recognised as ideas, rather than as 'truth', he writes: 'My point is not that everything is bad but that everything is dangerous, which is not exactly the same as bad' (Foucault, 1997: 256). As such, our critical eye should not only be trained on 'the powerful', because all ideas – our own included – are potentially dangerous.

Above I noted that it is possible to read Andreotti's work as if it implies that complex social structures and systems that create and maintain exploitation exist in some objective sense. It is worth making clear that this second sense of critical is also present when she writes:

> Criticality, in this context, does not refer to the dominant notion that something is right or wrong, biased or unbiased, true or false. It is an attempt to understand the origins of assumptions and implications. In this sense, critical literacy is not about 'unveiling' the 'truth' for the learners, but about providing the space for them to reflect on their context and their own and others' epistemological and ontological assumptions (2006: 49; see also 2010: 246–248).

Andreotti suggests that there have been some pedagogic initiatives based on this kind of analysis (such as Through Other Eyes) but in general the link between this thinking and educational practice has been weak. This may in fact understate the influence of this kind of thinking, at least in terms of curriculum documents: for example, both the Irish primary school History curriculum and the proposed (but not implemented) Politics and Society syllabus for upper second-level Irish education are based on precisely this kind of poststructuralist thinking (see Tormey, 2006; National Council for Curriculum and Assessment, 2009).

This second account of 'critical' is not without its critics. This kind of thinking has been regarded by some as quite sterile in that it can be hard to justify any action if one does not have some stable reference point (some 'truth') against which to justify it. This is the point the German sociologist and philosopher Jürgen Habermas raises in relation to Foucault's work when he asks '...why fight at all?' (1994: 96). Dillon (2003) too wonders if such 'critical thinking' accounts in development studies and development education are better at critiquing other people's practices rather than finding plausible bases for acting. Not everyone would agree with this position, however. Foucault actually argues that his perspective does not promote apathy but instead leads to 'hyper- and pessimistic activism' (1997: 256); since all actions are an articulation of power, all actions or inactions are, in a sense, activism. His aim is that such activism is constantly self-critical. Andreotti, similarly, refers to hyper self-reflexivity (2007: 75).

Corbridge (1998) goes much further in his critique, arguing that, in development studies, many of those who claim to be influenced by Foucault's approach actually do little more than rhetorically caricaturise perspectives they disagree with (as being inauthentic, urban, consumerist, monstrous, utilitarian – we could add technocratic, colonial, imperialist and Eurocentric to the list). Far from subjecting themselves to the same critical gaze that they direct towards others, he argues, they often uncritically proposed alternative ideas based on romanticised versions of subalterns, social majorities and soil cultures. As the Indian philosopher of Science Meera Nanda has put it, a 'radical xenophilia of Western intellectuals has minimised the theoretical space for a critical assessment of non-Western cultures' (2002: 215; see also Andreotti, 2007: 71–72).

To summarise the argument so far, within social sciences, we find two different meanings of the term 'critical thinking'. One emphasises that exploitative social and economic systems and structures objectively exist and that they are 'hidden' by ideological systems that make the current social system appear fair, God-given, just, normal or inevitable. In particular the role of human sciences (such as Economics or Development Studies) in generating apparently objective (but, in reality, ideological) knowledge is identified. In this context, 'critical thinking' means making clear that these ideas do not represent the truth about exploitation, but in fact they hide the truth. This approach has been criticised as being authoritarian. I have referred to it elsewhere as 'socially critical' development education (Batteson and Tormey, 2011). The second way of conceptualising the term 'critical' begins from a similar position in that it argues that ideas can be dangerous and that the ideas developed or used within social and human sciences merit particular attention. However it emphasises that there is no truth that is knowable outside the context of relations of power, and so our goal cannot be to expose 'the truth' but can only be to locate ideas in social and historical context. The supposedly emancipatory ideas of the apparently 'powerless' should not be exempted from this analysis. This approach has been criticised for failing to provide a positive basis for action and it has also been argued that, in practice, proponents often fail to adequately turn their critical gaze back on themselves. I have referred to this as 'critical thinking' development education (Batteson and Tormey, 2011).

To restate what was said in the introduction, the goal here is not to identify 'the best' meaning of the term critical but to allow each meaning to act as a counterpoint to the other. Each perspective provides us with a set of questions that can be offered to the other perspective. The exploration in this section so far has focussed on the goal or aim of 'critical thinking' (i.e., whether it aims to uncover the truth or to historicise and contextualise different perspectives). In doing so, I have drawn on social and political philosophy to inform this exploration. Yet I am conscious that the debates between these two perspectives are only possible because they share so much in common – their discourses overlap much more than they conflict. If we limit ourselves to these perspectives we limit what is thinkable and knowable about critical thinking. For that reason it is interesting to juxtapose a rather different approach to understanding what it means to be 'critical'.

It is notable that development education tends to draw on political philosophy for inspiration more than, say, educational psychology: for illustration purposes, a search for the name 'Freire' in the articles published in the development education journal *Policy and Practice: A Development Education Review* gives 33 citations, while a search for 'Piaget' elicits one, and a search for 'Vygotsky' elicits only two. Yet, the study of critical thinking has been an incredibly vibrant area in Psychology and Educational Psychology, and has a great deal to offer to development education debates. In neglecting the psychological literature, development education probably differs little from other aspects of educational studies that have expressed an interest in the concept of critical thinking. Kuhn has argued that 'the burgeoning critical thinking movement in education has proceeded with little apparent contribution from contemporary cognitive development research' (1999: 16). In order to redress this imbalance, it is to psychological accounts of critical thinking that I now turn.

Psychological accounts of critical thinking

If philosophical accounts of critical thinking often focus on the goal, psychological accounts tend to focus on the process. Magno (2010) has recently reviewed the various psychological definitions of critical thinking, and has shown that they tend to focus on systematic thinking aimed at making, understanding and evaluating arguments, detecting bias or perspective, and evaluating claims against evidence. An operational definition is supplied by Beyer (1984) who sees ten discrete skills as being at the core of critical thinking:

- Distinguishing between facts and value claims;
- Determining the reliability of a claim or of a source;

- Determining the accuracy of a statement;
- Distinguishing between warranted and unwarranted claims;
- Distinguishing relevant from irrelevant information, claims, or reasons;
- Detecting bias;
- Identifying stated and unstated assumptions;
- Identifying ambiguous or equivocal claims or arguments;
- Recognising logical inconsistencies or fallacies in a line of reasoning;
- Determining the strength of an argument.

The way this list of skills has been formulated can, of course, be critiqued from a political philosophical perspective. First, 'detecting bias' implies the possibility of a statement that is without bias (a 'truth'). Certainly, from Foucault's perspective, this would be problematic. Secondly, the list implies certain rules for identifying what constitutes the 'truth' (it should be logically consistent, based upon a logical argument and facts or evidence and so on). Again, from Foucault's perspective we should not simply accept these rules as being 'the' rules which produce a universal truth, but rather see them as the rules of a particular discourse (Foucault, 1991: 46–47). Yet, his own approach was not to abandon this kind of critical thinking but to turn it on itself – a kind of critical attitude turned to critical thinking, so to speak (Foucault, 1991). If we can live with some ambiguity as to the goals of critical thinking, then the practices identified within the cognitive research perspective appear to still fit reasonably well with both of the political philosophical positions already discussed.

If we then turn the gaze in the opposite direction and ask how the two philosophical perspectives on critical thinking look from a psychological standpoint, two things are evident.

- First, these perspectives do not present much that psychological science would recognise as evidence. Essentially, when faced with the question: 'What works when teaching critical thinking?', a psychological perspective will attempt to answer this with reference to both experimental and observational research, while the more philosophical approaches will instead ask, 'What is meant by "work", who defines it, and in what social and historical context?' Certainly, questioning the question can be seen as interesting and valid, but answering it may also be worth a shot.
- Secondly, it appears that both of the versions of critical thinking explored so far appear essentially similar in that both of them iden-

> tify that critical thinking involves recognising ideas as being mental objects, that is to say they are recognised as *representations* of reality rather than being reality-in-itself. Critical thinking then, from this perspective, involves mental work with ideas or 'thinking about thinking'. In cognitive sciences, this is generally known as 'metacognition' (Kuhn, 1999: 17).

The term metacognition refers to 'knowledge about the nature of people as cognisers, about the nature of different cognitive tasks, and about possible strategies that can be applied to the solution of different tasks. It also includes executive skills for monitoring and regulating one's cognitive activities' (Flavell, 1999: 21). Despite 30 years of research, metacognition remains something of a fuzzy concept (Flavell, 1981: 37; Zohar, 1999; McCormick, 2003: 82). This is in part because it draws on two distinct psychological research traditions: a developmental psychology tradition, building on Piaget's work on 'reflection' (which is, incidentally, why one might have expected more than a single reference to Piaget in the pages of *Policy and Practice – a Development Education Review*), and an information processing perspective which has tended to focus on what people know about and how they control their own process of learning, memorising and recalling (Jaušovec, 2008: 47; Tarricone, 2011). Metacognition can be thought of as a type of internal conversation in which someone asks questions about their own thinking, such as: 'What is my goal?', 'What are my criteria of judgement as to how well I succeed?', 'Where did this goal and these criteria come from?', 'What is my context and what resources do I have?', 'What sort of strategies or practices have previously worked in this kind of context?', 'Is my strategy working?', 'If so why and if not, why not?', 'How could I do things differently?', 'How well did I do?'.

If metacognition is important for development education because critical thinking is metacognitive work, it is also important because it is tied to the 'action' dimension. This action dimension is understood, in psychological terms, as a problem of 'transfer', that is, the desire to have learners take what they have learned in one context (a workshop or a classroom) and to apply it or use it in a different context (which might be a different class, the ballot box or when shopping). Bransford and Schwartz (1999) argue that, while it is typically assumed transfer is a normal and natural part of 'education' (as distinct from 'training'), transfer has been found to be remarkably difficult to achieve, and knowledge and skills tend to be highly contextualised such that people are much more likely to remember things, use strategies or engage in practices in contexts similar to those in which they have previously learned them. Bransford and Schwartz (1999) have argued that there is substantial evidence that an emphasis on metacognition in learning has been shown to increase transfer. This is not to suggest, of course, that transfer from education into lived practice is *only* a question of metacognition. Much of my recent research has been on emotional dimensions of teaching and learning (Corcoran and Tormey, 2010, 2012a, 2012b, 2012c) precisely because emotion is also important in relation to the motivation, will and assurance to take action. My point here is just that metacognition seems to be an important part of the transfer puzzle.

Thinking of critical thinking as metacognition is potentially quite fruitful for development education because the psychological research evidence suggests that metacognition can be learned and can itself be transferred from context to context. Of course, we want to be careful here. As Foucault would remind us, what constituted evidence within a psychological domain is set by the standards of knowledge production within that discourse. This can be situated socially and historically and alternative ways of producing knowledge can be identified. Nonetheless, accepting that the evidence is produced within a discourse, does not mean we should simply dismiss it.

Veenman's (2011) review of the psychological evidence suggests there are three principles which are fundamental to effective instruction in metacognitive skills: they are (a) the synthesis position (which means that metacognition should be imbedded into real thinking tasks), (b) informed instruction (meaning learners should be clear that development of metacognitive skills is a goal and is likely to be of benefit) and (c) prolonged instruction. Alexander and Murphy have argued that metacognitive training should also adequately address transfer to new situations (1998: 32) (see also van Gelder [2005] for another way of formulating these implications).

What would this mean for development education?

- First, it would mean that we would pay attention to the notion that critical thinking is metacognitive and therefore our focus is on thinking about mental objects, that is ideas and practices that constitute ways of viewing and being in the world. From a Foucauldian perspective we might ask where these ideas and practices come from, who holds them, what contexts they are developed in and what other ways of viewing the world were available at that time.

From a socially critical perspective we might ask whose interests are served by particular sets of ideas. Nonetheless, in both cases, we would pay attention to the notion that our goal is to see ideas as ideas, to think about our thinking. Various techniques have been found to be useful in helping people to recognise ideas as mental objects including visualising techniques, like argument mapping or concept mapping (McAleese, 1998; van Gelder, 2005) and self-verbalisation and self-questioning (Janssen, 2002).

- Second, it implies that we should be explicit that we are trying to get learners to reflect upon their thinking, about what skills in specific we are trying to teach, and about why these skills are valuable. Relevant skills might include those identified by Beyer (1984) which were described above. For example, in the case of 'detecting bias', we might be explicit with learners that this is the goal before getting them to practice it.
- Third, we can say that these skills should not be taught as isolated or stand-alone skills, but should be integrated into the content matter that informs development education. Thinking skills can be practiced when there is material to be worked with.
- Fourth, we can say that people should be afforded opportunities to practice a learned skill in different contexts. If they start by 'detecting bias' in a text on Hugo Chávez, for instance, they should have the opportunity to practice the same skill in other contexts (texts on different topics) and with different types of texts (advertisements, articles, news, videos etc.)
- Fifth, we will need learners to have prolonged exposure to such opportunities. The implication here is that short workshops of a few hours or a few days are unlikely to be effective in achieving critical thinking goals. It could be argued, by implication, that working within the formal educational sector is likely to provide more opportunities for successful development of critical thinking – metacognitive skills. This, however, raises issues about the possibilities and limits of working within formal educational structures.

Conclusion

Critical thinking is seen as central to development education. Insofar as there is debate within development education as to what this means, that debate can be regarded as dominated by political and social philosophical discourses. Like all discourses, these can be seen to have both possibilities and limits. On a positive note, they provide an analytical language which can help us to evaluate development education practice (such as, for example, in terms of whether it is 'soft', 'socially critical' or 'critical thinking') and also allows us to be sensitised to potential danger with each approach (whether a 'socially critical' approach is being dogmatic, for example, or whether a 'critical thinking' approach is being rhetorical or uncritical with respect to some positions).

One way to explore the limitations of a particular discourse is to compare it with another, which makes possible different ways of viewing the world. With respect to the notion of 'critical' I have tried to do that by comparing political philosophical perspectives with each other but also by comparing them to a more psychological perspective. The aim is not to suggest that the psychological perspective is better – like all others it can be critiqued – but simply to suggest that comparing different perspectives allows the possibilities and limitations of each to be grasped. One possibility of the psychological perspective is that it can provide an evidence base which can inform our development education practice. This evidence, in turn, provides some interesting bases for evaluating or critiquing our practices.

References

Alexander, P A and Murphy, P K (1998) 'The research base for APA's learner-centred psychological principles' in N M Lambert and B L McCombs (eds) *How Students Learn: Reforming Schools through Learner-Centered Education*, Washington DC: American Psychological Association.

Andreotti, V (2006) 'Soft versus critical global citizenship education', *Policy & Practice: A Development Education Review*, Vol. 3, pp. 40–51.

Andreotti, V (2007) 'An ethical engagement with the Other: Spivak's ideas on education', *Critical Literacy, Theories and Practices*, 1(1), pp. 69–79.

Andreotti, V (2010) 'Post-colonial and post-critical "global citizenship education"' in G Elliot, C Fourali and S Issler (eds) *Education and Social Change, Connecting Local and Global Perspectives*, New York: Continuum.

Batteson, T J and Tormey, R (2011) 'Introduction: Development education and initial teacher education' in T J Batteson and R Tormey (eds) *Teaching Global Perspectives: Introducing Student Teachers to Development Education*, Dublin: Liffey Press.

Beyer, B K (1984) 'Improving thinking skills – Practical approaches', *The Phi Delta Kappan*, 65(8), pp. 556–560.

Bransford, J and Schwartz, D (1999) 'Rethinking transfer: A simple proposal with multiple implications', *Review of Research in Education*, Vol. 24, pp. 61–100.

Carr, W and Kemmis, S (1986) *Becoming Critical: Education, Knowledge and Action Research*, London: Falmer Press.

Clegg, S R (1989) *Frameworks of Power*, London: Sage.

Corbridge, S (1998) '"Beneath the pavement only soil": The poverty of post-development', *The Journal of Development Studies*, 34(6), pp. 138–148.

Corcoran, R P and Tormey, R (2010) 'Teacher education, emotional competencies and development education', *Procedia – Social and Behavioral Sciences*, Vol. 2, pp. 2448–2457.

Corcoran, R P and Tormey, R (2012a) 'Assessing emotional intelligence and its impact in caring professions: The value of a mixed methods approach in emotional intelligence work with teachers' in A Di Fabio (ed.) *Emotional Intelligence: New Perspectives and Application*, Rijeka: InTech.

Corcoran, R P and Tormey, R (2012b) *Developing Emotionally Competent Teachers: Emotional Intelligence and Pre-Service Teacher Education*, UK: Lang Publishing.

Corcoran, R P and Tormey, R (2012c) 'How emotionally intelligent are pre-service teachers?', *Teaching and Teacher Education*, Vol. 28, pp. 750–759.

Dillon, E (2003) 'Development studies and development education: Some questions in the light of post-development theory' in R Tormey (ed.) *Teaching Social Justice, Intercultural and Development Education Perspectives on Education's Context, Content and Methods*, Limerick and Dublin: CEDR and Ireland Aid.

Doggett, R and Phelan, F (2012) 'The times they are a changing: What role for development education in times of economic crisis', *Policy and Practice: A Development Education Review*, Vol. 14, pp. 85–99.

Egan, A (2012) 'The elephant in the room: Towards a discourse on development education and corporate power', *Policy and Practice: A Development Education Review*, Vol. 14, pp. 45–63.

Flavell, J H (1981) 'Cognitive monitoring' in W P Dickson (ed.) *Children's Oral Communication Skills*, New York: Academic Press.

Flavell, J H (1999) 'Cognitive development: Children's knowledge about the Mind', *Annual Review of Psychology*, Vol. 50, pp. 21–45.

Foucault, M (1991) 'What is enlightenment?' in P Rabinow (ed.) *The Foucault Reader: An Introduction to Foucault's Thought*, Harmondsworth: Penguin.

Foucault, M (1997) *Ethics: Essential Works of Foucault 1954–1984*, Harmondsworth: Penguin.

Freire, P (1970) *Pedagogy of the Oppressed*, Harmondsworth: Penguin.

Freire, P (1999) *Pedagogy of Hope: Reliving Pedagogy of the Oppressed*, New York: Continuum Books.

Gallie, W B (1955–1956) 'Essentially contested concepts', *Proceedings of the Aristotelian Society*, Vol. 56, pp. 167–198.

Habermas, J (1994) 'Some questions concerning the theory of power: Foucault again' in M Kelly (ed.) *Critique and Power: Recasting the Foucault – Habermas Debate*, Cambridge, MA: MIT Press.

Hinchion, C and Hennessy, J (2009) 'Reading other worlds, reading my world', *Policy & Practice: A Development Education Review*, Vol. 9, pp. 7–22.

Janssen, T (2002) 'Instruction in self-questioning as a literary reading strategy: An exploration of empirical research', *Educational Studies in Language and Literature*, Vol. 2, pp. 95–120.

Jaušovec, N (2008) 'Metacognition: A psychophysiological perspective' in M F Shaughnessy, M V J Veenman and C K Kennedy (eds) *Meta-Cognition: A Recent Review of Research, Theory, and Perspectives*, New York: Nova Publishers.

Kuhn, D (1999) 'A developmental model of critical thinking', *Educational Researcher*, 28(2), March, pp. 16–25.

Magno, C (2010) 'The role of metacognitive skills in developing critical thinking', *Metacognition and Learning*, 5(2), pp. 137–156.

Mahadeo, M (2009) 'Increasing/enhancing public awareness of international development issues: A comparative working analysis of formal and informal educational methodology and practice in Northern Ireland', *Policy and Practice: A Development Education Review*, Vol. 8, pp. 16–27.

McAleese, R (1998) 'The knowledge arena as an extension to the concept map: Reflection in action', *Interactive Learning Environments*, 6(x), pp. 1–22.

McCarthy, T (1990) 'The critique of impure reason: Foucault and the Frankfurt School', *Political Theory*, 18(3), pp. 437–469.

McCormick, C B (2003) 'Metacognition and learning' in W M Reynolds and G E Miller (eds) *Handbook of Psychology, Volume 7, Educational Psychology*, Hoboken, NJ: John Wiley & Sons, Inc.

Nanda, M (2002) 'Do the marginalised valorise the margins? Exploring the dangers of difference' in K Saunders (ed.) *Feminist Post-Development Thought, Rethinking Modernity, Post-colonialism and Representation*, London: Zed Books.

National Council for Curriculum and Assessment (2009) *Politics and Society: Draft Syllabus for Consultation*, Dublin: National Council for Curriculum and Assessment.

O'Sullivan, D (1999) 'Educational disadvantage: Excavating theoretical frameworks' in K Fahy (ed.) *Strategies to Address Educational Disadvantage*, Galway: Community Workers Co-operative.

O'Sullivan, D (2005) *Cultural Politics and Irish Education since the 1950s*, Dublin: Institute of Public Administration.

Rabinow, P (1991) 'Introduction' in P Rabinow (ed.) *The Foucault Reader: An Introduction to Foucault's Thought*, Harmondsworth: Penguin.

Spivak, G C (1988) 'Can the subaltern speak?' in C Nelson and L Grossberg (eds) *Marxism and the Interpretation of Culture*, Chicago: University of Illinois Press, pp. 271–313.

Tarricone, P (2011) *The Taxonomy of Metacognition*, Hove: Psychology Press.

Tormey, R (2003) 'Development education and critical thinking' in R Tormey (ed.) *Teaching Social Justice, Intercultural and Development Education Perspectives on Education's, Context, Content and Methods*, Limerick and Dublin: CEDR and Ireland Aid.

Tormey, R (2006) 'The construction of national identity through primary school history: The Irish case', *British Journal of Sociology of Education*, 27(3), pp. 311–324.

Tormey, R and Gleeson, J (2012) 'The gendering of global citizenship: Findings from a large-scale quantitative study on global citizenship education experiences', *Gender and Education*, 24(6), pp. 627–645.

van Gelder, T J (2005) 'Teaching critical thinking: some lessons from cognitive science', *College Teaching*, Vol. 53, pp. 41–46.

Veenman, M V J (2011) 'Learning to self-monitor and self-regulate' in R E Mayer and PA Alexander (eds) *Handbook of Research on Learning and Instruction*, New York: Routledge, pp. 197–218.

Zohar, A (1999) 'Teachers: Metacognitive knowledge and the instruction of higher order thinking', *Teaching and Teacher Education*, Vol. 15, pp. 413–429.

Part II
Development Education Sectors

6

Young People and Development: The Role of Global Youth Work in Engagement and Learning

Paul Adams

Introduction

In this chapter I will outline the definitions and principles of what is known as global youth work and relate this to learning and development in the wider youth work sector. I will also look at how global youth work has been interpreted and what makes it distinctive, in terms of its approach, agenda and intended outcomes; be it young people's personal, social and political development or awareness of global development issues. Historically many local government youth services and voluntary and community sector organisations in the UK and Ireland have explored global issues with young people through international work, including youth exchanges, links and intercultural learning as distinct curriculum areas. However this work has always been constrained by the limited funding available and a lack of understanding of the value of this work as a core activity at a strategic level within the youth work and development education (DE) sectors and government departments. This chapter will identify some of the perceived differences between global youth work and school-based development education in regard to aims and methodology, in particular youth work's principle of 'voluntarism' and a desire to be 'action focused' involving the active participation of young people in curriculum design and delivery.

Global youth work and development education

Development education approaches to work with young people have often focused on the classroom and drawn on an understanding of the value of experiential learning (Kolb, 1984). For example the use of group work, role play and simulation games (see the *Global Dimension* website, Think Global, 2013). Much of this work takes place within the formal context of school, with associated standards of pupil behaviour and limited scope for critical questioning of the status quo, authority and power within these structures (Elias, 1976). This approach reflects the belief that to reach a wide youth audience schools are the most direct and economical route, where work can be undertaken in a structured environment and learning outcomes can be controlled and measured in line with national curricula. However it could be suggested that there is limited scope for the implementation of the principles and methodologies of 'popular education' or education for 'critical consciousness' as advocated by John Dewey (1933) and Paulo Freire (1972), amongst others, in this Western, European school setting in which young people are often subjected to a directive approach involving low levels of meaningful participation (Arnstein, 1969; Hart, 1992). Farthing (2012: 3) suggests, participation is 'a process where young people, as active citizens, take part in, express views on, and have decision-making power about issues that affect them'.

We know that not all young people are engaged with learning at school but they can still benefit from and contribute to development education in informal settings. This is reflected in the work of the development agency Y Care International which has found that:

> [T]he majority of the young people we work with in the UK and Ireland are from marginalised backgrounds. As these young people are not reached through the formal education sector, we believe that global youth work is a far more relevant tool than development education (Y Care International, 2013).

This approach is evident in Y Care's innovative 'Guns, Gang and Knives' project with gang members, and the 'Global Youth Work Behind Bars' project with young offenders (see http://www.ycareinternational.org). I propose that a youth work approach closely resembles the empowering methodologies advocated by educationalists such as Freire, as youth work takes place in an informal community context, where voluntary participation can lead to a more equal relationship between the learner and educator (Rogers, 1969). This has the potential to empower young people, and for the aims and aspirations of development education to truly flourish.

Global youth work is a form of development education. However, what distinguishes global youth work from DE is that it starts from young people's own perspectives and experiences and develops a negotiated agenda for learning. Global youth work also focuses primarily on the impact of globalisation on the lives of young people and communities rather than education about the *development* and *underdevelopment* of countries (DEA, 2007). Although development education shares many of the values and principles that underpin effective youth work, it often has its own agenda from the outset, linked to specific campaigns or concerns and has historically taken place in more formal educational settings. As Y Care puts it: 'what distinguishes global youth work from development education is its focus on young people taking action – it empowers them to make a decision to do something positive about the issues they learn about' (Y Care International, 2013).

Youth work principles

Tony Jeffs and Mark Smith suggest 'informal education' is the main distinguishing feature of youth work and youth workers should be concerned with:

- Focusing on young people
- Emphasising voluntary participation and relationships
- Committing to association
- Being friendly and informal, and acting with integrity
- The education and, more broadly the welfare of young people (Jeffs and Smith, 2005).

The elements that make youth work a distinctive and powerful form of education are reflected in the established definitions of youth work; where the content of the curriculum is less important than the principles of dialogue, voluntarism and participation. The English National Youth Agency (NYA, 2013) defines the purpose of youth work as to: 'facilitate and support young people's growth through dependence to interdependence, by encouraging their personal and social development and enabling them to have a voice, influence and place in their communities and society'. This definition goes further to suggest that:

> Youth Work offers both 'planned' (non-formal) 'and spontaneous' (informal) opportunities for people to learn through experience about self, others and society. Youth Work occurs when young people learn by interacting with their peers and others, share a range of new experiences which extend, challenge and excite the

individual, and have opportunities for reflection, planning and action (NYA, 2013).

This is reflected in the Republic of Ireland where the Youth Work Act 2001 states youth work to be: 'a planned programme of education designed for the purpose of aiding and enhancing the personal and social development of young persons through their voluntary participation' (Department of Children and Youth Affairs, 2001: 7). Williamson (2007) usefully summarises the key elements of youth work, suggesting that it is often portrayed as follows:

- Its goals relate to the personal and social development of young people;
- Its methods are embedded in personal relationships and experiential learning;
- Its values are based on voluntarism, working from the interests of young people and winning their consent rather than coercing their compliance (2007: 38).

This 'winning of young people's consent' and therefore their participation in a conversation, activity or a programme is key to youth work; an educational process which is based on relationships and dialogue, where the principle of voluntary engagement is central. It has been suggested by Jeffs and Smith (2005) and others that it is this 'experiential learning' that underpins youth work, and similarly development education places some emphasis on this approach. It is this approach that is primarily based on the assumption that: 'we can act upon our experiences rather than simply having them. It is this process of drawing out meaning from experience, often through reflection and discussion with others, which extends and deepens that experience, freeing us to learn from it' (Crosby, 2005: 54).

One of the central roles of the youth worker is to enable the young person to reflect upon, and consequently learn from, their day to day personal experiences. Youth workers should be proactive and seek to initiate and facilitate experiences which young people will learn from. Jeffs and Smith (2005) propose that education can be viewed on a spectrum, from a more idealistic 'conversation based' informal education ('free association' youth work) to a 'negotiated curriculum' ('non-formal' structured programmes of activity), towards the set curriculum of formal education (e.g. secondary school). Global youth work can be seen to be located between the 'informal' and 'non-formal'.

Definitions of global youth work offered by development agencies and others (Think Global for example) emphasise the *informal educational* nature of the work. However the manner in which much of the work with young people is delivered is centred on the *non-formal*, where there is a structure and is organised by the educator (youth worker) to specific ends (Ord, 2007).

Approaches to global youth work

The development of the term global youth work can be traced back to 1995 and the *World of Difference* report by Bourn and McCollum. This research report aimed to 'give an overview of development education within youth work in the UK' (1995: 6), and concluded that 'rather than promoting development education within youth work, one should be using the phrase "making global connections and promoting global perspectives"' (Ibid.: 94). This was the first step towards the notion of a distinctive 'global youth work' rather than development education with young people in the UK. In Figure 6.1 I have indicated the different types of work with young people that have an international or global dimension, and which have given rise to the concept of global youth work. All of these approaches have a global dimension

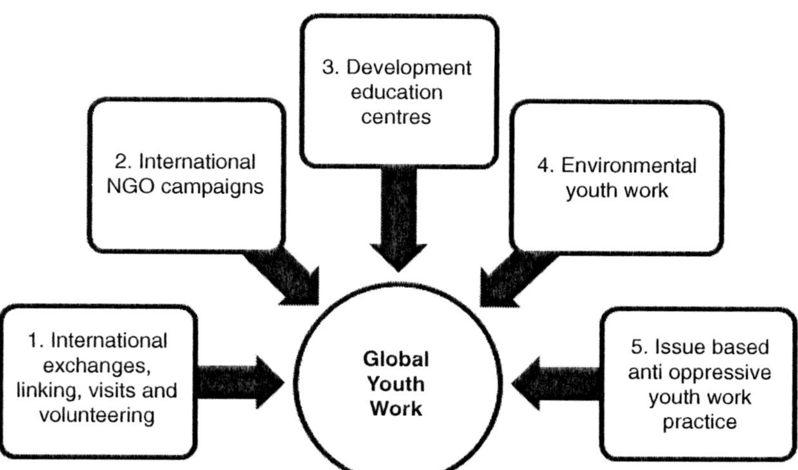

Figure 6.1 Global youth work conceptual model
Source: Adams, 2014.

but not all reflect the values of that which would later be termed 'global youth work'.

If we look at these areas, we can identify their contribution to the development of global youth work:

International exchanges, linking, visits and volunteering have essentially been about the mobility of young people and the resulting personal and social development and intercultural learning that takes place as a result (Commonwealth Youth Exchange Council [CYEC], 2013). There is a long history of these types of approaches within youth work organisations in the UK and Ireland and they continue to be delivered often based on historical, community or individual links with particular countries e.g. within the Commonwealth by members of black and minority ethnic (BME) communities.

International non-governmental organisation (NGO) campaigns have again contained an element of awareness raising, aimed at engaging young people in fundraising and or contributing to specific campaigns. A powerful example of this was the Make Poverty History campaign in 2005.

A relatively small number of development education centres in the UK and Ireland have organised youth work events, projects and workshops to engage young people in development education and curriculum-led activities, alongside the loan of educational resources to local youth workers. Some have developed more strategic responses in recent times for example the Global Youth Work Partnership East Midlands (GYWPEM) which involves a range of organisations in regional youth work events and training.

Environmental issues have long been a concern for some youth workers; in particular those in voluntary sector youth work organisations such as the Scouts and Woodcraft Folk, where this is reflected in their missions and programmes. Moreover, some environmental organisations such as Friends of the Earth have engaged in awareness raising work within the youth sector toward engaging young people with messages about sustainability, lifestyle choices and specific campaigns.

There has been a long and rich history of 'issue-based' anti-oppressive practice in the youth work sector. Anti-racist and anti-sexist approaches in particular have an inherent international dimension linked closely to the discrimination faced by young people from BME communities and young women (see Chauhan, 1989; Batsleer, 2013). From the 1960s we also saw a focus on sexuality and disability as distinct foci of youth work practice (Davies, 1999) and these again have often drawn on experiences, models, inspiration and solidarity from across the world. An anti-discriminatory approach is also reflected in the key principles and National Occupational Standards of youth work including 'value equality of opportunity and diversity, challenging oppression and discrimination' (LSI, 2012: 42).

The Development Education Association (DEA), now Think Global, set out a definition and a range of principles of global youth work in a *Global Youth Work Training and Practice Manual*. It states that global youth work:

- [S]tarts from young people's everyday experiences;
- engages them in critical analysis of local and global influences on their lives and communities;
- raises awareness of globalisation, the world's history and rich diversity of peoples, particularly in relation to issues of justice and equity;
- encourages young people to explore the relationships and links between their personal lives and the local and global communities;
- seeks young people's active participation to build alliances and create change, locally and globally (DEA, 2007: 21).

The emphasis on globalisation as the key term seeks to replace terms such as international work, international dimension to youth work or development education with young people. It has sought to place global youth work firmly in the tradition of youth work, aligning it with the principles of informal education with an added emphasis on young people taking action and recognising an unequal process of globalisation. These principles are supported within the Republic of Ireland by McCrea and Sheehan (2008) whom, whilst utilising the term development education, suggest that:

> [D]evelopment education places young people at the heart of the learning process. It starts with their experiences, perspectives and ideas and provides them with an opportunity to explore and take action on issues which are important to them and it shares many of the same principles as good youth work. These include starting with and valuing young people's own views, learning through participation and promoting equality, responsibility and mutual respect (McCrea and Sheehan, 2008: 53, 55).

Figure 6.2 Global dimension in youth work
Source: Based on Woolley, 2009: 22.

Woolley's *Global Dimension in Youth Work* (2009) model seeks to explain the elements which are essential to the understanding and delivery of global youth work. He suggests that three essential components are required to be in place to ensure that a comprehensive picture is offered which adheres to the key principles of global youth work.

To paraphrase Woolley, *global issues* are essentially the content or topic to be addressed with young people such as HIV/AIDS or child labour, which have both a local and global dimension. *Global perspectives* are about the inclusion of voices of peoples from the 'global south', whether they are in the UK or elsewhere (this can be linked to elements of issue-based anti-oppressive youth work mentioned earlier). *Global experiences* are concerned with the creation of experiences of a 'global' nature, for example youth exchanges, international trips or linking people by utilising technology like Skype. Any of these in isolation can be valuable for young people's personal and social development, but all elements need to be addressed to result in global youth work's desired outcomes, as identified by the DEA:

Knowledge and understanding – young people may develop knowledge and critical understanding of:

- local, national and global societies and cultures;
- the global dimensions of the world around them;
- the role of human rights locally and globally;
- the impact of personal or local action on global events.

Skills – young people may develop the ability to:

- analyse issues critically;
- carry out enquiries;
- challenge their own and others' attitudes;
- build alliances;
- show empathy;
- participate in activities.

Attitudes – young people may develop attitudes that demonstrate:

- self-respect;
- self-awareness;
- support for justice and fairness;
- open-mindedness;
- a global perspective on their world;
- an orientation toward action (DEA, 2007: 25).

In 2010 the DEA's Global Youth Action (GYA) programme developed a model of global youth work based on a youth action approach. The Centre for Social Action (2007: 5) define youth action as a 'way of supporting young people to develop and lead' and 'giving young people opportunities to play a key role in the design, delivery and evaluation of projects' including peer education. The GYA programme was instrumental in the development of a reflective practice model titled Connect, Challenge, Change (CCC). The CCC model could be seen as an attempt to make sense of the practice of global youth work in a substantial Global Youth Action programme over five years. The project suggested:

> [W]e help *connect* young people to the global issues that matter to them. We support them to make the connections between the personal, local and global, and to connect with peers who share their passions and concerns. We encourage young people to *challenge* themselves, to gain a more critical understanding of the world around them, and to challenge inequality and injustice. We support young people to plan and take action to bring about positive *change* towards a more just and sustainable world (DEA, 2010a: 3).

The CCC model appears to reflect a simplified version of Kolb's (1984) or Lewin's (1951) Learning Cycle, where there is an *experience* (global connections identified/engineered by the youth worker), which

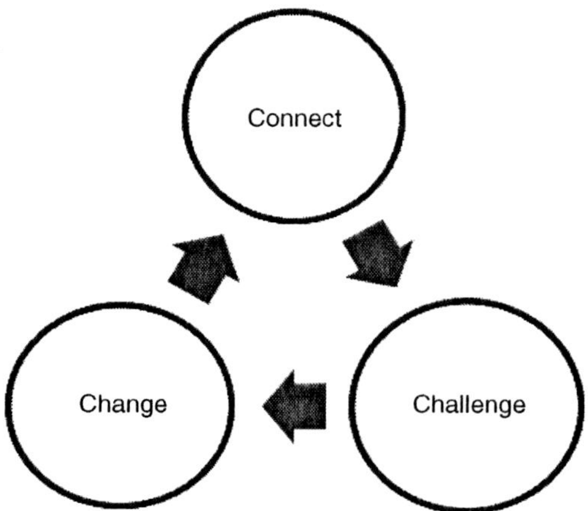

Figure 6.3 Connect Challenge Change model
Source: DEA, 2010a: 3.

leads to *reflection* (challenge) and is followed by *action* (change). All stages are seen to be essential to the learning process although the change stage is seen to be a key element in moving beyond raising awareness to personal or collective action. Uninformed action in itself is not sufficient; involving young people in action (e.g. campaign 'stunts') without first making emotional and intellectual connections to their personal lives and local concerns will reduce the likelihood of a deep reflective process and meaningful learning taking place. This is supported in part by the research of Devlin and Tierney whose findings suggest that for young people it is often 'difficult to make the connection with their own lives. Where there was any success in doing so, it most frequently involved making connections with the lives and circumstances of other young people, and in relatively tangible ways' (2010: 7).

This simple CCC model may be helpful for youth workers in planning interventions with young people. The DEA (2010b) discussed the origins and potential impact of this model in a research study which found that the CCC model 'provides an accessible framework and language and a "learning journey" design tool for global youth work in an outcomes-driven age. Focussing on the "how to" helps to integrate conceptualisation, learning progression and action' (DEA, 2010b: 3).

The practice of global youth work

In 2011 a small scale piece of qualitative research to map global youth work concluded that the focus on project work and curriculum resources suggests a mostly (but not exclusively) *ad hoc*, funding-led approach to practice (Adams, 2011). This is in contrast to an integrated approach as advocated by policy briefings such as *Young People in a Global Society* (2002), which stated that 'principal youth officers, senior managers and decision makers need to build on the practice of individual motivated youth workers and the interests of young people, and develop organisational policy frameworks [that] develop youth service/organisational mission/curriculum statements that include global youth work' (DEA, 2002: 9). For some global youth work is still seen as a 'curriculum area' (Woolley's 'global issues') equivalent to sexual health, sport or arts work for instance, which is addressed at various times in a youth work programme rather than as an *underpinning global dimension* to all curriculum areas. This view is underlined in Devlin and Tierney's (2010) work in which they suggest 'a focus on programmes – at all levels within the youth work sector – can at times work against the development of integrated understandings and responses' (2010: 8). This focus on the content and delivery (programmes) can distract from a strategic approach to the integration of global youth work in mainstream practice.

The 2011 study asked a sample of people who identified themselves as being involved in, or who have an interest in, global youth work what they felt were the most important aims of global youth work to be in order of priority (Adams, 2011). The largest proportion of respondents felt that 'to develop/empower the individual young person' was the most important aim of global youth work, reflecting the distinct youth work nature of the approach and perhaps in contrast to the broader aims of development education. The second largest response identified the need 'to challenge young people's attitudes/assumptions about others and the world around them'. The third significant choice was 'to increase young people's knowledge of development and globalisation issues, e.g. fair trade, climate change' (Adams, 2011: 8).

Based on these responses it appears that the skills and attitudes considered necessary to be an effective global youth work practitioner are not dissimilar to those of an effective youth worker, who engages young people in dialogue and some form of non-formal education (e.g. project work), which leads to personal or collective action in line with the National Occupational Standards for youth work (LSI, 2012). The research confirmed that there was little evidence of what can strictly be defined as informal education in the global youth work sector. Some workers stated that they deliver 'one-off' activities, but even these seem to have a method, content and outcome in mind after (or even before) an initial conversation with young people (Adams, 2011). 'Fundamentally, youth work with individuals and groups stems from negotiation and mutual agreement', which does not often occur in the formal education setting (Merton et al., 2004). And as one respondent stated during the 2011 qualitative study: 'ultimately global youth work is a vehicle for youth work to take place. It must be about young people and enabling their personal and social development rather than any other external agenda' (Adams, 2011: 7).

Global youth work, non-formal or informal, is based on a negotiated curriculum as a point of principle because engagement in youth work is voluntary and young people can walk away if they feel an encounter has no immediate connection to them and is not interesting or attractive. Consequently this increases the efforts required by the worker to ensure that any intervention is relevant and engaging. The practice of non-formal education is increasingly reflected by the current nature of youth work practice in local and commissioned youth services (Adams, 2011: 34). This type of practice increasingly requires youth workers to utilise structured work with young people, which results in evidence of progression and attainment, rather than informal education approaches, for example media or arts projects. According to the National Youth Agency (2007): 'Youth work offers both planned and spontaneous opportunities for people to learn through experience about self, others and society'. However, it is increasingly the *targeted* groups which are prioritised, recognised and rewarded within youth services. Ironically global youth work practice, rather than the theory, may be more in tune with this context.

It may also be useful to locate global youth work in relation to an established model of youth work, in particular Hurley and Treacy's (1993) *Models of Youth Work – Sociological Framework* which identifies a typology of youth work. In Hurley and Treacy's model the role of the youth worker ranges from character building, personal development, critical social education to radical social change. The expected outcomes of this activity will differ according to the perspective or paradigm adopted, consciously or subconsciously. Global youth work is aligned to a more radical *Critical Social Education* model where:

- Youth work has the positive intention of transferring power to young people;

- Relationship with young people is undertaken with a view to 'engaging' them as partners;
- Youth worker adopts the role of 'problem poser';
- Young people actively involved in identifying, exploring and understanding issues of concern to them;
- Two way process of mutual dialogue between young people and adults;
- Action is the result of analysis and reflection (Hurley and Treacy, 1993: 41–43).

Hurley and Treacy suggest the 'outcomes for young people' of this model include:

- Young people have developed the ability to analyse and assess alternatives;
- the capacity to define 'their position' in their world and the skills to act to change it if they sought to;
- Young people are aware of the inequities which institutions promote;
- Young people are active in mobilising groups at a local level to seek changes within existing structures.

According to Hurley and Treacy (1993: 44) the 'outcomes for society' might result in institutions undergoing 'internal structural change to respond to demands for change'. This model is reflected in the stated aims and principles of global youth work, for instance young people developing the necessary skills, knowledge and attitudes to: 'take action locally to combat the negative effects of globalisation and enhance the positive by developing and supporting ethical alliances and partnerships between young people, organisations and networks in the UK and across the world' (DEA, 2007: 24).

Professional youth work training

Nationally recognised, professional youth work has existed in the UK since the early 1960s, and now the National (Joint Negotiating Committee [JNC]) Qualification, validated by the National Youth Agency in England, requires an Honours Degree delivered via one of the 58 professional training routes (NYA, 2013). In 2002 it was recommended in the *Young People in Global Society* document (DEA, 2002: 7) that 'initial training courses in higher education need to: Recognise the skills, knowledge and experiences required to develop global youth work through curriculum content and placements, including youth work curriculum design and delivery as well as analysis'.

Indeed the criteria for professional youth work training have gone some way to recognise the value of the global dimension in the skills and knowledge which should be possessed by youth workers. For those advocating global youth work the anticipation has been that this will lead to a more 'globally aware' set of professionals emerging from professionally validated programmes/courses, who will in turn implement programmes with young people – including some of the most difficult to reach – with 'global' messages. However there has been little research to measure this impact as yet, other than the work of Sallah (2008: 3) who concluded in *The State of Global Youth Work in Higher Education Institutions (HEIs)* summary report that 'ways of working with young people that address the global dimension are understood variously'. He identified 'four main classifications: namely Development Education, Concept and Process of Globalisation, Global Youth Work and Global Citizenship' and that '90% of respondents from HEIs said that GYW is covered within their institution' (43 out of a possible 50 HEIs were contacted).

Importantly there are now references to the global context to youth work within the National Occupational Standards (NOS) for Youth Work (LSI, 2012). Reference to the NOS learning outcomes and assessment is an essential requirement for validation of *professional* youth work training routes in the UK. This is in addition to the Higher Education *Subject benchmark statement: Youth and community work, Quality Assurance Agency* (*QAA*) (2009), essential for *academic* validation in higher education in England. If we look at each in turn we can identify the integration of the global dimension.

The National Occupational Standards for Youth Work (LSI, 2012) specify that youth workers should be able to: 'engage with communities to promote the interests and contributions of young people'. The knowledge and understanding required is: 'how local, regional, national and global issues and activities can impact upon each other, including how local activities relate to the wider context, and vice versa' (p. 25). The standards locate the global dimension within the arena of citizenship and youth workers are asked to: 'encourage young people to broaden their horizons to be active citizens' and be able to 'explore constructively with young people the concept of citizenship including its relevance at local, national, international and global levels; promote an awareness of the wider local, national and global communities, and explore and identify the benefits of involvement with these' and 'explore with young people the global context to personal, local and national decisions and actions' (p. 40). The knowledge and understanding required includes: 'what is meant by effective citizenship, including its relation to families, local communities, local and national government, and international and global affairs' (p. 41).

The *Subject benchmark statement: Youth and community work* (QAA, 2009: 13) states that the 'approaches to learning and development' should include:

> global learning, environmental learning and theological or faith-sensitive learning, using characteristic methods of informal education, which require practitioners to locate their practice within a matrix of power dynamics across local, global and faith divides, citizenship learning, collaborative and open enquiry and political education.

As might be expected there is little detail in these standards and benchmarks as to how these areas should be addressed in the HEI curriculum or in youth work practice per se, leading to the variance in delivery identified by Sallah (2008). Although subject to monitoring, periodic review and revalidation, HEIs and other training providers are free to interpret these standards and benchmarks as they see fit. So whilst the integration of a global dimension into these standards and professional requirements is to be welcomed there is little evidence that these developments have resulted in an increased awareness of the importance of a global dimension amongst youth work professionals, or whether this has resulted in a significant change to youth work practice.

Local 'non-professional' training, some with accreditation validated by the National Open College Network, have been offered by global youth work projects over a number of years, including; Think Global and Global Youth Work Partnership East Midlands in England, Centre for Global Education in Northern Ireland and Cyfanfyd in Wales. In addition Y Care International has worked with the YMCA George Williams' College to develop a stand alone, credit bearing 'Certificate in Global Youth Work', one of the few offered in the UK to date. This training has been offered as a professional development opportunity for interested youth workers but this is not on a scale which will have a significant impact on mainstream youth work practice. Interestingly these organisations are not youth work organisations, and are located in the voluntary and community (charity) sector, which tend not to employ professionally (JNC) qualified youth work staff, nor are they required to adhere to National Occupational Standards for youth work. In the UK these programmes have, until recently, largely been supported by the Department for International Development and other grant aid providers like the Big Lottery Fund. The government sources are, as always, subject to the whim of policy and unsurprisingly global youth work, by its very nature a youth action focused, form of critical pedagogy, is not a current government priority.

Conclusion

In theoretical terms global youth work can be identified as a form of *Critical Social Education*, employing a youth action approach, concerned with increasing young people's capacity to effect change at a personal and structural level, by contributing to local, national and global communities whilst developing their own social capital. Global youth work requires, and desires, high levels of participation by young people in the design and focus of non-formal activities, unlike more mainstream school-based development education where the curriculum and delivery is largely set externally by the provider and funding sources. Within global youth work the outcomes for the young people themselves are important, unlike youth campaigns, and can include critical thinking skills which contribute to a more holistic understanding of globalisation and development issues.

Global youth work offers non-formal educational opportunities for often marginalised young people outside of the formal education system. It often employs experiential learning approaches and its 'action focused' approach to utilising young people's energy and enthusiasm, supports their personal and social development in line with youth work's core principles. Historically youth work organisations have addressed elements of *Global Issues* and *Global Perspectives*, in relation to issues of equality and diversity and anti-discriminatory practice and offered *Global Experiences* in the form of youth exchanges and links, within the youth work curriculum. The informal, voluntary, organic, negotiated nature of youth work and the lack of predetermined learning goals can be perceived as a lack of focus or rigour by funders, formal educators and government departments, leading to marginalisation of the work, especially in times of austerity. But these principles can be understood as the strengths of global youth work, the ability to engage often disadvantaged young people in flexible, relevant learning about the world and their place in it, by supporting them to take action to change it.

References

Adams, P (2011) *A Mapping of Global Youth Work*, London: Think Global.

Adams, P (2014) 'Young people and development: The role of global youth work in engagement and learning' in S McCloskey (ed.) *Development Education in Policy and Practice*, Basingstoke, Hampshire: Palgrave Macmillan.

Arnstein, S R (1969) 'A ladder of citizen participation', *Journal of the American Planning Association*, 35(4), July 1969, pp. 216–224.

Batsleer, J (2013) *Youth Working with Girls and Young Women in Community Settings*, Surrey: Ashgate.

Bourn, D and McCollum, A (1995) *A World of Difference – Making Global Connections in Youth Work*, London: DEA.

Butters, S and Newell, S (1978) *Realities of Training: A Review of the Training of Adults Who Volunteer to Work With Young People in the Youth and Community Services*, Leicester: National Youth Bureau.

Centre for Social Action (2007) *How Youth Action Volunteering Enhances the Social Capital of Young People and Their Communities*, Leicester: De Montfort University.

Chauhan, V (1989) *Beyond Steel Bands 'n' Samosas: Black Young People in the Youth Service*, Leicester: National Youth Bureau.

Commonwealth Youth Exchange Council (CYEC) (2013) *Youth Exchanges*, available: http://www.cyec.org.uk/exchanges/youth-exchanges (accessed 13 March 2013).

Crosby, M (2005) 'Working with people as an informal educator' in L Deer Richardson and M Wolfe, *Principles and Practice of Informal Education*, London: Routledge Farmer, p. 54.

Davies, B (1999) *The History of the Youth Service in England*, Leicester: Youth Work Press.

Development Education Association (DEA) (2002) *Young People in a Global Society*, London: DEA.

DEA (2007) *Global Youth Work Practice Training and Resource Manual*, London: DEA.

DEA (2010a) *Connect, Challenge, Change – A Practical Guide to Global Youth Work*, London: DEA.

DEA (2010b) *Global Youth Action Evaluation Summary*, available: http://www.think-global.org.uk/resources/item.asp?d=2113 (accessed 13 March 2013).

Department of Children and Youth Affairs (2001) *Youth Work Act*, available: http://www.dcya.gov.ie/viewdoc.asp?fn=%2Fdocuments%2Fyouthaffairs%2Fpolicies.htm (accessed 12 May 2013).

Devlin, M and Tierney, H (2010) *Standpoints Attitudes of Young People and Youth Workers to Development and Global Justice Issues*, Dublin: National Youth Council of Ireland.

Dewey, J (1933) *How We Think. A Restatement of the Relation of Reflective Thinking to the Educative Process* (Revised edition), Boston: D. C. Heath.

Elias, J L (1976) *Conscientization and Deschooling: Freire's and Illich's Proposals for Reshaping Society*, Philadelphia: Westminster Press.

Farthing, R. (2012) 'Why youth participation? Some justifications and critiques of youth participation using New Labour's youth policies as a case study', *Youth and Policy*, No. 109, September 2012, pp. 71–97, available: http://www.youthandpolicy.org/ (accessed 12 May 2013).

Freire, P (1972) *Pedagogy of the Oppressed*, Harmondsworth: Penguin.

Friends of the Earth (2013) *What We Stand For*, available: http://www.foe.co.uk/what_we_do/about_us/friends_earth_values_beliefs.html (accessed 13 March 2013).

Global Youth Work Partnership East Midlands (GYWPEM) (2013) available: http://www.gywpem.org.uk/Default.aspx (accessed 17 March 2013).

Hart, R. (1992) *Children's Participation: From Tokenism to Citizenship*, Florence: UNICEF International Child Development Centre.

Hurley, L and Treacy, D (1993) *Models of Youth Work – Sociological Framework*, Dublin: Irish Youth Work Press.

Jeffs, T and Smith, M (2005) *Informal Education – Conversation, Democracy and Learning*, Nottingham: Education Heretics Press.

Kolb, D A (1984) *Experiential Learning: Experience as the Source of Learning and Development*, Englewood Cliffs, New Jersey: Prentice-Hall.

Lewin, K (1951) *Field Theory in Social Sciences*, London: Harper Row.

Learning and Skills Improvement Service (2012*) Youth Work National Occupational Standards*, available: http://www.excellencegateway.org.uk/node/61 (accessed 23 March 2013).

Make Poverty History (2005), available: http://www.makepovertyhistory.org/takeaction/ (accessed 13 March 2013).

McCrea, N and Sheehan, J (2008) 'Going global: Good practice guidelines for development education in youth work', *Youth Studies Ireland*, 3(1), pp. 52–67.

Merton, B et al. (2004) *An Evaluation of the Impact of Youth Work in England*, Youth Affairs Unit De Montfort University, Research Report RR606, Leicester: De Montfort Expertise Ltd.

National Youth Agency (2007) *The NYA Guide to Youth Work in England*, available: http://nya.org.uk/catalogue/workforce-1/nya-guide-to-youth-work-and-youth-services (accessed 10 January 2014), p. 5.

NYA (2013) *What is Youth Work?* available: http://www.nya.org.uk/workforce-and-training/want-to-work-in-youth-work#What is youth work? (accessed 23 March 2013).

Ord, J (2007) *Youth Work Process, Product and Practice: Creating an Authentic Curriculum in Work with Young People*, Exeter: Russell House Publishing.

QAA (2009) *Subject Benchmark Statement: Youth and Community Work*, available: http://www.qaa.ac.uk/Publications/InformationAndGuidance/Pages/Subject-benchmark-statement-Youth-and-community-work.aspx (accessed 23 March 2013).

Rogers, C (1969) *Freedom to Learn: A View of What Education Might Become*, Columbus, OH: Merrill.

Sallah, M (2008) *The State of Global Youth Work in Higher Education Institution (HEIs)*, Leicester: De Montfort University.

Scouts (2013) *What We Do*, available: http://scouts.org.uk/home/ (accessed 23 March 2013).

Think Global (2013) *Global Dimension ... the World in Your Classroom*, available: http://globaldimension.org.uk/ (accessed 23 March 2013).

Williamson, H (2007) 'Youth work in a changing policy environment' in R Harrison et al. (ed.) *Leading Work With Young People*, London: Sage, p. 38.

Woodcraft Folk (2013) *About Woodcraft Folk*, available: http://woodcraft.org.uk/ (accessed 13 March 2013).

Woolley, G (2009) 'The global dimension in youth work: A conceptual model', Global Education Derby, available: http://files.invosis.com/ged/20110203013740683_wrhqrpmtiwj.pdf (accessed 22 January 2014).

Woolley, G and Valdivia, R (2011) *The Processes and Outcomes of Global Youth Work*, available: http://www.gywpem.org.uk/Downloads.aspx (accessed 17 March 2013).

Y Care International (2013) *About Global Youth Work*, available: http://www.ycareinternational.org/810/what-is-global-youth-work/about-global-youth-work.html (accessed 13 March 2013).

7

Moving Beyond Boundaries: Development Education in Initial Teacher Education

Fionnuala Waldron

Introduction

Teacher education has undergone something akin to a revolution in Ireland in the past few years. Consigned for decades to the torpid backwaters of national policy where it was intermittently prodded and nudged by government reports and critical commentary, it was generally left to its own devices, responding as best it could to the changing needs of Irish society and the developing knowledge-base of education, pedagogy and children's learning. More recently, policy initiatives, which instituted new regulatory procedures and structures, have led to a period of sustained focus on the processes and outcomes of initial teacher education (ITE). Having come late to the international table of sectoral review and reform, Ireland has avoided some of the market-led, competency-driven excesses evident in other more diverse systems (Smith, 2012). Premised on a view of teacher education as a continuum of lifelong learning, teacher education policy in Ireland has drawn on key theories and discourses in teacher education around reflective and inquiry-oriented practice, collaborative learning communities and situated learning (Teaching Council, 2011).

While the reform agenda is ambitious, it is being rolled out in the context of an economic recession which has resulted in the reduction of resources for teacher education, an increased emphasis on the link between education and the economy and a consequent growth in the dominance of the neoliberal agenda in education. This resurgence of neoliberalism is evident in Ireland and internationally in the increased emphasis on accountability, a prioritisation of STEM (Science, Technology, Engineering and Mathematics) education over other areas and a growing emphasis on performativity as a discourse of improvement. Within teacher education in Ireland, it is evident in the increased control and surveillance of teacher education programmes by regulatory bodies and the consequent lessening of autonomy for university-based teacher education institutions, coupled with a move towards commercialisation and privatisation in provision (Smith, 2012).

While recognising these constraints, the current focus on reform in the sector has provided teacher educators with the opportunity to review our work and to radically rethink what we do and how we do it. It has prompted us to engage with key and emergent issues in teacher education in a sustained way and to endeavour to build programmes that are characterised by deep modes of engagement. Among those issues are questions around the relationship between initial teacher education and development education (DE) and the responsibility of educators to 'care about', as opposed to 'care for', global justice (Noddings, 2005). This chapter is written from the perspective of an Irish teacher educator struggling to engage with the complex challenges which development education presents. In seeking to construct a practice that negotiates the spaces between the familiar discourses of initial teacher education in mainstream programmes and the disruptive possibilities of development education, I hope to bring to the surface some questions and 'provoking absences' and 'engage with possibilities not yet found' (Phelan and Sumsion, 2008: 3).

Given the importance of context in enabling us to 'face reality' as 'we collectively imagine ways to move beyond boundaries' (hooks, 1994: 207), I will begin by sketching in broad terms the practice of development education across the formal education landscape in which initial teacher education operates where problems of definition are played out in contradictory practice. I will then consider some 'troublesome' spaces where DE and ITE intersect which offer both the prospect of transformation and the risk of domestication and suggest how teacher educators might forge a holistic approach to development education within initial teacher education without sacrificing its critical and counter-hegemonic stance.

Understanding the broader context: Sketching the contradictory spaces of policy and practice

The exponential growth in 'adjectival' educations in the last 30 years is a manifestation of an increased focus on educational responses to issues of equality, justice, power and environment (Davies et al., 2005:

77). However, the range of terms used to name the development education space raises issues of definition (Bourn, 2008; Hogan and Tormey, 2008). Educations such as human rights education, global citizenship education and education for sustainable development are generally seen as related educations or subsumed within the broader 'global' focus of development while multicultural and intercultural education are generally seen as providing the 'local' dimension. The proliferation of terms and their interchangeability can result in a lack of clarity, subverting education to the needs of particular agendas (Bourn, 2008: 11).

Across the range of educations in this space, distinctions are drawn between conceptualisations and approaches that are seen as deriving from a liberal, humanistic vision, generally categorised as *soft* and *critical* approaches that have a more radical transformative agenda. Rooted in the discourse of modernisation, soft development education privileges Western/European trajectories and ideologies of development as normal and universal, locating the causes of poverty in the lack of resources and infrastructure in countries of the global South. In general, actions that derive from this conceptualisation are motivated by humanitarian ideals and by the personal desire to 'make a difference' (Andreotti, 2006: 45–47). Critical development education, on the other hand, requires a shift in focus that acknowledges the learner's complicity in structures and relations of domination and confronts the Western-centric power of definition inherent in the notion of the 'benevolent inclusion of the Other' (Mignolo, 2000: 742). While both Bourn (2011) and Andreotti (2006) note the need for a range of responses to issues of development, limiting educational responses to 'soft' interpretations can compromise the extent to which education can enable learners to engage with systemic change in areas such as climate change/climate justice education (Kavanagh et al., 2012).

In their critique of the global dimension in education in the UK, Mannion et al. (2011) identify what they describe as the 'curricular global turn' in education where the mainstreaming of global citizenship education represents an official response to the perceived 'challenge of preparing students for life in a global society and work in a global economy' (p. 449). Calling for educators to critically interrogate the view of globalisation embedded in official discourse, Mannion et al. argue that it presents globalisation as 'given' and 'fixed' rather than constructed and changeable and depoliticises the field of student engagement (Mannion et al., 2011: 450). As constructed, they argue, global citizenship education pursues a political project that is rooted in a local rather than a global agenda, which fails to problematise Western development and locates the 'responsible' citizen in an apolitical space defined by economics and culture (p. 451). Indeed, the primacy of the economic and cultural over the political is noted also in Bryan's (2010) critique of social and educational policy responses to cultural diversity in Ireland where business-oriented 'corporate multiculturalism' and celebratory interculturalism define immigrants as deserving of welcome 'so long as they represent an economic and cultural benefit to the state' (Bryan, 2010: 260). Finding a formal home for justice-oriented models of education in state policy may resolve little if it represents co-option to the state's neoliberal agenda. Indeed, as is evident in the literature, at the level of implementation such models can play host to contradictory practices antagonistic towards their core aims.

Recent studies suggest that 'soft' approaches to development education are characteristic of the practice of Irish teachers. Consistent with such approaches, children and young people are more likely to encounter views of development: that privilege models of economic development characteristic of the global North; that fail to problematise or historicise the power inequalities inherent in North/South relations; and that promote individual humanitarian engagement as the default response to manifestations of global inequality. Despite its good intentions, such practice tends to domesticate the idea of action, focusing largely on fundraising and promoting a charity response to issues of justice (Bryan and Bracken, 2011: 264; Waldron et al., 2011: 51, 52). This de-limiting of learners' potential fields of action towards individualised, depoliticised and safe modes of engagement is evident also in citizenship education and human rights education (Waldron, 2004; Waldron et al., 2011) embodying Westheimer and Kahne's (2004) model of the 'personally responsible citizen' and Flowers' (2004) idea of 'preservative' human rights education (Westheimer and Kahne, 2004; Flowers, 2004).

Despite positive dispositions, systemic constraints related to teacher capacity, time and resources present barriers to practice (Gleeson et al., 2007; Dillon and O'Shea, 2009; Bryan and Bracken, 2011). In the absence of dedicated spaces for development education within state curricula, the perception that the curriculum is overcrowded militates against any concerted focus on development education beyond a superficial engagement under the guise of cross-curricular integration. Thus, development education is, at the same time, everywhere and nowhere, reduced to an 'add-development-and-stir' model (Bryan and

Bracken, 2011: 259) or subject to a superficial integration that is more accidental than planned (Waldron et al., 2011: 36).

Not surprisingly, research findings in relation to ITE mirror many of the problems found in schools and indicate the difficulties in translating positive dispositions towards DE into practice (Robbins et al., 2003; McCormack and O'Flaherty, 2010; Bryan and Bracken, 2011). School culture, teachers' expectations, curriculum constraints, time limitations and supervision by college tutors are among the factors cited as barriers to teaching. Students see their knowledge as inadequate and identify classroom management and 'fitting in' as early-career priorities (McCormack and O'Flaherty, 2010: 1336). Similar to the practice of in-service teachers, the evidence suggests the dominance of 'soft' forms of development education, oriented towards awareness-raising and characterised by charity-oriented models of activism (Fitzgerald, 2007a; Bryan and Bracken, 2011: 141–143).

Superficial engagement runs the risk of reproducing existing relations of domination rather than challenging them, confirming the aid-giver/aid-recipient binarised conceptualisation of North/South relations and perpetuating the trope of 'caring for' the 'less fortunate' other as the appropriate response to global poverty. Disrupting that discourse requires that ITE provides students with learning experiences that shift their way of reading the world, enabling them to recognise their own positionality and deconstruct the meta-narratives of progress, development and power. It requires that student teachers come to 'care about' inequalities of power, recognition and distribution and that they recognise the role of structures and systems in perpetrating and maintaining them.

For initial teacher education, then, it is not a case of simply doing 'more of the same' or of adding a global gloss to an already crowded space. Rather, what is needed is to develop a practice that recognises the particular context of ITE, that engages with its dilemmas as well as its possibilities, and that identifies the troublesome spaces where taken-for-granted ways of seeing the world can be interrogated and challenged.

Teacher education as an 'archaeology of the self': Disrupting embedded constructions of normality

Writing about her practice as a teacher educator over twenty years ago, Suzanne M. Wilson used Frances H. Burnett's children's novel, *The Secret Garden*, as a metaphor for teacher education. Locating student teachers' prior experiences and resultant beliefs as part of that secret garden, Wilson argued for the opportunity to work together with her students to reveal the constructed nature of those taken-for-granted beliefs about teaching and learning, about knowledge and about education, which, she suggested, in many cases act as barriers to change. 'I want them', she wrote, 'to learn how to look at themselves' (Wilson, 1990: 208). Wilson's plea to look beneath the surface of student teachers' experiences has continued to resonate with teacher educators.

Lortie (1975) coined the now paradigmatic phrase 'the apprenticeship of observation' to capture the formative impact of student teachers' years of schooling on their thinking, an 'apprenticeship' that provides student teachers with 'insider knowledge' in relation to their future lives as teachers and a tendency to see their individual experiences as typical (Holt-Reynolds, 1992). These lay theories, perceptions, values, attitudes and beliefs that arise from student teachers' prior experiences as learners in the system can be remarkably enduring and difficult to shift. Their persistence prompted Darling-Hammond (2006) to name the 'apprenticeship of observation' as one of the three 'perennial challenges in learning to teach', with the other two challenges being those of enactment and the inherent complexity of teaching (p. 35). Teacher education programmes in general accept the idea that lay theories and assumptions about being a teacher should be critically interrogated as a core dimension of student teacher learning with a view to enabling students to subject those previously submerged habits of thought to conscious scrutiny.

Where issues of diversity are concerned, theorists have recognised the need for student teachers to engage in 'autobiographical exploration, reflection, and critical self-analysis', examining their identities, identifications and attachments (Villegas and Lucas, 2002: 22) and deconstructing prevailing narratives of normativity (Banks, 2011; Cochran-Smith, 2012). Andreotti's call for learners to engage in a deep interrogation of their co-implication in the systems, structures, power relations and assumptions that underpin global justice issues (Andreotti, 2006) requires a similar focus on subjectivities, positionality and embedded emotions. Given the continuing focus within teacher education on the critical interrogation of student teachers' attitudes, perceptions and beliefs, it could be argued that, from the perspective of development education, teacher education programmes that embrace the idea of such interrogation provide a welcoming environment. While, on the surface, such practice suggests a coming together of the processes of teacher education and critical development education, and, indeed, other forms of justice-oriented education, that hospitable environment cannot be taken for granted.

An inherent danger in the growing dominance of inquiry and reflective practice as the normalising discourse of teacher education, particularly in light of the increasing influence of neoliberalism on national policy, is its potential to depoliticise and individualise the interrogative process in relation to student teachers' deeply held assumptions about how the world of education works. The interrogation of lay theories and beliefs becomes the mode through which student teachers are initiated into a discourse of continuous improvement of professional practice tied to an over-arching meta-narrative of accountability rather than the kind of genealogical critique that might give insight into our co-implication in structures, processes and relations of domination locally and globally. Teaching and learning, and the sites in which they are practiced, become apolitical and neutral spaces with little connection to issues of justice and recognition except when they present as 'problems' to be resolved by more effective teaching. Reflection becomes an acritical process of self-improvement and an 'evocation of educational individualism' (Boler, 1999: 177). In an Irish context, despite the occasional use of the term 'critical' potentially suggesting a politically-oriented process, the focus is overwhelmingly on the interrogation of practice with a view towards its improvement (see, for example, Conway et al., 2009: 202; Teaching Council, 2011: 23).

Moving from an individualised to a collective space does not necessarily alter the focus on the professionalisation of reflection as a tool for improvement nor move it beyond the instrumentality of accountability-led notions of school reform (Cochran-Smith, 2012: 46–48). It could be argued that what is needed are parallel spaces of critical inquiry and reflection that engage with issues of power, positionality and justice in a range of contexts from the local to the global. However, such paralleling risks the creation of 'safe' depoliticised spaces of practice and 'unsafe' spaces where student teachers' subjectivities and emotions are challenged. Education, however, is neither 'safe' nor neutral; it is always political and the centrality of emotions to the practice of teaching is increasingly recognised, with experiences of teaching and learning constructing at times 'an emotional tightrope' for both learner and teacher (Corcoran, 2012: 147). The challenge presented by development education to initial teacher education, however, is not simply one of space and time, but whether teacher educators are prepared to embrace the risk, ambiguity and uncertainty and share in 'the students' vulnerability and suffering' (Boler, 1999: 188).

Boler's (1999) conceptualisation of a 'pedagogy of discomfort' offers a radical reconceptualisation of that space which has the potential to 'disrupt' deeply held assumptions about the world and how it works (Bryan, 2011: 261), enabling learners to 'see differently' (Boler, 1999: 176). She defines a 'pedagogy of discomfort' as 'both an invitation to inquiry as well as a call to action', though the action itself and its direction remain open (Boler, 1999: 176). Critical of the lack of 'collective accountability' characteristic of 'individualized self-reflection', Boler argues for the development of an historicised ethics which enables us to recognise our emotional patterns of selectivity: when we select to engage in passive 'spectating' removed from the field of action, which allows us to abdicate responsibility; and when, through 'collective witnessing', we take responsibility and recognise our co-implication (p. 186). Imagining critical reflection as a 'pedagogy of discomfort' provides teacher education with the possibility of reclaiming the radical possibilities of reflection as an open-ended and collective process of 'becoming' teachers and 'becoming' teacher educators.

Moving from individual to systemic change

The idea that student teachers should engage with systemic critique, which is seen as a key component of DE, is not new territory for initial teacher education. Indeed, as noted by Zeichner and Flessner (2009), claiming a social justice agenda has become commonplace across the sector, representing a normalising process that brings with it the danger of a loss of meaning (Ibid.: 25). Given the near-hegemonic status of such approaches, which presuppose engagement with systemic critique of structural inequalities, and in light of the limitations in the practice of DE identified earlier, it is pertinent to ask whether the transformation inherent in the transition from an individualised, humanistic response to development issues to a systems-led political response is realisable in an ITE context?

A transnational study that examined the development of beliefs consistent with a commitment to teach for social justice gives interesting insight into student teacher development over the course of initial teacher education in the United States, New Zealand and Ireland (Cochran-Smith et al., 2012). The study locates itself within a view of social justice that incorporates the goals of redistribution and recognition and a belief that teacher education should prepare 'teachers who are committed to, and know how to, teach for social justice' (Ibid.: 174). Despite the different contexts in which the research was carried out, significant similarities emerged in the findings supporting the contention that teaching for social justice represents an important cross-cultural concept in initial teacher education (p. 189). Across all three sites, student teachers on entry were most likely to believe in and agree with those items that relate to their practice as individual teachers engaging with individual students in their classrooms and least likely to believe in and agree with those items that focused on the wider structures and processes that constructed inequalities in the first place. On exit, the study found a 'modest, but very clear cross-site shift' in student teachers' beliefs from an individualistic to a structural perspective, recognising the inequitable impact of social structures and processes on different groups of students based on categories such as race, class, ethnicity and language (p. 191).

As noted by Cochran-Smith et al. this focus on the individual on entry is hardly surprising and is consistent with the common desire amongst teachers and student teachers to 'make a difference' and with Westheimer and Kahne's (2004) model of the 'personally responsible' citizen. Given the focus on action within development education, it is worth noting that the shift towards systemic understanding included movement towards the idea of activism as part of a wider collective challenge to systemic inequalities (Cochran-Smith et al., 2012: 191). While this study suggests that teacher education programmes are effecting 'modest' change in student teachers' perspectives on social justice over time, it acknowledges that more research is needed to reveal the change processes at work and any impact on subsequent classroom practice (Ibid.: 193).

It is reasonable to suggest that part of that process of change includes opportunities for students to engage with challenging and 'troublesome knowledge' (Meyer and Land, 2003: 2). In calling for critical teacher education as a response to globalisation, Apple (2011) argues the need for teacher education to engage student teachers with 'powerful' theory around global inequalities, distributive justice and the politics of recognition which would enable them to engage in systematic critique, understand the socio-historical processes that shape global structures and relations and their own implicatedness in maintaining those structures. Apple provides a telling autobiographical account of the transformative impact of 'powerful' critical theory on his identity as a teacher, enabling him to understand more fully the implications of own class background, which had positioned him intellectually as 'less than', and providing him with the possibility of agency. 'Learning and using *powerful* theory, especially powerful *critical* theories, in essence, became a counterhegemonic act' (Apple, 2011: 228). Given the proliferation of justice-related educations within an already crowded space and the power of the neoliberal agenda in teacher education, how do you locate DE within the mainstream, while maintaining its counter-hegemonic power as a site of 'troublesome knowledge'? How do you counter the potential co-optive effect of mainstreaming (Liddy, 2011: 28) and the reductive tendencies inherent in over-generalised approaches to educations such as education for social justice in ITE (Zeichner and Flessner, 2009)?

Looking at core concepts that are shared across different kinds of justice-oriented education with a view to maximising their potential to effect change provides one response to issues of over-crowding and fragmentation. Fitzgerald (2007b), for example, developed a shared conceptual framework which identified common themes, values and skills across intercultural education and development education. Others have looked at core concepts that underpin different approaches to environmental education with a view to mainstreaming them (Hogan and Tormey, 2008). Still others have noted synergies between human rights education and the social and situated pedagogies of child education (Waldron and Ruane, 2010: 217). While this work brings greater clarity and connectedness to these related areas of education, identifying shared elements of DE and of ITE which could be considered as potentially generative of change is of key importance. Deegan (2012) suggests the power of *threshold concepts* (Meyer and Land, 2003) for transformative ITE. Likened to a 'portal' that can open up a new way of thinking, threshold concepts can transform thinking around 'subject matter, subject landscape, or even world view' (Meyer and Land, 2003: 1). Figure 7.1 suggests the shared space that threshold concepts would inhabit in the emerging framework.

Not all important concepts are threshold concepts and the idea itself is one that loses its power by over-generalisation. However, while identifying shared threshold concepts requires greater elaboration than is possible here, the following concepts suggest themselves as transformative in their impact on student teachers' worldviews and of straddling a shared conceptual space between ITE and DE: education as inherently political; knowledge as incomplete, constructed, situated and plural; understanding of hegemony and counter-hegemony; constructions of normativity and difference; banking education; voice and agency. Many of these concepts are drawn from the 'powerful' critical theory

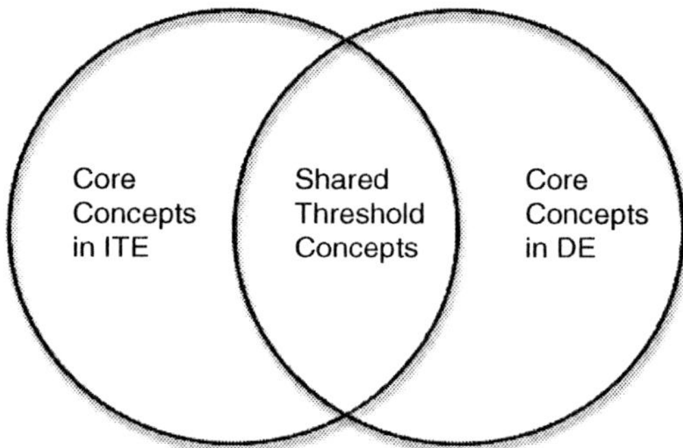

Figure 7.1 Mainstreaming development education through threshold concepts
Source: Meyer and Land, 2003.

identified by Apple, and are part of the mainstream theoretical landscape of initial teacher education. It is essential also to engage with such theory in ways that avoid the traditional critique of ITE as overly theoretical, and that recognise the complexity of the theory/practice relationship, if the limitations of practice in schools and in ITE identified earlier in the chapter are to be challenged. Are there ways of 'doing theory' that avoid the theory/practice dichotomy?

Capturing the agentic space: Crossing boundaries of theory and action

While few ITE programmes adhere to the theory-to-practice model at the centre of traditional critique, the theory/practice dynamic is still recognised as one of the core dilemmas of teacher education. The growing hegemonic status of socio-cultural epistemologies of student teacher learning, new conceptualisations of practitioner knowledge and a return to Deweyan principles are among some of the discernible influences on the current conceptual mapping of this space in ITE. Models such as Korthagen's 'realistic' teacher education which are premised on a practice/theory/practice approach see the relationship as a dynamic and iterative looping between experience and reflection, informed by theoretical insights (Korthagen, 2001, 2012). The recognition of teaching as a complex and messy activity, characterised by uncertainty, ambiguity and contingency has raised the need within teacher education to facilitate a continuous dialogic negotiation of the theory/practice interface, making the tacit visible and digging deep into the assumptions underpinning taken-for-granted and routinised practice.

Immersive school experiences are set in the context of ongoing reflection while interactive, participatory seminars integrate pedagogy and knowledge-in-teaching with an understanding of the socio-cultural contexts of teaching; in addition, meta-reflective and inquiry-based practices such as journaling, lesson study and case studies which are sensitive to the affective dimensions of teaching and learning are increasingly characteristic of the sector. If implemented consistently such practices should result in teachers who are caring, responsive, insightful and versatile, being able to build on those 'teachable moments' which offer the possibility of authentic learning. But what of the engagement with 'powerful theory' which transformed Michael Apple's view of the world? How is that best conceptualised as part of the practice/theory/practice 'dance' of 'radical interconnectedness' (Selby, 2001)?

One way of thinking about it would be to extend the contexts for school experience to include placement in countries of the global South. Combined with critical reflection on the experience and on student teachers' beliefs and values relating to global issues, such experiences can result in deep learning (Kambutu and Nganga, 2008; Ryan, 2011). Ryan (2011) acknowledges that such placements may not be for everyone but argues the possibility of a 'multiplier effect' in colleges and schools (p. 48). Given the research that suggests the importance of student teachers' wider experiences of other cultures and contexts (Leavy, 2005; Clarke and Drudy, 2006; Holden and Hicks, 2007; McCormack and O'Flaherty, 2010), extending opportunities for such experiences is worth considering, provided they avoid the pitfalls of school immersion schemes, such as being seen simply as opportunities for self-enhancement and cultural tourism (Bryan and Bracken, 2011: 244). Others have argued for critical literacy as an approach towards sustained engagement with global issues in a teacher education context (Andreotti, 2006; Bryan, 2011; Bryan and Bracken, 2011). Bryan's account of using a critical media literacy framework with an elective group of post-graduate student teachers and master's level students illustrates the potential of this approach to 'disrupt' embedded ways of thinking about the world (Bryan, 2011).

If DE is to have a systemic impact on ITE, however, it needs to leave the relatively protected space of student choice and join the mainstream. The Development and Intercultural Education (DICE) project offers a current model for mainstreaming at a systemic level. Since

2004, the DICE project has worked to embed development and intercultural education in mainstream ITE programmes. Funded by Irish Aid, the overseas development arm of the Department of Foreign Affairs, DICE provides dedicated lecturers, organises a support network for sharing good practice and supports ongoing research in the area. DICE lecturers work with students in mandatory and elective spaces, while endeavouring to integrate development and intercultural perspectives more widely across programme modules and other aspects of student life. While no large-scale study of its impact has been undertaken, a recent small-scale study indicated the following outcomes: growth in positive dispositions, an improved awareness of global issues and concepts and increased knowledge of DE teaching methodologies; however, the dominance of ethical consumerism, 'helping' actions and charity-based responses in conceptualisations of action suggest the ongoing influence of 'soft' models of DE. It is worth noting in this regard that at the time of the study student exposure to DICE modules was limited and, indeed, the study found qualitative differences in the understanding of students who received a short mandatory programme and those who chose a longer elective programme which covered global issues in more depth (Fitzgerald, 2007a).

The framework for development presented below (Figure 7.2) was developed as part of the DICE project in St Patrick's College, Drumcondra and attempts to enact the transformative potential of DE in an ITE context. The model is progressively spiralled, while, at the same time, embodying the dynamic and recursive 'dance' between

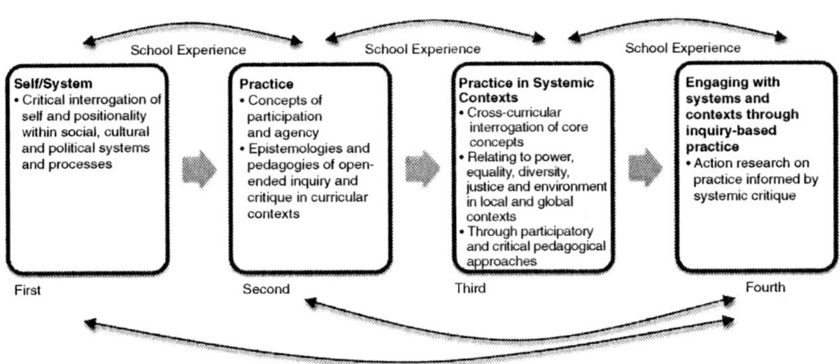

Figure 7.2 Four-stage framework for DE in initial teacher education
Source: Centre for Human Rights and Citizenship Education, St Patrick's College.

self/system, theory/practice and local/global contexts across the four years of the programme. In the first stage, the focus on the critical interrogation of student teachers' positionalities, and their structural embeddedness in historically-rooted systems of culture, society and economy, aims to 'disrupt' existing narratives and patterns of thinking. The second stage focuses on threshold concepts relating to participation, voice and agency in the context of social constructivist and inquiry-based approaches to learning and their pedagogical realisation in key curricular contexts such as the teaching of history, geography and social, personal and health education. In stage three, students engage in cross-curricular explorations of key issues relating to: global and local systemic inequalities of power and resources, sustainable environments and communities, issues of discrimination and recognition and discourses of normativity. In the final stage, student teachers deepen their understanding of curriculum and pedagogy-in-action through school-based action-research which draws on their emergent capacities for systemic critique. Each stage engages in an ongoing dialogue with school-based experience.

While the stages conform to years in terms of the programme, the arrows are indicative of the ongoing 'dance' between the ideas and processes characteristic of each stage throughout the duration of the programme, presenting a model that engages the student teacher in a continuous process of negotiation between current patterns of thought/action and emergent ideas in the process of becoming a teacher.

Conclusion

The idea that DE is 'comfortable' with 'discomfort' and committed to a process of open-ended critical enquiry presents a provocative counter-narrative to prevailing discourses of accountability and performativity in education in general and to the growing dominance in ITE of outcomes-related and competency-based regulatory frameworks. In seeking to bring development education in from the margins of initial teacher education, I have argued that we need to counter the tendency towards superficiality and depoliticisation that can accompany integration into mainstream curricula. While 'soft' development education has its place, it can lead to practices within education that reinforce, rather than challenge, existing structures, processes and relations of domination. For such practice to change, student teachers need learning opportunities where they can interrogate their own roles within those structures and develop their capacities to engage in systemic critique and action. I have suggested the presence of 'troublesome spaces' within the practice of initial teacher education where such opportunities could be carved out.

Engaging with the possibilities of critical reflection provides one of those spaces. Undoubtedly the 'reflective turn' in teacher education holds within it the promise of transformation if rescued from the embrace of the performance enhancement agenda. Boler's 'pedagogy of discomfort' provides one way of reimagining that space, moving beyond the limits of individual reflection, to engage with the 'ambiguous self' and the silences and omissions that mask oppressive structures through the power of 'collective witnessing' (Boler, 1999: 184). Identifying a range of threshold concepts that resonate across the domains of ITE and DE provides a second space where student teachers can encounter 'troublesome knowledge' that can unlock different ways of seeing the world. Finally, in the context of a growing recognition of the complexity of the 'dance' between theory and practice, I suggested a possible framework to enable student teachers to navigate between the disruptive potential of these troublesome spaces and the ambiguities, uncertainties and complexities of practice in the context of a mainstream initial teacher education programme.

Moving beyond the boundaries between teacher education and development education, between what 'is' and what is 'becoming' requires naming possible starting points, 'fragments of possibilities that offer potential escape-routes from the tired recycling of the same old concerns' (Phelan and Sumsion, 2008: 13). In taking as my perspective that of the teacher educator working through key 'perennial challenges' (Darling-Hammond, 2006: 35), I hope I have identified some of those fragments, and contributed them to the collective imaginary.

References

Andreotti, V (2006) 'Soft versus critical global citizenship education', *Policy and Practice: A Development Education Review*, Vol. 3, Autumn 2006, pp. 40–51, available: http://www.developmenteducationreview.com/issue3-focus4

Apple, M W (2011) 'Global crises, social justice and teacher education', *Journal of Teacher Education*, 62(2), pp. 222–234.

Banks, J A (2011) 'Citizenship education and diversity: Implications for teacher education', *Journal of Teacher* Education, 52(5), pp. 5–16.

Boler, M (1999) *Feeling Power: Emotions and Education*, New York: Routledge.

Bourn, D (2011) 'Discourses and practices around development education: From learning about development to critical global pedagogy', *Policy and Practice:*

A Development Education Review, Vol. 3, Autumn 2006, pp. 40–51, available: http://www.developmenteducationreview.com/issue 12-focus1

Bourn, D (2008) 'Introduction', *Development Education: Debates and Dialogue*, London: Institute of Education, University of London, pp. 1–17.

Bryan, A (2010) 'Corporate multiculturalism, diversity management, and positive interculturalism in Irish schools and society', *Irish Educational Studies*, 29(3), pp. 253–269.

Bryan, A (2011) 'Disrupting a passion for ignorance: Exploring development themes using a critical (media) literacy framework' in T J Batteson and R Tormey (eds) *Teaching Global Perspectives: Introducing Student Teachers to Development Education*, Dublin: The Liffey Press, pp. 259–272.

Bryan, A and Bracken, M (2011) *Learning to Read the World? Teaching and Learning About Global Citizenship and International Development in Post-Primary Schools*, Limerick: Irish Aid.

Clarke, M and Drudy, S (2006) 'Teaching for diversity, social justice and global awareness', *European Journal of Teacher Education*, 29(3), pp. 371–386.

Cochran-Smith, M (2012) 'Trends and challenges in teacher education: National and international perspectives' in F Waldron, J Smith, M Fitzpatrick and T Dooley (eds) *Re-imagining Initial Teacher Education: Perspectives on Transformation*, Dublin: Liffey Press, pp. 29–53.

Cochran-Smith, M, Ludlow, L, Ell, F, O'Leary, M and Enterline, S (2012) 'Learning to teach for social justice as a cross cultural concept: Findings from three countries', *European Journal of Educational Research*, 1(2), pp. 171–198.

Conway, P F, Murphy, R, Rath, A and Hall, K (2009) *Learning to Teach and its Implications for the Continuum of Teacher Education: A Nine-Country Cross-National Study*, Maynooth: The Teaching Council.

Corcoran, D (2012) 'Constructivism made visible in contingency: Learning to teach mathematics in a community of practice' in F Waldron, J Smith, M Fitzpatrick and T Dooley (eds) *Re-imagining Initial Teacher Education: Perspectives on Transformation*, Dublin: The Liffey Press, pp. 135–154.

Darling-Hammond, L (2006) *Powerful Teacher Education: Lessons from Exemplary Programs*, San Francisco: John Wiley and Sons.

Davies, I, Evans, M and Reid, A (2005) 'Globalising citizenship education? A critique of "global education" and "citizenship education"', *British Journal of Educational Studies*, 53(1), pp. 66–89.

Deegan, J G (2012) 'Bridging being and becoming: Teacher education programmes in the Republic of Ireland' in F Waldron, J Smith, M Fitzpatrick and T Dooley (eds) *Re-imagining Initial Teacher Education: Perspectives on Transformation*, Dublin: The Liffey Press, pp. 179–200.

Dillon, S and O'Shea, M (2009) *From the College to the Classroom: The Impact of DICE Courses on the Inclusion of Development Education and Intercultural Education in the Primary Classroom*, Dublin: DICE Project.

Fitzgerald, H (2007a) *Analysis of the Impact of DICE modules on Initial Teacher Education on Students' Knowledge and Views of the Global Dimension in Education*, Dublin: DICE Project.

Fitzgerald, H (2007b) *The Relationship between Development Education and Intercultural Education in Initial Teacher Education*, Dublin: DICE Project.

Flowers, N (2004) 'How to define human rights education? A complex answer to a simple question' in V B Georgi and M Seberich (eds) *International Perspectives in Human Rights Education*, Gütersloh: Bertelsmann Foundation Publishers, pp. 105–127.

Gleeson, J, King, P, O'Driscoll, S and Tormey, R (2007) *Development Education in Irish Post-Primary Schools: Knowledge, Attitudes and Activism*, Limerick: Shannon Curriculum Development Centre, Curriculum Evaluation and Policy Research Unit, University of Limerick and Irish Aid.

Hogan, D and Tormey, R (2008) 'A perspective on the relationship between development education and education for sustainable development', *Policy and Practice: A Development Education Review*, Vol. 6, Spring 2008, pp. 5–16, available: http://www.developmenteducationreview.com/issue6-focus1

Holden, C and Hicks, D (2007) 'Making global connections: The knowledge, understanding and motivation of trainee teachers', *Teaching and Teacher Education*, 23, pp. 13–23.

Holt-Reynolds, D (1992) 'Personal history-based beliefs as relevant prior knowledge in course work', *American Educational Research Journal*, 26, pp. 160–189.

hooks, b (1994) *Teaching to Transgress: Education as the Practice of Freedom*, New York: Routledge.

Kambutu, J and Nganga, L (2008) 'In these uncertain times: Educators build cultural awareness through planned international experiences', *Teaching and Teacher Education*, 24, pp. 939–951.

Kavanagh, R, Waldron, F, Ruane, B and Oberman, R (2012) 'Education, climate change and climate justice: Irish perspectives', paper presented at the American Educational Research Conference, April 2012, Vancouver, available: http://www.ideaonline.ie/sites/default/files/Kavanagh_Waldron_Ruane_and_Oberman_Paper.pdf

Korthagen, F A (2001) 'Building a realistic teacher education program' in F A Korthagen, J Kessels, B Koster, B Lagerwerf and T Wubbels (eds) *Linking Practice and Theory: The Pedagogy of Realistic Teacher Education*, Mahwah: Lawrence Erlbaum Associates, pp. 69–87.

Korthagen, F A (2012) 'Linking practice, theory and person in teacher education' in F Waldron, J Smith, M Fitzpatrick and T Dooley (eds) *Re-imagining Initial Teacher Education: Perspectives on Transformation*, Dublin: The Liffey Press, pp. 117–134.

Leavy, A (2005) '"When I meet them I talk to them": The challenges of diversity for preservice teacher education', *Irish Educational Studies*, 24(2), pp. 159–177.

Liddy, M (2011) 'Mainstreaming education for sustainable development: Obstacles or opportunities' in T J Batteson and R Tormey (eds) *Teaching Global Perspectives: Introducing Student Teachers to Development Education*, Dublin: The Liffey Press, pp. 23–42.

Lortie, D C (1975) *Schoolteacher: A Sociological Study*, Chicago: University of Chicago Press.

Mannion, G, Biesta, G, Priestley, M and Ross, H (2011) 'The global dimension in education and education for global citizenship: Genealogy and critique', *Globalisation, Societies and Education*, 9(3–4), pp. 443–456.

McCormack, O and O'Flaherty, J (2010) 'An examination of pre-service teachers' attitudes towards the inclusion of development education into Irish post-primary schools', *Teaching and Teacher Education*, 26, pp. 1332–1339.

Meyer, J and Land, R (2003) *Threshold Concepts and Troublesome Knowledge: Linkages to Ways of Thinking and Practising within the Disciplines*, Edinburgh: Economic and Social Research Council.

Mignolo, W (2000) 'The many faces of cosmo-polis: Border thinking and critical cosmopolitanism', *Public Culture*, 12(3), pp. 721–748.

Noddings, N (2005) 'Global citizenship: Promises and problems' in N Noddings (ed.) *Educating Citizens for Global Awareness*, New York: Teachers College Press, pp. 1–21.

Phelan, A and Sumsion, J (2008) 'Introduction: Lines of articulation and lines of flight in teacher education' in A Phelan and J Sumsion (eds) *Critical Readings in Teacher Education: Provoking Absences*, Rotterdam: Sense Publishers, pp. 1–15.

Robbins, M, Francis, L J and Elliott, E (2003) 'Attitudes toward education for global citizenship among trainee teachers', *Research in Education*, 69, pp. 93–98.

Ryan, A (2011) 'Integrating experiential and academic learning in teacher preparation for development education', *Irish Educational Studies*, 31(1), pp. 35–50.

Selby, D (2001) 'The signature of the whole: Radical interconnectedness and its implications for global and environmental education' in E V O'Sullivan, A Morrell and M O'Connor (eds) *Expanding the Boundaries of Transformative Learning*, New York: Palgrave, pp. 77–94.

Smith, J (2012) 'Initial teacher education in Ireland: Transformation in a policy context' in F Waldron, J Smith, M Fitzpatrick and T Dooley (eds) *Re-imagining Initial Teacher Education: Perspectives on Transformation*, Dublin: The Liffey Press, pp. 74–97.

Teaching Council (2011) *Initial Teacher Education: Criteria and Guidelines for Programme Providers*, Maynooth: The Teaching Council.

Villegas, A M and Lucas, T (2002) 'Preparing culturally responsive teachers: Rethinking the curriculum', *Journal of Teacher Education*, 53(1), pp. 20–32.

Waldron, F (2004) 'Making the Irish: Identity and citizenship in the primary curriculum' in C Sugrue (ed.) *Ideology and Curriculum: Irish Experienced, International Perspectives*, Dublin: The Liffey Press, pp. 122–140.

Waldron, F, Kavanagh, A, Kavanagh, R, Maunsell, C, Oberman, R, O'Reilly, M, et al. (2011) *Teachers, Human Rights and Human Rights Education: Knowledge, Perspectives and Practices of Primary School Teachers in Ireland*, Dublin: The Centre for Human Rights and Citizenship Education.

Waldron, F and Ruane, B (2010) 'Conclusion' in F Waldron and B Ruane (eds) *Human Rights Education: Reflections on Theory and Practice*, Dublin: The Liffey Press, pp. 215–219.

Westheimer, J and Kahne, J (2004) 'What kind of citizen? The politics of educating for democracy', *American Educational Research Journal*, 41(2), pp. 237–269.

Wilson, S M (1990) 'The secret garden of teacher education', *The Phi Delta Kappan*, 72(3), pp. 204–209.

Zeichner, K and Flessner, R (2009) 'Educating teachers for social justice' in K M Zeichner (ed.) *Teacher Education and the Struggle for Social Justice*, New York: Routledge, pp. 24–43.

8
Strengthening Development Education Practice in the Higher Education Sector: Re-imagining Research

Su-ming Khoo

Introduction

This chapter examines the case for development education research, explores the relationship between research and development education in the higher education sector and considers the implications for development education capacity and practice. It suggests a number of ways in which research enhances development education capacity, but argues that 'research' and the academic contribution need to be reimagined to address problematic divides. Boyer's reimagination of 'scholarships' reconnects research to an ecology of practice comprising engagement, inter-disciplinary collaboration and teaching. However, 'engagement' is not necessarily synonymous with 'compliance'. The situation of public higher education is discussed and the chapter concludes with some reflections about global visions of research and the particular relevance of critical, defiant, humanistic and rights-based versions of development education for a sector facing into globalisation, crisis and the pressures of relentless reform.

Reconnecting scholarships and reimagining research

The Oxford English Dictionary defines 'research' as 'systematic investigation or inquiry aimed at contributing to knowledge of a theory, topic, etc., by careful consideration, observation, or study of a subject'. This definition associates 'research' with originality, rigour and an academic setting, stating that more contemporary usage denotes research as 'original critical or scientific investigation carried out under the auspices of an academic or other institution'. Instead of seeing tertiary institutions as being merely synonymous with 'research', this contribution argues for explicit scrutiny of the academic contribution, and calls for an analysis that 'un-thinks' (Wallerstein, 2001) divisive traditional assumptions – between academic theory and practice, between tertiary education institutions and the wider public, between research and teaching, and between the different disciplines that contribute to development education capacity and practice. The reimagination of research beyond these divides requires 'research' to be recontextualised in an ecology of academic work that reconnects the work, or 'scholarship', of research to other 'scholarships' of engagement, interdisciplinarity and teaching (see Boyer, 1990, 1996).

This concrete and holistic approach serves the knowledge and pedagogical bases of development education, and informs a more nuanced case for it. Integrating research with teaching, engagement and interdisciplinary dialogue broadens the actors and audiences of development education to involve disciplines and professions, policy-makers and the public as well as 'teachers' and 'students'. While this vision obviously involves the key constituency of teacher education, it is certainly not limited to it, extending to all the disciplines offered by comprehensive higher education – the arts, social sciences, medical and health sciences, law, engineering, business studies and so on. Thus reimagined, research enables an evolving and critical understanding of the meanings and purposes of development education, supports more comprehensive and creative practice, enables more appropriate and effective evaluations of practice, and engages policy-makers and the public.

The ideas about 'scholarships' in the plural and of 'engaged' research derive from the work of Ernest Boyer, former President of the Carnegie Foundation for the Advancement of Teaching. Boyer was asked to address the problem of research concentration in higher education and the accompanying devaluation of teaching. His much cited-book, *Scholarship Reconsidered* (1990), presented a manifesto for rethinking academic work, offering a schema of research, engagement, cross-disciplinary integration and teaching as types of academic work which could be equally recognised, valued and rewarded. These four distinct 'scholarships' were not opposed, but complementary, hence research, or 'the scholarship of discovery' was valued *in relation to*, not *over*, the other three 'scholarships'. The 'scholarship of integration' makes interdisciplinary connections, contextualises specialised knowledge, 'illuminates' data and educates non-specialists.

The 'scholarship of application' seeks relevance by applying knowledge 'responsibly' to address important social problems. This relevance agenda was recast as 'the scholarship of engagement' in a later article (Boyer, 1996) addressing the question of higher education's relevance to society. Economic crisis and austerity have amplified the pressure on higher education institutions on this point as politicians, policymakers, the media and the public increasingly demand that the sector justify its public funding and prove its relevance. In Boyer's vision, 'engagement' reached out to the local civic sphere, to connect '...the rich resources of the university to our most pressing social, civic, and ethical problems, to our children, to our schools, to our teachers, and to our cities' (1996: 11). Boyer's ideas about integrated scholarship and the engaged university revisit the roots of the nineteenth-century 'Humboldtian' ideal of the modern research university. This model aspired to achieve the highest form of knowledge and scholarship for society through a blend of active intellectual engagement, sound judgment and moral feeling (*Wissenschaft*), achieved through the freedom of teaching (*lehrfreiheit*) and learning (*lernfreiheit*) (Perkin, 2006: 177).

Teachers and students were understood to be united in the common pursuit of knowledge and learning, driven by moral and practical problems requiring the application of disciplinary knowledge. The engagement agenda reflects a contemporary insistence that academic knowledge be relevant to the public, and relevance involves doing more than just pushing out research products towards a general public. The 'scholarship of teaching' does not merely transmit knowledge, but extends and transforms it (Boyer, 1990). Interactions between academia and the public must move in both directions and it might seem obvious that engaged teaching and students provide key links (Vannini and Milne, forthcoming). Student research, volunteering and civic engagement provide crossovers between research and teaching, and between academia and the public, offering examples of a broader ideal of knowledge exchange, translation and mobilisation. Student expertise increasingly contributes to the creation and spread of innovative and collaborative research products, and this mode of engagement is enhanced by the growth of the mature and non-traditional student constituency and the introduction of more flexible teaching and learning formats.

Kenway and Fahey suggest that the research imagination should not necessarily be confined to a localised and 'compliant' role and they choose to highlight researchers with 'defiant global research imaginations' (2009: 10). Doreen Massey's contribution to Kenway and Fahey's volume suggests a different research imagination to Boyer's localised and communitarian vision of academic civic engagement, engaging 'responsibility over distance' in our 'hugely interconnected world'. For Massey, globalisation is neither unitary nor monologic (see also Munck, 2007). The neoliberal form of globalisation may be dominant, but there are also ethical alternatives which ask 'why are we responsible?' Massey travels globally to teach and research, and her experiences cause her to 'learn more than what she teaches' (2009: 76, 79). Kenway and Fahey speak up for a research imagination that engages in less familiar ways of thinking, and allows creative and 'fresh flights of thought'. The 'travelling research imagination' occurs when disciplinary and geographical boundaries are crossed, sparking 'an intellectually or politically transgressive sensibility'. A globalised research imagination casts research in a larger frame and critically engages global logics and trends. In the case of development education research, this brings to bear much wider perspectives on education and development policy and practice. Contrarian and transgressive views 'dig within the national' and generate a different sense of the implications of global policies and trends (2009: 13, 22).

Applying the scholarship of integration to development education

The 'scholarship of integration' takes an inter-disciplinary approach to research. 'Development' is by nature a problem and policy-oriented field involving inter-disciplinary approaches and a travelling research imagination. The two words 'development' and 'education' have come together in the term 'development education', but the worlds of development research, educational research and development education research have yet to consolidate firm common ground. Development education research is still a relatively small and nascent field of research, mainly comprising descriptive studies *on* or *about* development education, with relatively weak connections to research in the mainstream of educational or development studies. For example, Regan and Sinclair (2006) raise questions about the nature of development education in their key development education resource while Borg, Hayden and Regan's chapter in that resource tries to show how 'human development' fits in with development education. The concept of 'human development' is much debated in development studies, however Borg, Hayden and Regan elide discussion about human development in theory or practice, in favour of descriptive examples of inspiring projects and ideas for student engagement.

Research studies on global education and global citizenship education do overlap with development education and are more routinely inter-disciplinary in content, moving across education, philosophy, political science, sociology and policy studies. Mainstream development studies focuses more on 'the development of education', dominated by a somewhat uncritical and hegemonic emphasis on the quantitative expansion of formal educational provision. My own experiences in trying to bring together the worlds of development education and development studies, and development research and development education (Khoo, 2006; Khoo et al., 2007) have pointed to rights-based approaches and human development and capabilities as the most promising routes to inter-disciplinarity and perhaps even transdisciplinarity, drawing together and consolidating development research, law, gender studies, research on food, health, education and security (e.g. Khoo and Lehane, 2008; Khoo, 2012; on inter-disciplinarity see Sumner and Tribe, 2008: 53–76).

It would be welcome to see development education research closing the gap with research in development studies, and this convergence looks more likely as the focus and approach of development studies shifts. Sumner and Tribe (2008: 19) state that the concerns of development studies extend beyond developing countries since poverty and wealth exist in every country. Debates about the meaning of development and the concerns with economic development, wellbeing and progress are applicable in any setting. A recent blog on the Irish Development Education Association website criticises the domestic media for badly framing the issues of overseas aid, ignoring the links to injustice within Ireland (IDEA, 2012b). But the debate is not only about injustice, it is about crises of development. Debt injustice, imposed policy austerity and widening inequalities have been central to dilemmas of development for several decades since the advent of structural adjustment programmes and policy conditionality.

The public in Ireland can be engaged in a deeper and more nuanced discussion on overseas aid, development and justice, and it is arguably development education's role to engage this public discussion. The questioning of priorities for overseas aid, given Ireland's and many other 'developed' countries' recent experiences of deep economic austerity and social crises means that the debates have already moved beyond academic research in development studies to the broader public realm. Development ethics, debates about justice and grounded global sensibilities (Massey, 2009: 80) offer key substantive connections across different disciplines, pointing to a common ground where development ethics, educational ethics and development education research ethics are questioned and debated. Ethics, justice and a grounded approach to globalisation (Massey, 2009; Munck, 2010) offer a theoretical and practical focus for thinking about development education. Ethics must inform how research is conducted, and the ethics of the development education community itself are also up for debate (cf. Sumner and Tribe, 2008).

The context and problematique for development education research

The Irish Development Education Association (IDEA, 2012a) defines development education capacity broadly, as a '...holistic approach to professional development that encompasses networking activities, research and communications as well as training'. In practice, this translates into five main areas: 1) organisational management, 2) development education knowledge and skills, 3) networking and coordination, 4) quality and impact, and 5) policy and research. All of these areas can potentially benefit from interaction with the tertiary education sector, though we might expect the tertiary education institutions to contribute research in particular, adding to the knowledge base and informing policy.

Research also enables a greater understanding of quality and impact and widens opportunities for networking. Development education research, which can be defined as research *on*, *about* or *for* development education, is generally thought to represent only a small element of development education practice. Even if systematic knowledge and learning are arguably always *somewhere* in the background, research is not usually acknowledged as a primary input, objective or outcome of most development education practice. Research activity, disciplinary specialisation, professional education and the principle of *academic freedom* underlie the particular contribution of the higher education sector. This mix enables higher education to offer a space where different stakeholders and interests can meet and explore different approaches and orientations as well as deeper and more controversial ideas and debates. Research in the academic context can include policy-driven and short-term 'outputs' such as commissioned policy work or evaluations, but is not confined to them. The role of academic research is also to contribute to practice and policy learning over a longer time frame and in a wider societal context.

The relevance of human rights

The transdisciplinary norms of human rights are currently used by many different actors for imaginative advocacy and problem-solving around the issues of globalisation. Former President of Ireland and UN High Commissioner for Human Rights, Mary Robinson argues that human rights offer a form of ethical globalisation (*Realizing Rights*, no date). More polemically, O'Connell (2007) argues that human rights necessarily involve taking a stand against dominant forms of neoliberal globalisation. Steiner (2002) suggests that human rights has moved beyond the narrowly defined scholarly field, to offer a set of norms, as a 'lens' through which diverse issues such as development, gender, terrorism, religion or even pandemics can be viewed. He calls for tertiary-level institutions to play a critical role in fostering the study and teaching of human rights as '[f]ew institutions other than the university are positioned to undertake such work' (2002: 317).

Research universities play a critical role in the global human rights movement because they are uniquely positioned for critical and interdisciplinary debate and there is a fundamental fit between the '...basic tenets of the international [human rights] instruments – freedoms of belief, inquiry, advocacy and association' and the foundational values of the university itself (Steiner, 2002: 318). Development educators should support this by continuing to demand that tertiary-level institutions deploy their traditions of academic freedom, scholarship and autonomy together with the wide spectrum of disciplinary knowledge required to approach ethical globalisation and human rights contextually and concretely. A safe and enabling milieu is needed for conversations about conflicting versus common values and their relation to universal rights to proceed. Research, teaching and the engagement agenda can be channelled towards widening such conversations, extending across a wide range of disciplinary, professional and practice activities.

Shifting landscapes of development education

The landscape of development education has undergone major transformations over the past two decades and great changes have been experienced by each of the major relevant 'sectors' or players – higher education, development and development education. Development education has only recently emerged as a recognisable constituency or sector-in-itself with the capability to articulate its own specific knowledge needs.

The period between the late 1990s and 2008 was one of particularly rapid growth and change, punctuated by increased government commitments, more policy engagement and programmatic action in Ireland, the UK and across Europe. Development education became more strongly linked with official aid policy as the UK and Irish governments issued White Papers on International Development (Secretary of State for International Development (UK), 1997; Government of Ireland, 2006). The Irish government became active in setting up Global Education Network Europe (GENE), a network of ministries, agencies and national bodies involved in funding and policy-making in the field of global education (Fiedler et al., 2011: 45).

The Council of Europe's Resolution on 'Development Education and Raising European Public Awareness of Development Cooperation' (2001) also led to support for CONCORD (the European NGO confederation for relief and development) a Europe-wide consortium of development non-governmental organisations (NGOs), to create the DEEEP (Developing Europeans' Engagement for the Eradication of Global Poverty) programme. To summarise, development education efforts became more aligned with official, governmental development assistance programmes. As government funding and policy engagement for development increased, the argument was made for public awareness and support measures to be ramped up, moving development education and support activities from the margins of NGO campaigning, fundraising and informal education into a mainstream of official aid policy, public communication and citizen education. An ambitious agenda began to emerge around mainstreaming and the professionalisation of development education.

Academic support for development education increased (Bourn, 2007), in a context where postgraduate 'fourth level' higher education and research activity were growing and academic development studies and development research were becoming more established, although in Ireland this was from a fairly low base, if compared to the UK. Elements of a research agenda began to tentatively emerge, in an atmosphere of greater policy centralisation, engagement and dialogue between development education practitioners, academics, development practitioners and government. As the development education sector professionalised, the demand increased for opportunities and professional career paths into, and out of, higher education. The sector has called for the Irish government to continue funding high-quality research, to prioritise under-researched areas and to support more effective research dissemination and impact (Fiedler et al., 2011).

Development education in 'hard times' – an ethical response to globalisation as the 'economisation' of knowledge

Development education and research are currently entangled in much wider contestations about the values and purposes of education and even of knowledge itself. The higher education sector has found itself particularly embroiled as a key actor within a global 'knowledge economy' in the throes of deep crisis and contradictions. The research agenda is part and parcel of a broader drama of growth, crises and reform of higher education institutions (HEIs) which were given a central role in 'helping Europe meet its goals' according to the European Union's 'Lisbon Agenda' for a global knowledge economy (EUA, 2007). The Lisbon vision was for Europe to become '...the most competitive and dynamic knowledge-based economy in the world, capable of sustainable economic growth with more and better jobs and greater social cohesion' (European Parliament, 2000).

The noted failure of the Lisbon Strategy (Wyplosz, 2010) has not put an end to the waves of reforms hitting higher education, but have intensified their impacts and contradictions, while spurring the university sector to respond by restating a 'common vision'. There is a wish for universities to perform more and wider roles in the 'knowledge society', providing more discipline-based education, professional training and fundamental as well as applied and profitable research. There is recognition that higher education institutions are diverse and should retain their autonomy. It is also acknowledged that they have a public responsibility for promoting social equity and an inclusive society (EUA, 2007: 2). Yet the contradictions are large, as the main political imperatives are for rationalisation, downsizing and more centralised control even as political support and financial resources are being pulled away from the sector. The pressure for international competitiveness has led to an increased emphasis on performance management, institutional branding and global market positioning, with Irish tertiary education institutions desperately seeking, and locked into, maintaining, 'world class' status while competing for their market share of students. Their research activities increasingly eschew traditional scholarly values of academic freedom, in favour of 'impact', market values and competitive global league tables. Political efforts to restructure the national higher education 'landscape' have intensified institutional uncertainty and competition since the vision anticipates corporate merger-style changes, with fewer, larger institutions, greater economies of scale and concern with 'critical mass' (HEA, 2012).

While profitability and markets have become more important, reform for its own sake, increased managerialism and audit culture are also ascendant as ideological-cultural norms in themselves, recreating once-collegial and peer-oriented academia as a 'disenchanted' and hierarchical lifeworld. Lock and Martins criticise the European knowledge economy for restricting the citizen to a very minimal interpretation of 'citizenism' that '...humanizes capitalism, renders it more just and gives it a "supplemental soul"' (2009: 160). The European model advances notions of 'active citizenship' based upon the 'competent, active citizen', a compliant citizen imaginary that is essentially based upon depoliticised and functional understandings of citizenship and citizen education (Biesta, 2009: 146).

An exploration of research within higher education policy and practice (Khoo et al., 2007) suggested several different possible scenarios and models for the globalisation of research, teaching and engagement. At the start of the current crisis, Khoo and Lehane (2008) argued that development educators must critically engage with the globalisation of Irish HEIs as a matter of urgency. We argued that development education presented an important corrective to an increasingly instrumental, dehumanised and economistic vision of global education. For development education to play this role, however, it must reimagine itself defiantly, as a tool for contesting globalisation (Munck, 2007). With increasing pressure on academic researchers and educators to be reform takers and adopt market values and measures, development education can still offer an important alternative for those interested in defending diversity, inclusiveness and other fundamental educational and developmental purposes. To act from, and for, development education entails actively creating, and participating in grounded globalisation, experiencing defiant and critical spaces of reflection (Andreotti, 2010), where globalisation is contested. Development education represents a tradition of critical pedagogical commitments and continues to offer non-coercive spaces for reflective and critical thinking, where commitments to the values of humanity, solidarity, diverse voices and meaningful participation can continue to be explored.

Key research debates

A meta-analysis of development education research in Ireland identified three main debates dominating the research field (Fiedler et al., 2011: 6). Firstly, there was a struggle to find clear demarcation lines between governmental needs (particularly for public information about its Official Development Assistance or ODA) and development education seen as a broader educational process, but also to identify points of convergence between these two purposes. A second, related debate was how development education is (or should be) positioned within ODA programming and the overall paradigm of international development. Sumner and Tribe (2008) note that within development studies, understandings of 'development' generally shifted from describing long-term societal transformations to prescribing a shorter-term 'impact agenda' by the 1990s. This shift forced to the surface hard questions about how educational efforts targeted at a domestic public could be said to contribute to the achievement of narrowly defined development goals in ODA recipient countries. This, in turn, pushed forward the third main research debate about the fundamental implications and impact of 'mainstreaming' development education.

Development education had its historical origins and social roots in non-governmental or civil society activism of the 1970s (e.g. Dillon, 2009). Some civil society actors, especially those from an activist or campaigning background, saw 'mainstreaming' and professionalisation as de-radicalising, or 'de-clawing' the project of development education (Bryan, 2011). By the end of the 1990s, development education had become increasingly embedded in mainstream educational and political institutions and settings, including government departments, primary and secondary schools, universities and colleges, youth programmes and trade unions. This posed an uncomfortable challenge for development educators who remained faithful to their radical political and educational roots, even as they sought to maximise the growing opportunities to spread and institutionalise more development education activities.

Irish development education research can be seen to fall into seven broad research themes, as listed in Table 8.1. We might note that this research agenda does not include the examination of the role, purpose, content or context of 'research' itself. Practitioners who do not consciously see themselves as 'researchers' find 'research' to be a particularly inscrutable and abstract category. From the academic side of the fence, research is so central to the everyday academic world that it has 'the invisibility of the obvious' (Kenway and Fahey, 2009: 7). There is also ambivalence towards research because it dominates academia's prestige economy, generating anxiety around unhealthy academic individualism and competition, to the neglect of teaching and student needs, shared academic culture and collegiality.

Table 8.1 Themes in Irish development education research

Development education research themes
1. Description of development education provision (formal and non-formal).
2. Identification of opportunities for integrating development education within the formal curriculum at post-primary level.
3. Exploration of attitudes, understandings and engagement with development education.
4. Examination of representations of development issues and policies in the formal curriculum and in the wider public domain.
5. Examination of the status and perceptions of citizenship education.
6. Identification of challenges and constraints associated with development education provision.
7. Evaluation of development education teaching and learning methodologies.

Source: Adapted from Fiedler et al. (2011: 8).

Development education in hard times: Responses to economic crisis in the West

At the end of 2008, economic crisis and budget austerity caused development education activities across Europe to shift from an expansionary to a contractionary, survivalist mode. Austerity and budget defensiveness have intensified managerialist tendencies, pushing development and development education towards an almost exclusive concern with 'impact' and 'value-for-money'. Official political discourse in both the UK and Ireland emphasised the difficulties of maintaining aid commitments in the face of cuts to other budget sectors and austerity for the electorate. In the UK broad government support for public education and awareness-raising was replaced by an emphasis on evaluation, 'results' and 'development impact' (Khoo, 2011a). Projects which failed to meet these criteria were terminated and no new funding was made available for broader development awareness programmes. One UK-based development education centre which had its grant terminated saw this as an indication of '...a new and deep scepticism about development awareness'. As '...the link between development awareness in the UK and poverty reduction overseas is at best unproven...we are under no illusion; DfID's support for our work has changed' (Knowles, 2011).

The current UK position on development education shows a major shift in the assumptions, intentions and approach to development education towards an increased emphasis on benefits to the learner, and the underpinning disposition to promote '...the potential of trade, wealth creation and economic development to build a freer, more prosperous world' (O'Brien, 2011). Previous efforts under New Labour to stimulate and coordinate development education could be interpreted as taking a Keynesian or 'demand-side' approach, using public investment in educational infrastructure and shared understanding to support collective or public benefits, broadly defined. The current Conservative-Liberal Democrat policy regime appears to have shifted towards neoclassical orthodoxy, preferring deregulated 'supply side' activities that roll back the state and allow 'markets' (meaning schools and teachers) to shape development education. Teachers and parents are seen as private individuals, who like (and will fundraise for) popular activities such as school linking and volunteering.

The current period (2008–) of economic crisis in the West (Pilling, 2012) makes it rather difficult to think about the future, but the Fiedler, Bryan and Bracken report (2011) has signposted a research agenda for future development education in Ireland. The research agenda they have identified fits with some of the proposals advanced in this chapter for development education research as integrated scholarship. There is still a dearth of fundamental research on the history and theory of development education. There is a need for integration, meaning cross-disciplinary dialogue and learning between educationists, development studies specialists, historians, political scientists, sociologists, theologians and so on, as well as the obvious engagement with the policy and social context and with the agenda of relevance and impact. In the absence of dialogue, what we can observe happening is direct policy transfer, for example of evaluation frameworks from development studies to development education practice.

The missing dialogue needs to engage the relevant cross-disciplinary, political and ethical debates about the meanings and purposes of development, education and development education. Key topics include research on the debates and controversies surrounding the relationship between the state and civil society and the early contributions of social movements (e.g. O'Sullivan, 2007); about the societal context for development education; the routes for dissemination and learning from the research that has been produced; the disciplinary division between development education and development studies and the role of higher education. More research is also needed on how the scholarship of teaching communicates or extends what researchers already know, and how this shapes the researchers and research agenda of the future.

There are six main problems which set a challenging scenario for those interested in an ethical and transformative vision of global higher education (see also Khoo, 2011b). Core resources and support for development education in particular, and for research and the tertiary sector in general, are low, volatile and declining. The current academic monitoring and reward structures encourage trade-offs, not integration of scholarships and those academics who have attempted an integrated approach have faced considerable difficulties and disincentives (Huber, 2004). Media and political pressure discourage public support for academic freedom and for defiant and global visions of scholarship. The tertiary institutions themselves are far too preoccupied with problems of financing, competition and relentless reforms from above to clarify what they stand for. Overall, the policy community is facing 'hard times' for higher education (Walker, 2006). Compliant and risk-averse versions of education prevail in such times, as human capital theory and the imperatives of the knowledge economy make it hard to justify education in democratic, educational or non-economistic terms.

Conclusion: Pluralising global educational and developmental futures

This chapter concludes that higher education has something valuable to offer development education, but development education has something important to offer higher education in return. Development education is a powerful tool for engaging an ethical reimagination of higher education in the current era of globalised and managed (dis-)engagement. The track record of limited, conditional and volatile support for development education research does not mean that there is no case for a wider and more integrated conception of development education research that moves beyond research *on* development education, to encompass questions of what it is broadly *about*, and what it is *for*, when integrated into an ecology of cross-disciplinary and engaged scholarship. North-South collaborative research offers important spaces and examples of partnerships in teaching, training and research that engages with development issues (see Nakabugo et al., 2010). Development education research, thus broadly conceived, merits core support not only from official development assistance programmes, but from third-level institutions, from development education practitioners, from the education and development sectors generally, and from the whole gamut of disciplines and professions represented at tertiary institutions.

Nandy (2000) suggests that universities play a pivotal role, especially in postcolonial societies, by enabling cultural resistance and recovery through a democratisation of knowledge (see also Delanty, 2001). The main responsibility of tertiary education is to 'pluralize the future by pluralizing knowledge in the present', providing 'a better, more honest range of options – material, ideational, and normative – for human beings and societies to choose from' (Nandy, 2000: 122). Gidley (2000: 236, 237) suggests that higher education can break out of globalisation's vicious circles, if inspired human agency and a sense of higher coherence are allowed to come in to underpin attempts to solve the problems of the future. She contends that those of us in the tertiary education sector, '...[a]cademics, administrators and students alike need to become creatively courageous in reinventing universities if we are to become the creators of transformed futures and not just creatures of the past' (2000: 238).

Courage, creativity and a different kind of critical mass are needed to effectively challenge the new political economy of market-rational globalisation, and to recover the possibility of alternative futures. Tertiary education can only play its proper critical role with regard to ethical development (Qizilbash, 1996) and human rights (Steiner, 2002), by purposefully diversifying and simultaneously integrating the spaces of research, teaching and engagement. Their democratic and democratising role requires the engagement of a wider public in the production of knowledge about, and practice of, a public pedagogy of human rights (see Giroux, 2003). They play a role in keeping the possibility of democratic futures open, where the quality of human lives, social justice and human freedom can be freely and authentically decided (see Delanty, 2001). In response to the hollow and 'metallic' language of educational reform advanced by managed discourses of education and governance (Fielding, 1999), development educators might choose to counterpose human rights concepts of answerability and constructive accountability (Freedman, 2003).

Bourn suggests that we should be more aware of the fundamental distinction between 'learning about development' and 'critical global pedagogy' – a distinction which invokes the connections between theory and practice (2011). The bulk of commissioned and published research on development education tends to centre around professional and formal-sector approaches to development education in the global North. Yet some of the most interesting and inspiring examples of critical global pedagogy in practice come from movements for direct democracy in the global South which reposition education centrally in a broader reclamation of politics. Developments across Latin America include the '*horizontalidad*' movement in Argentina which followed the financial crisis of 2001 (Sitrin, 2007), the Cuban model (McCloskey, 2011) and the Zapatista programme of alternative tertiary education in Chiapas, Mexico (Khoo and Walsh, forthcoming).

These Latin American examples provide interesting points of comparison with many examples of popular education for resistance and transformation in India (e.g. Kapoor, 2004, 2007) and transformative research and education in South Africa (Hoppers, 2009; SANPAD, no date). These diverse examples point to the possibilities of a travelling and global research imaginary that engages with educational and knowledge alternatives, including informal, indigenous, adult and vocational visions of education which attempt to redefine development on alternative terms that directly challenge, or offer alternatives to, the dominant global neoliberal consensus (King, 1998; Fasheh and Pimparé, 2006; Khoo and Walsh, forthcoming). In these cases, there is much that the North can learn *from*, and not just *about*, development in the South and take heart from the promise of defiant and critical development education practice for alternative, ethical versions of globalised education.

References

Andreotti, V (2010) 'Global education in the "21st century": Two perspectives on the "post-" of modernism', *International Journal of Development Education and Global Learning*, 2(2), pp. 5–22.

Biesta, G J J (2009) 'What kind of citizenship for European higher education? Beyond the competent active citizen', *European Educational Research Journal*, 8(2), pp. 146–158.

Borg, B, Hayden, I and Regan C (2006) 'Human development – where do we fit in?' in C Regan (ed.) *80:20 Development in an Unequal World*, Dublin: 80:20 Educating and Acting for a Better World, pp. 121–140.

Bourn, D (2007) 'Building academic support for development education', *Policy and Practice: A Development Education Review*, Vol. 5, Autumn 2007, pp. 31–42.

Bourn, D (2011) 'Discourses and practices around development education: From learning about development to critical global pedagogy', *Policy and Practice: A Development Education Review*, Vol. 13, Autumn 2011, pp. 11–29, available: http://www.developmenteducationreview.com/issue13-focus1 (accessed 8 February 2013).

Boyer, E (1990) *Scholarship Reconsidered: Priorities of the Professoriate*, Stanford: Carnegie Foundation for the Advancement of Teaching.

Boyer, E (1996) 'The scholarship of engagement', *Journal of Public Service and Outreach*, 1(1), pp. 11–20.

Bryan, A (2011) 'Another cog in the anti-politics machine? The "de-clawing" of development education', *Policy and Practice: A Development Education Review*, Vol. 12, Spring 2011, pp. 1–14, available: http://www.developmenteducation-review.com/issue12-editorial (accessed 8 February 2013).

Council of Europe (2001) 'Development education and raising European public awareness of development cooperation', 13323/01DEVGEN 157, November 2001.

Delanty, G (2001) *Challenging Knowledge: The University in a Knowledge Society*, Buckingham, UK: Open University Press.

Dillon, S (2009) *Trócaire and Development Education: Remembering the Past, Signposting the Future*, Kildare: Trócaire.

European Parliament (2000) 'Lisbon European Council 23 and 24 March 2000 Presidency Conclusions', available: http://www.europarl.europa.eu/summits/lis1_en.htm#a (accessed 8 February 2013).

EUA (European University Association) (2007) 'Lisbon Declaration: Europe's Universities beyond 2010: Diversity with a common purpose', Brussels: European University Association, available: http://www.eua.be/fileadmin/user_upload/files/Lisbon_Convention/Lisbon_Declaration.pdf (accessed 8 February 2013).

Fasheh, M and Pimparé, S (2006) *Emerging and Re-emerging Learning Communities: Old Wisdoms and New Initiatives From Around the World*, Paris: UNESCO November (ED-2006/WS/16), pp. 6–11.

Fiedler, M, Bracken, M and Bryan, A (2011) *Mapping the Past, Charting the Future: A Review of Irish Government's Engagement with Development Education and a Meta-Analysis of Development Education Research in Ireland*, available: http://www.irishaid.gov.ie/media/irishaid/allwebsitemedia/20newsandpublications/publicationpdfsenglish/deac-research-report-2011-mapping-the-past-charting-the-future.pdf (accessed 9 April 2013).

Fielding, M (1999) 'Target setting, policy pathology and student perspectives: Learning to labour in new Times', *Cambridge Journal of Education*, Vol. 29, pp. 277–287.

Freedman, L (2003) 'Averting international death and disability: Human rights, constructive accountability and maternal mortality in the Dominican Republic', *International Journal of Gynaecology and Obstetrics*, Vol. 82, pp. 111–114.

Gidley, J (2000) 'Unveiling the human face of university futures' in S Inayatullah and J Gidley (eds) *The University in Transformation: Global Perspectives on the Futures of the University*, Westport, CT: Bergin and Garvey.

Giroux, H (2003) 'Public pedagogy and the politics of resistance: Notes on a critical theory of educational struggle', *Educational Philosophy and Theory*, 35(1), pp. 5–16.

Government of Ireland (2006) *White Paper on Irish Aid*, available: http://www.dfa.ie/uploads/documents/Irish%20Aid/temp/white%20paper%20on%20irish%20aid%202006.pdf (accessed 8 February 2013).

HEA (Higher Education Authority) (2012) 'Completing the landscape process for Irish higher education', Dublin: Higher Education Authority.

Hoppers, C O (2009) 'Development education at the transition from the modern triage society to a moral and cognitive reconstruction of citizenship', keynote address at the *International Conference on Critical Thinking and Development Education: Moving from evaluation to research*, NUI Galway, 3rd–4th October 2009, available: http://www.nuigalway.ie/dern/documents/prof_catherine_hoppers.pdf (accessed 8 February 2013).

Huber, M Taylor (2004) *Balancing Acts: The Scholarship of Teaching and Learning in Academic Careers*, Stylus Publishing: Sterling, VA.

Irish Development Education Association (IDEA) (2012a) 'Towards a Stronger and More Effective DE Sector Capacity Development Plan 2013–2015', Dublin: 19 September 2012, available http://www.ideaonline.ie/content/towards-stronger-and-more-effective-de-sector-final-cd-plan-available (accessed 9 April 2013).

Irish Development Education Association (IDEA) (2012b) 'Something Worth Learning About? Why We Need Development Education Now More Than Ever', Dublin, 8 November 2012, available http://www.ideaonline.ie/content/something-worth-learning-about-why-we-need-development-education-now-more-ever (accessed 9 April 2013).

Kapoor, D (2007) 'Subaltern social movement learning and the decolonization of space in India', *International Education*, 37(1), pp. 10–41.

Kapoor, D (2004) 'Popular education and social movements in India: State responses to constructive resistance for social justice', *Convergence*, 37(2), pp. 55–63.

Kenway, J and Fahey, J (eds) (2009) *Globalizing the Research Imagination*, London and New York: Routledge.

Khoo, S (2012) 'Educating within culture and human rights: What can a capabilities approach add?' in K Hashemi and L Briskman (eds) *NAM Year Book on Human Rights and Cultural diversity: Cultures in Support of Humanity*, Vol. 1, Tehran: Non-aligned Movement Center for Human Rights and Cultural Diversity, pp. 444–475.

Khoo, S (2011a) 'The shifting policy landscape of development education', *Policy and Practice: A Development Education Review*, Issue 13, Autumn 2011, pp. 1–10, available: http://www.developmenteducationreview.com/issue13-editorial (accessed 8 February 2013).

Khoo, S (2011b) 'Ethical globalisation or privileged internationalisation? Exploring global citizenship and internationalisation in Irish and Canadian universities', *Globalisation, Societies, Education*, 9(3–4), pp. 337–353.

Khoo, S (2006) 'Development education, citizenship and civic engagement at third level and beyond – Capacity building for development education in third level education', *Policy and Practice: A Development Education Review*, Issue 3, Special Issue on 'Citizenship', pp. 26–39.

Khoo S, Healy C and Coate K (2007) 'Development education and development research – Contradictory or complementary?' *Policy and Practice: A Development Education Review*, Issue 5, Autumn 2007, pp. 5–19.

Khoo, S and Lehane, O (2008) 'Globalisation and the re-imagination of research, teaching and learning in Irish higher education', *Policy and Practice: A Development Education Review*, Issue 7, Autumn 2008, pp. 18–34.

Khoo, S and Walsh, A (forthcoming) 'Regenerating education from below: Critical pedagogy in alternative development niches', *British Journal of Sociology of Education*.

King, L (ed.) (1998) *Reflecting Visions: New Perspectives on Adult Education for Indigenous Peoples*, Waikato: UNESCO: Institute for Education, The University of Waikato.

Knowles, E (2011) 'DFID's changing funding and policy priorities', *Irish Newsletter for Development Education Exchange (INDEX)*, Dublin: Comhlámh.

Lock, G and Martins, H (2009) 'The European universities, citizenship and its limits: What won't solve the problems of our time', *European Educational Research Journal*, 8, pp. 159–174.

Massey, D (2009) 'Responsibilities over distance', in J Kenway and J Fahey (eds) *Globalizing the Research Imagination*, London and New York: Routledge, pp. 73–85.

McCloskey, S (2011) 'Cuba's model of development: Lessons for global education', *Policy and Practice: A Development Education Review*, Vol. 13, Autumn 2011, pp. 84–98, available: http://www.developmenteducationreview.com/issue13-viewpoint2 (accessed 8 February 2013).

Munck, R (2010) 'Civic engagement and global citizenship in a university context: Core business or desirable add-on?', *Arts and Humanities in Higher Education*, 9(1), pp. 31–41.

Munck, R (2007) *Globalisation and Contestation*, London: Routledge.

Nakabugo, M, Barrett, E, McEvoy, P and Munck, R (2010) 'Best practice in North-South research relationships in higher education: The Irish African partnership model', *Policy and Practice: A Development Education Review*, Vol. 10, Spring 2010, pp. 89–98.

Nandy, A (2000) 'Recovery of indigenous knowledge and dissenting futures of the university', in S Inayatullah and J Gidley (eds) *The University in Transformation: Global Perspectives on the Futures of the University*, Westport, CT: Bergin and Garvey.

O'Brien, S (2011) 'The Department for International Development's Approach to Development Education', *Policy & Practice: A Development Education Review*, Vol. 13, Autumn 2011, pp. 62–66, available: http://www.developmenteducationreview.com/issue13-perspectives1

O'Connell, P (2007) 'On reconciling irreconcilables: Neo-liberal globalisation and human rights', *Human Rights Law Review*, 7(3) pp. 483–509.

O'Sullivan, K (2007) 'Biafra to Lomé: The evolution of Irish government policy on official development assistance, 1969–1975', *Irish Studies in International Affairs*, Vol. 18, pp. 91–107.

Perkin, H (2006) 'History of universities', in J Forest and P Altbach (eds) *International Handbook of Higher Education: Part One Global Themes and Contemporary Challenges*, Dordrecht: Springer, pp. 159–205.

Pilling, D (2012) 'Capitalism in crisis: Perilous path to prosperity', *Financial Times*, 16 January 2012, available: http://www.ft.com/cms/s/0/1d92589a-3090-11e1-9436-00144feabdc0.html#axzz2PCROwvbo (accessed 1 April 2013).

Qizilbash, M (1996) 'Ethical development', *World Development*, Vol. 24, pp. 1209–1221.

Realizing Rights: The Ethical Globalisation Initiative, 'What is ethical globalisation?', available: http://www.realizingrights.org (accessed 18 July 2008).

Regan, C and Sinclair, S (2006) 'Engaging development – learning for a better future?', in C Regan (ed.) *80:20 Development in an Unequal World*, Dublin: 80:20 Educating and Acting for a Better World, pp. 107–120.

SANPAD (South Africa Netherlands research Programme on Alternatives in Development) (no date), available: http://www.sanpad.org.za/sanpad2011/ (accessed 9 April 2013).

Secretary of State for International Development (UK) (1997) *Eliminating World Poverty: A Challenge for the 21st Century: White Paper on International Development*, London: DFID, http://webarchive.nationalarchives.gov.uk/+/http://www.dfid.gov.uk/policieandpriorities/files/whitepaper1997.pdf (accessed 8 February 2013).

Sitrin, M (2007) 'Ruptures in imagination: Horizontalism, autogestion and affective politics in Argentina', *Policy & Practice: A Development Education Review*, Vol. 5, Autumn 2007, pp. 43–53.

Steiner, H (2002) 'The university's critical role in the human rights movement', *Harvard Human Rights Journal*, Vol. 15, Spring, pp. 317–328.

Sumner, A and Tribe, M (2008) *International Development Studies: Theories and Methods in Research and Practice*, London: Sage.

Vannini, P and Milne, L (forthcoming) 'Public ethnography as innovative learning – an in-depth statement', available: http://publicethnography.net/projects/public-ethnography-innovative-learning-depth-statement (accessed 8 February 2013).

Walker, M (2006) *Higher Education Pedagogies*, Maidenhead: Open University Press.

Wallerstein, I (2nd ed.) (2001) *Unthinking Social Science: The Limits of Nineteenth Century Paradigms*, Philadelphia: Temple University Press.

Wyplosz, C (2010) 'The failure of the Lisbon strategy', *Vox: Research-based Policy Analysis and Commentary from Leading Economists*, 12 January 2010, available: http://www.voxeu.org/article/failure-lisbon-strategy (accessed 8 February 2013).

Part III

Development Education and Sustainable Development

9

Striking a Faustian Bargain? Development Education, Education for Sustainable Development and the Economic Growth Agenda

David Selby and Fumiyo Kagawa

Introduction

Faustus is writ large in European mythology. A sixteenth-century German astronomer, he is reputed to have sold his soul to the devil for unlimited power. In modern English parlance, to 'strike a Faustian bargain' is to be willing to make questionable sacrifices for knowledge or power or influence, closing one's eyes to the consequences.

This chapter will ask whether the interrelated and overlapping fields of development education and education for sustainable development are in the process of striking a Faustian bargain. Each field draws significant inspiration from a radical, status quo critical, value system of transformative intent with respect to the human condition and the human/nature relationship. But, are there signs within each field of a compromising of values and trimming of the original vision in light of the economic growth agenda and global marketplace? And, if so, is that happening by commission, by oversight borne of sleeping immersion in current orthodoxies, or by studied omission?

Falling in or out with the growth agenda?

The recent global financial meltdown has occasioned yet another wave of frenzied action to revitalise the oversized and overstretched global economic growth machine (Kingsnorth, 2011). 'One of the most striking features of the global financial crisis that emerged during 2008', writes Jackson (2009: 68), 'was the degree of consensus that the overriding priority was to re-invigorate economic growth. From the International Monetary Fund to the United Nations Environment Programme, from political parties across the political spectrum, and from within both liberal and coordinated market economies, the call was for mechanisms that would "kick-start" economic growth again'. Governments, banks, corporations, as well as the multilateral and bilateral banking and development agencies related to the United Nations system, have gone on to canvass and enact all kinds of initiatives intended to stimulate (or avoid hampering) further and faster growth. These include: swingeing reductions in public expenditure and services (Public Services International Research Unit, multi-dated), reinvigorated drives towards privatisation (Seeking Alpha, 2011), decentralisation of the locus of control away from government (Fedelino, 2010) and otherwise shrinking governmental latitude to shield the vulnerable from often times deleterious market forces (Wall, 2012).

All of this is happening in the name of the global marketplace; of ensuring virility in an era of global competitiveness predicated on unending growth. Affluent societies and peoples, in particular, have become so transfixed by the idea of economic growth that it has taken on the proportions of delusional realism. Capitalist realism, argues Mark Fisher (2009: 2), has become such an ideological malaise that there is a 'widespread sense that not only is capitalism the only viable political and economic system, but that it is now impossible even to *imagine* a coherent alternative to it' [italics in original].

As Clive Hamilton (2010: 32) sees it, we have become immured in 'growth fetishism'. Hamilton adds that:

> In affluent societies, religious value seems now to be invested in the most profane object, growth of the economy, which at the individual level takes the form of the accumulation of material goods. Our political leaders and commentators believe that it has magical powers that provide the answer to every problem. Growth alone will save the poor. If inequality causes concern, a rising tide lifts all boats. Growth will solve unemployment. If we want better schools and more hospitals then economic growth will provide. And if the environment is in decline then higher growth will generate the means to fix it. Whatever the social problem, the answer is always more growth (2010: 33).

The reference to growth as an article of quasi-religious faith is echoed by Bob Lloyd (2009: 516) who sees close parallels between the 'God delusion' as interrogated by Richard Dawkins (2006) and what he calls the 'growth delusion' – 'the irrational insistence on endless growth as a non negotiable axiom, by a large proportion of the world's population'. Those with the temerity to demur are 'denigrated as aberrant spoilsports' (Lloyd, 2009: 517) and characterised as 'opponents of progress' wishing us back to a cave dwelling existence (Hamilton, 2010: 34). Viable alternatives are not there to countenance; they are banished from the landscape.

Economic growth goes hand in glove with economic globalisation; what Carlos Torres (2009: 14) calls 'globalization from above'. This involves the ongoing neoliberal systemisation of the world as a marketplace through the opening of national economic borders, the creation of huge regional markets, the acceleration and intensification of financial exchange especially through electronic communication, the burgeoning role of the corporate sector, and the diminution of the power and sway of the nation state in determining policy priorities and legislating (Wells et al., 1998; Hall, 2002: 36; Rizvi, 2004; Torres, 2009: 14).

This hegemonic form of globalisation is resisted by 'globalization from below' – the myriad more or less interconnected expressions globally of social and environmental justice activism and indigenous cultural resistance (Hawken, 2007; Torres, 2009: 15; Selby and Kagawa, 2011). In response, the embrace of humanistic values remains largely tokenistic within neoliberal discourse (Chossudovsky, 1997; Stromquist, 2002). 'The trouble', writes Hossay (2006: 120) 'is, increasingly, the only goals that matter are those defined by the market. Concerns over the health of the global ecosystem, justice, traditions, sacred beliefs, shared community, care and concern for fellow beings, are all left by the wayside'.

Within such a climate, there is the constant danger that those committed to 'globalization from below' can find themselves co-opted, seduced or swallowed up by the growth and globalisation agendas. Wanting to effect change, they feel themselves facing a dilemma of either trimming their agenda so as to have some say, sway and influence of a reformist nature within the prevailing climate or of adhering to a transformative, status quo critical standpoint which may well resign them to a position of peripheral, maverick influence. Do they opt for tampering with, and so, perhaps, bolstering the system, or stand by turning it around? A case in point is that of climate change advocates seeking purchase and influence in the corridors of power and so making the most persuasive case they can for green energy primarily based on its potential to make a significant contribution to continuous economic growth. They have chosen to do this when, all around them, lies abundant evidence that economic growth and consumerism are at the root of runaway climate change that is already damaging the lives of 325 million people per year (Global Humanitarian Forum, 2009; Hamilton, 2010). Advocacy of green energy is laudable but in making their case as persuasively as possible to the powers-that-be they accede to making protection of the climate secondary to growth. In so doing a kind of Faustian bargain is struck; a selling of the soul to the prevailing neoliberal worldview in return for some, likely ephemeral, purchase on policy. This pact prioritises a place at the table now, whatever the likely future dystopian consequences resulting from an adherence to the growth imperative. For probably similar reasons, leading environmental advocates have chosen to relinquish their public embrace of the intrinsic value of nature by adopting an instrumental growth-speak lexicon in which nature is described as 'natural capital', 'ecosystem services' and 'natural resources' (Selby and Kagawa, 2011).

The fields of development education and education for sustainable development can be considered educational expressions of 'globalization from below'. Are they similarly caught up in striking a Faustian bargain with the neoliberal powers-that-be?

Development education across Europe: What is said; what is not being said

Development education in Europe is a broad field embracing overlapping initiatives under various headings: development education and awareness raising (DEAR), global education, global development education, global learning, education for sustainable development, to name but a few. The European Consensus on Development states that:

> Development Education and Awareness Raising contribute to the eradication of poverty and to the promotion of sustainable development through public awareness raising and education approaches and activities that are based on values of human rights, social responsibility, gender equality and a sense of belonging to one world (*European Consensus on Development: The Contribution of Development Education and Awareness Raising*, 2007: 5).

Agnes Rajacic et al. (2010)'s comprehensive review of DEAR discerns six common threads across the field: development of critical understanding of issues, local through global; a concern for empowerment; a values bedrock of justice, inclusion, human rights and respect for others and the environment; a learner-centered, participatory pedagogy; a desire to effect informed engagement and advocacy; and a redressing of Eurocentrism through greater attention to Southern voices. Overall, the study points to an emerging tendency to move away from uncritical acceptance of an official development cooperation agenda to more critical engagement with development-related issues.

Such a transformative reorientation is welcome. However, what is largely missing from the DEAR discourse is explicit attention to issues of economic growth, neoliberal globalisation and consumerism which, according to many commentators, are deeply and devastatingly culpable for fomenting inequality, social injustice and the destruction of both ecosphere and ethnosphere (Chossudovsky, 1997; Hall, 2002; McGregor, 2003). A keyword search of three studies of development education in Europe (CONCORD/DEEEP, 2009; Krause, 2010; Rajacic et al., 2010) reveals that economic growth is barely mentioned, let alone problematised. Globalisation appears throughout the three studies, usually associated with the concept of 'interdependence', but seems taken as a given, an essentially unexceptional, non-complicit canvas against which social justice and environmental issues are treated. There is no mention in the studies of 'consumerism', although 'consumption' is sometimes identified as a development education theme.

Some expressions of development education adopt a heavily 'global skills' orientation which, in its formulation and overall tenor, seems to close down learning opportunities for sustained and forensic scrutiny of the complicity of the global marketplace. *Global Skills*, a manual produced by the Development Education Research Centre at the London Institute of Education, offers 'a framework that equips the UK workforce to make sense of the global society, with the appropriate skills to be active participants in the global society and economy of the twenty first century' (Bourn, 2008: 4). One passage summarises the 'generic skills in the context of globalisation' as 'communicating well and recognizing cultural and social difference, being able to respond to rapidly changing skills and knowledge needs, and being able to work in collaborative environments with people of different backgrounds' (Bourn, 2008: 24).

Development education, so rendered, looks by and large accepting of the neoliberal growth and globalisation model and seems primarily concerned with workforce preparation for technocratic competitive efficacy. Key global issues are explored but against a backdrop of imperturbable and incontrovertible economic globalisation. Social cohesion and multiculturalism – what the manual refers to as 'the recognition of cultural sensitivity in forms that are appropriate and relevant to upskilling the UK workforce' (Ibid.: 4) – matter but are conceived of as feeding into muscular economic performance. Where are the skills and capacities for resistance and transgression amidst a 'globe-speak' reflective of UK national imperatives?

These findings raise some important questions. First, why does a field with a core commitment to the eradication of global poverty and inequality through education largely shrink from explicitly addressing the interface between global poverty, social injustice and environmental devastation and what has been described as 'the powerful wave of neo-liberalism rolling over the planet' (Jickling and Wals, 2008: 2)? Effective treatment of causal relationships would seem to be a *sine qua non* of a thoroughgoing social justice agenda.

Following from this, does the field sufficiently deal with controversial issues that could be construed as indispensable for fostering 'informed citizen participation' and helping the learner 'learn how to learn'? A 2010 CONCORD/DEEEP study on development education in formal curricula in 29 European countries reveals 'a reluctance to address particular controversial issues that challenge our global society', pointing out that the theme of global terrorism never appears in curricula 'despite its constantly high profile and analysis in national media, and in government policies'. It may be included, the study speculates, under the topic of 'human security' but is never explicitly referenced (CONCORD/DEEEP, 2010: 16). The global growth economy and hyper-consumerism may occupy an analogous position. They may lie submerged under themes such as 'global poverty', 'global economy/markets and trade' and 'globalization' while not made explicit. But, why might that be?

Third, how can mal-development be treated unless consumerism is confronted head-on in learning programmes? There is no assurance in the programme descriptions reviewed that consumerism is interrogated. Or that, if it is present but inconspicuous, the treatment moves beyond reformist 'consumer awareness' (sustainable, responsible, ethical, green consumerism) to a critical treatment implicating 'consumption beyond dignified sufficiency' (McIntosh, 2008: 180) as complicit in global environmental and social breakdown. David Woodward and Andrew Simms (2006: 3) point out that 'Europe's levels of consumption amount to more than double its own domestic biocapacity, meaning that European lifestyles can only be sustained by depending on the natural resources and environmental services of other nations'. Why, then, is rampant consumerism given such minimal attention in development education programmes?

Fourth, what are the repercussions of the easy connect being made with the concept of 'education for sustainable development'? The CONCORD/DEEEP (2009: 13–14) study finds that development educators in 19 of the 29 countries surveyed use 'sustainable development' as an operative descriptor in learning programmes. But has the field embraced the concept too readily and uncritically? If so, why might that be?

Education for sustainable development: *sotto voce* on the neoliberal agenda

Tomorrow Today (UNESCO, 2010) is a collection of papers published to coincide with the mid-decade report to the UN General Assembly on the UN Decade of Education for Sustainable Development (2005–2014). As such, it provides something of a 'state of the art' policy and practice overview of a field garnering adherence and support from around the world. In an opening contribution to *Tomorrow Today*, Mark Richmond (2010: 19), asserts that ESD 'provides many of the questions and answers about what education should be about and what it should be for in the 21st century'. That said, it is interesting that across the contributions to the collection there is no thoroughgoing unpacking of the neoliberal agenda and its culpability for fomenting many of the issues that are ubiquitously touched upon in the collection, such as inequality, poverty, starvation, biodiversity loss and climate change. There is, then, space for a serious look at presenting consequences but little critical examination of root causes.

Across the collection, too, the inevitability of increased economic globalisation and the consequences for environmental and social sustainability are not called into question. While there are references to the importance of 'sustainable consumption', there is no direct reference to rampant consumerism in the metaphorical North and amongst elites in the metaphorical South and the part it plays in violating once-resilient communities and ecosystems. The global arms trade, a lucrative strand of globalisation (Hall, 2002: 37) is not mentioned. True, there are contributions expounding the positive benefits of green growth (Sangkyoo, 2010: 49) and outlining approaches to building a corporate social ethic (Fien and Maclean, 2010: 24) but absent are contributions embracing a root and branch critique of the global marketplace, its manifestations and impacts, and offering alternatives.

This same lacuna was observed by a UK spokesperson at the World Summit on Sustainable Development in Johannesburg in 2002. At the Summit there was no critical exploration of sustainable development:

> It was as if engaging in this discussion could potentially ruin the 'whole idea' and slow down its world-wide implementation. The focus of this international gathering, instead, seems to have been on how to *promote* education for sustainable development, and how to set standards, benchmarks, and control mechanisms to confidently assess progress towards its realization. Rather than discussing and exposing underlying ideologies, values and worldviews, the general consensus at the World Summit on Sustainable Development, and the many meetings that were organized in its slipstream, seemed to be that educators have passed the reflective stage, and that they must roll up their sleeves and start implementing! However, it can also be argued that at best they are implementing a chimera – a fanciful illusion – or worse. It could also be argued that many educators have become agents in the trend towards economic globalization (Jickling and Wals, 2008: 6).

How resonant is this with the neoliberal educational agenda of standards, benchmarks, testing and accountability!

The Bonn Declaration emerging from the UNESCO World Conference on Education for Sustainable Development, 2009, was in similar vein with two thirds of its text given over to a 'call for action' listing of concrete initiatives that policy-makers and practitioners should undertake. In its short preamble, there is reference to the global economic system. 'The global financial and economic crises', the text goes (UNESCO, 2009: 1), 'highlights the risks of unsustainable economic development models and practices based on short-term gains'. This is subsequently followed by the assertion that ESD 'is critical for the development of new economic thinking' (Ibid.: 2) but the reader is left wondering in what direction that thinking might lead. For John Huckle (2010) UNESCO-driven ESD is tantamount to 'business as usual' and supportive of the global treadmill of neoliberalism. The Bonn Declaration, Huckle asserts, 'ignores economic and political realities', 'locates the challenges facing humanity in values, rather than the political economy of sustainable societies', 'fails to specify what values, knowledge, skills and competencies might encourage sustainable living, participation in society, and decent work', and 'fails to suggest ways in which current economic thinking should change' (pp. 135–136). We need, he adds, 'to locate the barriers to sustainability in the structures and processes of global capitalism and recognise the limitations of dominant models of sustainable development and current proposals for new green deals' (Ibid.: 136).

There is a fundamental problem in education for sustainable development arising out of the continued reticence of its agencies and proponents to come clean about whether, for them, development connotes growth. The World Commission on Environment and Development report, *Our Common Future*, gave us the definition of sustainable development that has been rehearsed mantra-like in the past 25 years or so: 'development that meets the needs of the present without compromising the ability of future generations to meet their needs' (WCED, 1987: 43). The report proceeds to treat economic growth and sustainable development as largely consistent concepts (WCED, 1987: 44), a view compounded at the 1992 United Nations Conference on Environment and Development (Gutiérrez Perez and Pozo Llorente, 2005: 298) yet fails, as do most still reciting the 'Bruntland' formula, to reconcile the problems associated with a paradigm that conceives of a future that is 'axiomatically sustainable and able to grow' while being 'supported indefinitely by a finite Earth' (Lloyd, 2009: 516). 'It will be highly improbable to reconcile the objectives of poverty reduction and environmental sustainability if global growth remains the principal economic strategy', write Woodward and Simms (2006: n.p.). 'The scale of growth this model demands would generate unsupportable environmental costs; and the costs would fall disproportionately, and counter productively, on the poorest – the very people the growth is meant to benefit'.

A related problem concerns the melding of globalisation and sustainable development, a union that many sustainability educators appear to see as wholly unexceptional or advocate as desirable (see, for instance, Bourn, 2009). For Jickling and Wals (2008: 5), education for sustainable development is a policy-driven phenomenon propelled forward by the globalisation imperative. 'We view education for sustainable development', they write, 'as a product and carrier of globalizing forces' (2008: 18). As such it allies with allopoetic (neocolonial, externally driven and/or imposed) forms of development rather than autopoetic (locally-framed, self-generating, self-regulating) alternatives (Shiva, 2008: 14).

The field so far offers little by way of antidote to the growth machine by opening learning windows considering ideas for transition to slow growth, no growth and steady state economies (Daly, 1996; Victor, 2008) or for concretising those ideas through learning-in-community experimentation and practice. Critical theory prompts us to raise some important considerations when we find no-go areas and blind spots such as these:

- What is power? Who holds power? How is it used in the sustainability debate?
- The concept of 'false consciousness': the ways in which we may consent to domination and hegemony and accept taken-for-granted ideologies without realising we are doing so.
- The exploration of 'silences' or 'gaps' in the discourse; what is not 'up for discussion' may be even more important than what is (Springett, 2010: 80–81).

Sidestepping a Faustian bargain

We have reviewed the fields of development education and education for sustainable development. With the former, we are left wondering why neoliberal growth and globalisation are kept in the shadows when they are so clearly complicit in deepening poverty and injustice and harming the environment. With the latter, we are left pondering on the reluctance to confront growth fetishism in the name of sustainable development and why the field is so seemingly comfortable with the marketplace globalisation that so threatens sustainability prospects. With both fields, we ask ourselves why the exploration of alternatives to growth fails to receive the curricular and policy exposure the global condition would seem to merit.

Are there traces of a Faustian bargain here? Is the need to achieve purchase within educational systems increasingly wedded to the purposes of the global marketplace encouraging circumspection in identifying with status quo critical agendas? Is there an element of self-censorship amongst academic and non-governmental providers of development and sustainability learning programmes and resources as they gauge what development arms of government and others offering funding support are likely to countenance? Are alignment with prevailing orthodoxies and avoidance of the potentially risqué becoming consciously adopted strategies in relating to government and the formal sector? We have no answers to any of these questions, only hunches, and can only speculate, just as we encourage others to speculate and reflect.

With powerful forces wedded to the global marketplace, how might those committed to pursuing a transformative agenda sidestep the dangers of falling into a Faustian bargain? We close with some suggestions:

- ***Catalyse the 'shadow spaces'.*** Institutions have their formal dimensions and structures but also their 'shadow spaces': 'the relational spaces within organisations that cut across the formal organisational structures for learning and adaptation, and which relate to individual and social learning'. These spaces 'allow individuals or subgroups within organisations to experiment, imitate, communicate, learn and reflect on their actions in ways that can surpass formal processes within policy and organisational settings' (Pelling et al., 2008: 868). Consciously nurtured, the dynamism of the shadow space can inform the formal dimension. Transformative educators, we suggest, might do well to think more creatively and laterally about strategies for creative use of shadow spaces and for inducing spillover into the formal. These can be built into project design.
- ***Ask questions of and speak truth to power.*** From the platform, in the workshop, over an informal cup of tea or anywhere else, we can ask questions of power just as Delyse Springett, cited above does. Or, as Vanessa Andreotti (2006: 44) does: 'Whose interests are represented here? Is this an elitist project? Are we empowering the dominant group to remain in power? Are we doing enough to examine the local/global dimensions of our assumptions?' We can tease out and expose incongruities in mainstream thinking (for instance, between embracing, on the one hand, growth-oriented sustainable development and committing to tackling global inequality, on the other). We can follow David Woodward and Andrew Simms (2006: 5) in asking: 'why is [economic growth] the single overriding goal of every government, of every economy, the world over?'
- ***Capitalise on Trojan horses within the walls of mainstream thinking.*** Notions such as 'balance', presenting diverse perspectives and critical thinking are articles of faith within formal learning systems. The problem has been that the arms of the balancing scales have not extended far enough either side of the fulcrum, the diversity of perspective has been excessively constricted and the critical thinking not very wide or deep. But in the name of these articles of faith, the transformative educator can legitimately fold into learning resources and processes, critical examination of the growth machine and its impact, and exploration of alternatives.

- ***Don't see social entities as monolithic.*** We should regularly remind ourselves that no arm of government offering development education funding, no funding foundation, no educational system and no learning institution is made up of people uniformly wedded to one worldview. Diversity, difference and dissonance are everywhere! A critical stance towards the growth-oriented global marketplace can resonate in the most unexpected of quarters! Seeking to effect transformative change involves at one level developing and building outwards from a network of the sympathetic within and across institutions and systems. But we should note, too, that across the plethora of funding sources for development education and education for sustainable development, there are grant givers who signal their interest in supporting risk-taking, 'out of the box' thinking and radical interrogation of blind spots and assumptions as a precursor to policy innovation. Drawing from a diversity of funding sources is always preferable to dependency on a funding source monoculture but especially so for those pursuing (risking) a transformative status quo critical educational agenda.
- ***Return to first principles.*** In our discussion of education for sustainable development, we have described collective flight from first principles and root meanings at the World Summit of 2002. For those of us wishing to escape any Faustian bargain, a leitmotiv of our work has to be a return to first principles. Discussion of first principles and meanings is also a vital element in engaging with teachers, community leaders and members, and others with whom we work. Why are we committed to this? What values matter most to us, and why? What values, competencies and dispositions do we think will best realise the future, personal through global, that we are working for? Is anything we are doing or saying – or anything we are not doing or saying – tantamount to trimming on our worldview for short-term influence? If so, what are the attendant dangers and likely consequences? What should we do so as to better achieve a congruent way forward?

Conclusion

We write as critical friends of both development education and education for sustainable development. Ours is a well-disposed concern that two fields of status quo critical and transformative purpose are, through omission or commission, and with eyes wide shut, sailing too close to the twin agendas of economic growth and globalisation and are, like Faustus, in proximate danger of selling their souls. Our overarching purpose is to urge that economic growth and globalisation and their deleterious economic, environmental social and cultural effects be addressed head-on in the curricula and discourse of both fields. We also recommend that colleagues recognise the powerful and insidious nature of neoliberalism within educational institutions and systems and develop subtly effective forms of resistance and subversion that make space for learning of unalloyed transformative purpose.

References

Andreotti, V (2006) 'Soft versus critical global citizenship education', *Policy & Practice: A Development Education Review*, Vol. 3, Autumn 2006, pp. 40–51.

Bourn, D (2008) *Global Skills*, London: Learning and Skills Improvement Service.

Bourn, D (2009) 'Globalisation and sustainability: The challenges for education', *Environmental Scientist*, 18(1), pp. 12–14, 52.

Chossudovsky, M (1997) *The Globalisation of Poverty: Impacts of IMF and World Bank reforms*, London: Zed Books.

CONCORD/DEEEP (2007) *European Consensus on Development: The Contribution of Development Education and Awareness Raising*, available: http://www.deeep.org/fileadmin/user_upload/downloads/Consensus_on_DE/DE_Consensus-EN.pdf (accessed 1 December 2010).

CONCORD/DEEEP (2009) *Development Education and the School Curriculum in the European Union: A Report on the Status and Impact of Development Education in the Formal Education Sector and School Curriculum in Member States of the European Union*, available: http://www.deeep.org/schoolcurricula.html (accessed 1 December 2010).

Daly, H (1996) *Beyond Growth: The Economics of Sustainable Development*, Massachusetts: Beacon.

Dawkins, R (2006) *The God Delusion*, London: Bantam.

Fedelino, A (2010) *Making Fiscal Decentralization Work: Cross-country Experiences*, International Monetary Fund, 6 October.

Fien, J and Maclean, R (2010) 'The private sector and education for sustainable development' in UNESCO, *Tomorrow Today*, Paris: Tudor Rose, pp. 52–53.

Fisher, M (2009) *Capitalist Realism: Is There No Alternative?* Winchester: O Books.

Global Humanitarian Forum (2009) *The Anatomy of a Silent Crisis*, Geneva: Global Humanitarian Forum Impact Report.

Gutiérrez Perez, J and Pozo Llorente, M T (2005) '*Stuitifera Navis:* Institutional tensions, conceptual chaos, and professional uncertainty at the beginning of the decade of education for sustainable development', *Policy Futures in Education*, 3(3), pp. 296–308.

Hall, B (2002) 'The right to a new utopia: Adult learning and the changing world of work in an era of global capitalism' in E O' Sullivan, A Morrell and M A O'Connor (eds) *Expanding the Boundary of Transformative Learning*, New York: Palgrave, pp. 35–46.

Hamilton, C (2010) *Requiem for a Species: Why We Resist the Truth about Climate Change*, London: Earthscan.

Hawken, P (2007) *Blessed Unrest: How the Largest Movement in the World Came into Being and Why No One Saw It Coming*, London: Viking.

Hossay, P (2006) *Unsustainable: A Premier for Global Environmental and Social Justice*, London: Zed Books.

Huckle, J (2010) 'ESD and the current crisis of capitalism: Teaching beyond green new deals', *Journal of Education for Sustainable Development*, 4(1), pp. 135–142.

Jackson, T (2009) *Prosperity Without Growth? The Transition to the Sustainable Economy*, London: Sustainable Development Commission.

Jickling, B and Wals, A E J (2008) 'Globalization and environmental education', *Journal of Curriculum Studies*, 40(1), pp. 1–21.

Kingsnorth, P (2011) 'The economic collapse is a crisis of "bigness"', *The Guardian*, 25 September, available: http://www.guardian.co.uk/commentisfree/2011/sep/25/crisis-bigness-leopold-kohr?INTCMP=SRCH (accessed 22 March 2013).

Krause, J (2010) *European Development Education Monitoring Report: "DE Watch"*, available: http://www.deeep.org/dewatch.html (accessed 1 December 2010).

Lloyd, B (2009) 'The growth delusion', *Sustainability*, Vol. 1, pp. 516–536.

McGregor, S (2003) *Consumerism as Source of Structural Violence*, available: http://www.kon.org/hswp/archive/consumerism.html (accessed 24 February 2013).

McIntosh, A (2008) *Hell and High Water: Climate Change, Hope and the Human Condition*, Edinburgh: Birlinn.

Pelling, M, High, C, Dearing, J and Smith, D (2008) 'Shadow spaces for social learning: A relational understanding of adaptive capacity to climate change within organisations', *Environment and Planning*, Vol. 40, pp. 867–884.

Public Services International Research Unit (multi-dated) *Cuts Watch*, University of Greenwich: PSIRU, available: http://www.psiru.org/cutswatch (accessed 11 April 2013).

Rajacic, A, Surian, A, Fricke, H-J, Krause, J and Davis, P (2010) *DEAR in Europe ~ Recommendations for Future Interventions by the European Commission. Final Report of the 'Study on the Experience and Actions of the Main European Actors Active in the Field of Development Education and Awareness Raising'*, available: https://webgate.ec.europa.eu/fpfis/mwikis/aidco/index.php/DEAR_Final_report (accessed 24 February 2013).

Richmond, M (2010) 'Envisioning, coordinating and implementing the UN decade of education for sustainable development' in UNESCO, *Tomorrow Today*, Paris: Tudor Rose, pp. 19–22.

Rizvi, F (2004) 'Debating globalization and education after September 11', *Comparative Education*, 40(2), pp. 157–171.

Sangkyoo, K (2010) 'Unlocking the potential of ESD for green growth' in UNESCO, *Tomorrow Today*, Paris: Tudor Rose, pp. 49–51.

Seeking Alpha (2011) *Privatization Could Stimulate Economic Growth in Europe*, 22 December, available: http://seekingalpha.com/article/315581-privatization-could-stimulate-economic-growth-in-europe (accessed 11 April 2013).

Selby, D and Kagawa, F (2011) 'Climate change learning: Unleashing blessed unrest as the heating happens', *Green Teacher*, 94, Fall, pp. 3–15.

Shiva, V (2008) *Soil Not Oil: Climate Change, Peak Oil and Food Insecurity*, London: Zed.

Springett, D (2010) 'Education for sustainability in the business studies curriculum' in P Jones, D Selby and S Sterling (eds) *Sustainability Education: Perspectives and Practice Across Higher Education*, London: Earthscan, pp. 75–92.

Stromquist, N (2002) *Education in a Globalized World: The Connectivity of Economic Power, Technology, and Knowledge*, Oxford: Rowman and Littlefield Publishers.

Torres, C A (2009) *Education and Neoliberal Globalization*, New York: Routledge.

UNESCO (2009) *Bonn Declaration*, UNESCO World Conference on Education for Sustainable Development, 31 March–2 April 2009, available: http://www.esd-world-conference-2009.org/fileadmin/download/ESD2009_BonnDeclaration080409.pdf (accessed 24 February 2013).

UNESCO (2010) *Tomorrow Today*, Paris: Tudor Rose.

Victor, P (2008) *Managing Without Growth: Slower by Design Not Disaster*, Cheltenham: Edward Elgar.

Wall, K (2012) 'The end of the welfare state? How globalization is affecting state sovereignty', *Global Policy*, 17 August, available: http://www.globalpolicyjournal.com/blog/17/08/2012/end-welfare-state-how-globalization-affecting-state-sovereignty-0 (accessed 11 April 2013).

WCED (World Commission on Environment and Development) (1987) *Our Common Future*, Oxford: Oxford University Press.

Wells, A S, Carnochan, S, Slayton, J, Allen, R and Vasudeva, A (1998) 'Globalization and educational change' in A Hargreaves (ed.) *International Handbook of Educational Change*, Dordrecht: Kluwer Academic Publishers, pp. 322–348.

Woodward, D and Simms, A (2006) *Growth isn't Working: The Uneven Distribution of Benefits and Costs from Economic Growth*, London: New Economics Foundation, available: http://www.neweconomics.org/publications/growth-isn%E2%80%99t-working (accessed 24 February 2013).

10
Development Education and Climate Change

Glenn Strachan

Introduction

> Emissions of carbon dioxide from the burning of fossil fuels have ushered in a new epoch where human activities will largely determine the evolution of Earth's climate (National Research Council, 2011: 5).

The scientific debate around climate change has a substantial heritage. John Tyndall the nineteenth-century Irish physicist provided a step change in our understanding of the atmosphere by revealing that nitrogen and oxygen are transparent to both visible and infrared radiation, while other gases, including carbon dioxide, methane and water vapour, are transparent in the visible part of the spectrum, but partially opaque in the infrared part of the spectrum (Kolbert, 2007). This explained how increases in what became known as 'greenhouse gases' caused heat to be trapped by the Earth's atmosphere. The end of the twentieth century and the early twenty-first century have seen the scientific data from contemporary atmospheric measurements and historic ice core analysis combine with observed climatic changes around the world to support the notion that climate change is happening and that human activity is a primary cause (IPCC, Intergovernmental Panel on Climate Change, 2007a, 2007b).

There are those who contest this assessment with regard to the severity of climate change and particularly its anthropogenic nature (see The Heartland Institute at www.heartland.org, accessed 26 April 2013; Goreham, 2012). However NASA (National Aeronautics and Space Administration) presents evidence on its website to support the consensus that 'Ninety-seven percent of climate scientists agree that climate-warming trends over the past century are very likely due to human activities and most leading scientific organisations worldwide have issued public statements endorsing this position' (NASA).

This chapter on development education (DE) and climate change is written from the perspective that climate change is happening and that it is anthropogenic in nature. The human responses to climate change fall into two broad categories: one is the mitigation of the causes of climate change in order to prevent future adverse changes, and the second is the adaptation to the present impacts of climate change and to the future impacts that are already forecast. Accepting that the causes of climate change are anthropogenic has significance for DE in relation to the mitigation of climate change. The fact that certain economic, political and cultural activities can be linked to the causes of climate change opens the opportunity for DE to contribute to change in these areas. Equally, as increasing numbers of communities are confronted with being forced to change their lifestyles, livelihoods and in some cases their location as a result of climate change (Griswold, 2013), DE can contribute to understanding how populations need to adapt now and in the future. Figure 10.1 suggests the potential contribution of DE in helping to address climate change.

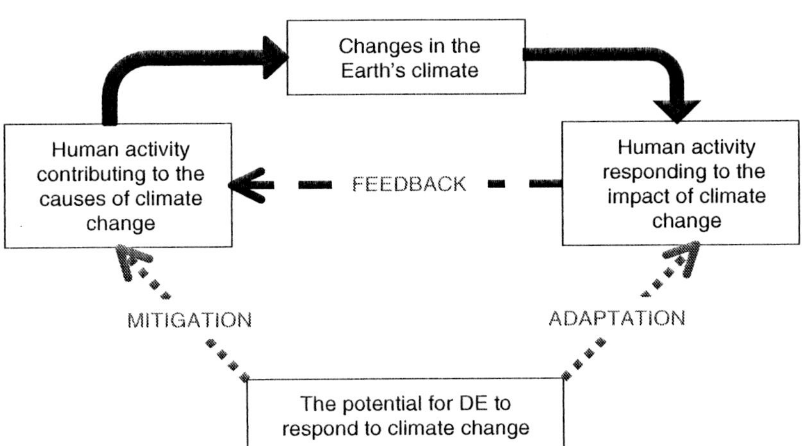

Figure 10.1 Connecting DE to the causes and impacts of climate change

This chapter will identify some of the impacts of climate change on people in different parts of the world, demonstrating that this global phenomenon requires a global perspective as part of the response. Although climate change is often discussed as a specific environmental problem, it will be discussed here in the context of a series of trends which indicate that the impact of human activity is now the major force shaping the future of planet Earth. The dominance of human influence on the planet has led Dutch scientist Paul Crutzen to propose that we are living in a new epoch called the 'Anthropocene' (Kolbert, 2007). The relevance of DE to the concept of the Anthropocene will be explored and the chapter will conclude by considering how integrating DE with education for sustainable development (ESD) enhances the impact that these forms of education can make on addressing the issues associated with climate change.

Climate change and development

> Climate change is expected to hit developing countries the hardest. Its effects – higher temperatures, changes in precipitation patterns, rising sea levels, and more frequent weather-related disasters – pose risks for agriculture, food, and water supplies. At stake are recent gains in the fight against poverty, hunger and disease, and the lives and livelihoods of billions of people in developing countries (World Bank, 2013).

> Above all else climate change is a human rights issue (UK Climate Change and Migration Coalition, 2012: 17).

Climate change has been compartmentalised as an environmental problem by some current governments and by most governments in the past, by placing the issue of climate change into government departments responsible for environmental or energy policy. The quotation above from the World Bank website is illustrative of the growing recognition that climate change is far more than just an environmental problem. The UK Climate Change Migration Coalition (UKCCMC) states that there is a need to constantly reiterate the phrase that 'climate change is a human rights issue' in order to 'break open the limitations of 20 years of defining climate change as solely an '"environmental" issue' (UKCCMC, 2012: 17).

By taking a more holistic view of climate change that encompasses both its causes and its impacts, it is possible to see climate change as a

Table 10.1 Millennium Development Goals and climate impacts

Millennium Development Goals	Climate Risks
MDG 1: Eradicate extreme poverty	Depleted livelihood assets, reduced economic growth, and undermined food security.
MDG 2: Achieve universal primary education	Reduced ability of children to participate in full-time education by loss of infrastructure, loss of livelihoods (forcing children to work), and displaced families.
MDG 3: Promote greater gender equality and empower women	Additional burdens on women's health and limited time to participate in decision-making and income-generating activities.
MDGs 4, 5 and 6: Reduce child mortality; improve maternal health; combat HIV/AIDS, malaria and other diseases	Greater prevalence of vector-borne and waterborne diseases, and heat-related mortality; declining food security, maternal health and availability of potable water.
MDG 7: Ensure environmental sustainability	Negatively impacted natural resources and productive ecosystems.

Source: Das, 2010: 15.

problem of equality and social justice linked to economics, livelihoods, migrations and other development related issues. Climate change threatens to reverse progress made in several areas relating to the Millennium Development Goals (MDGs) as illustrated in Table 10.1, which is taken from Das (2010) who was writing from the perspective of the Maldives in the Indian Ocean. The Maldives are one of a series of five atoll nations already affected by climate change, which Mark Lynas (2007) believes will not exist in the future as the sea level gradually continues to rise for centuries in response to changes resulting from the greenhouse gases that have already been emitted.

The global trend towards urbanisation deflects from the fact that the majority of the 1.4 billion poorest people in the world, who live on less than $1.25 per day, are mainly living in rural areas and dependent on agriculture for their livelihoods (Regan, 2012; IFAD, 2010). According to the International Fund for Agricultural Development (IFAD), 'agriculture is where climate change, food security and poverty reduction intersect' (IFAD, 2010: 10). IFAD emphasises the need to see climate change not as an isolated threat, but as a 'threat multiplier' increasing a range of livelihood threats and vulnerabilities. In countries reliant on rain-fed agriculture climate change exacerbates inequality as it is often rural women, who have fewer assets and less decision-making power, that are more exposed to the impacts of climate change than men. The integrated nature of the climate change threat requires an integrated adaptation strategy, which in agriculture dependent communities in the global South includes improving access to secure water supplies, adapting agricultural practices and improving weather forecasting to aid preparation for adverse conditions.

The South African National Climate Change Response Strategy (DEAT, 2004) presents a comprehensive approach to the challenges presented by climate change. The adaptation section of the Strategy identifies a series of interventions in specific areas; these include measures in health protection and promotion, water resource management, agriculture and biodiversity. Livelihoods in the poorest communities are already precarious without the added challenges of a changing climate which exacerbates other existing threats as identified by IFAD (2010). The impacts of climate change, such as major flooding, drought and crop failure, are already urgent challenges which require adaptation strategies and a rethinking of approaches to development in the regions that are affected. When livelihoods are completely undermined by climatic conditions the best option for survival may be to migrate. In Africa more people are migrating as a result of weather conditions than fleeing from wars (Griswold, 2013). Migration often means crossing borders, highlighting the international dimension of the impact of climate change and the need for a global perspective in managing these impacts. Communities in the poorer countries are currently experiencing the greater impacts of climate change and as a result they have to take the more radical steps in order to adapt to those impacts.

Wealthier countries in the global North are experiencing extreme weather events (Lynas, 2007), but these do not result in the same scale of devastation experienced by countries in the South (CIEH, 2008). In the short term wealth can offset the direct impacts of extreme weather or the indirect impacts resulting from social and economic disruption in other parts of the world. However, while wealthier countries appear to be suffering less detrimental impacts from climate change, they are contributing disproportionately to the causes. This is demonstrated by the correlation between high levels of wealth and high levels of greenhouse gas emissions as presented by Hertwich and Peters (2009) and the response from wealthier countries with regard to mitigating the causes of climate change which is generally characterised by less urgency than is indicated as necessary by the IPCC (2007a).

According to Steffan et al. (2005) certain human activities have become so pervasive and profound in their consequences that they affect the Earth at a global scale in complex, interactive and apparently accelerating ways and the most dramatic illustration of this is the human influence on the concentrations of greenhouse gases in the Earth's atmosphere. To understand the causes of climate change and the action required to mitigate those causes it is necessary to see climate change in the context of the human activities referred to by Steffan et al., who assert that 'over the past two centuries the interactions among population, technology and socio-political organisations have changed dramatically' (2005: 83).

The extent of the human impact, not just on the atmosphere but on the Earth's natural systems generally, is what led Paul Crutzen to suggest that we are now living in the Anthropocene (Kolbert, 2007). The Anthropocene is defined by the notion that people have become the dominant force shaping the future of planet Earth, rather than natural or extraterrestrial forces. The roots of this change can be traced back to the merchant capital accumulation in the fifteenth century followed by the industrial revolution from the mid-eighteenth century onwards. But it is the rapid acceleration in economic growth linked to globalisation since the mid-twentieth century which has taken the planet into the Anthropocene (Steffan et al., 2005). In *Global Change and the Earth System: A Planet Under Pressure*, Steffan et al. refer to a series of indicators linked to human activities that support the idea of people as the dominant force shaping the planet.

The trend in these indicators is relatively flat until the Anthropocene epoch at which point they embark on exponential growth, following a pattern set by the global population. After thousands of years of relatively slow growth the global population accelerated to five billion in 1988, six billion in 2000 and seven billion in 2011. This pattern has been followed by Anthropocene indicators such as the consumption of non-renewable resources, the use of agricultural fertilisers, the damming of rivers, water use, carbon dioxide and methane emissions, the loss of tropical forests, the loss of global biodiversity, and the increase in global Gross Domestic Product (GDP); they have all followed the exponential growth curve (Steffan et al., 2005). However, while these indicators have been recording exponential growth at a global level, disparities relating to the positive and negative impacts of this growth have been widening between global regions (Regan, 2012).

Exponential growth results from a fixed rate of increase over a regular time period, for example 3 percent per annum. The inherent danger in exponential growth is the way a relatively small increase can rapidly develop into a vast total, something that *The Limits to Growth* report tried to bring to the world's attention in the 1970s (Meadows et al., 1972). While a 3 percent increase per annum in, for example, a population, might seem quite modest, it results in a doubling of that population every 23 years, which is a long time in the life of a human, but not in the history of humankind. The same doubling principle applies to constant rates of growth in the use of resources or the emissions of gases. An increase in the growth rate results in a shorter doubling time, for example a 10 percent annual growth rate has a doubling time of just seven years. The reason the doubling time is important is because once a population or volume of gas has doubled the new total is greater than the sum of all previous doubling totals as demonstrated by the story of the grains of wheat on a chessboard in Box 10.1. A short doubling time results in growth quickly getting out of control. The impacts, both positive and negative, of the rapid growth in human activities are not equally distributed at a global level, a point emphasised by Steffan et al. (2005).

Focusing on a specific task such as reducing carbon dioxide emissions offers tangible actions for people to engage in when it comes to mitigating climate change. Although DE may appear as a less direct form of intervention, it is one aimed at long-term change in the economic, social, political and cultural fields through enhanced awareness and understanding about climate changes and by encouraging informed action to adapt to, and mitigate against, the current trends.

Development education for adaptation and mitigation

> Climate change challenges many of the basic assumptions of international development, refugee and human rights sectors and requires new thinking and approaches (UKCCMC, 2012: 2).

When viewed from the perspective of the Anthropocene the tasks associated with adaptation to, and mitigation of, climate change are hugely challenging. Changing livelihoods at local levels, shifting patterns of production and consumption both locally and globally, and coping with large-scale migrations all challenge existing power structures and established practices and have significant potential for conflict. In such circumstances education has a key role to play and DE

Box 10.1 The Wheat on the Chessboard

The Story of Wheat on the Chessboard

A long time ago in a distant land there lived a wise and skilful man who invented a game similar to chess that was played on a board with sixty-four squares. The Ruler of the distant land hugely enjoyed playing the game and decided to summon the Inventor to his palace in order to congratulate him on his invention. The meeting between the Ruler and the Inventor was so congenial the Ruler was moved to offer the Inventor a reward for creating such a wonderful game, and asked him to choose either land or gold. The Inventor thanked the Ruler, but explained that his requirements in life were simple and that all he wanted as a reward was wheat – one grain for the first square of his game-board, two grains for the second square, four grains for the third square and so on, doubling the grains of wheat on each successive square until the sixty-fourth square was reached.

When the Ruler heard what the Inventor wanted, he was not sure whether to be insulted at the rebuff to his generosity, or to be pleased that the Inventor, who had disappointed him by being rather a stupid man after all, wanted so little. He decided to give the Inventor what he had asked for and to dismiss him from his court. His servants were ordered to bring wheat from the Ruler's granaries and to comply precisely with the Inventor's request by placing one grain on the first square of the game-board and doubling the amount for each subsequent square.

As the wheat was counted out, the Ruler began to realise that he had underestimated the Inventor and the cleverness of his request. Over one thousand grains were required for the eleventh square, over one million for the twenty-first square and over one billion for the thirty-first square. Just halfway across the game-board the Ruler's granaries were empty, there was nothing left for even the mice to nibble, and the Ruler could not give the Inventor all that he had agreed to give him.

(It would have taken many times today's global wheat harvest to meet the requirements of square sixty-four. In modern mathematical script the amount can be written 2^{64} and the total amount of wheat would be in the region of 500 trillion tonnes.)

brings a particular approach to that role. The emergence of DE in the postcolonial period in the former European imperial powers involved in part the challenging of assumptions upon which the imperialist Eurocentric worldview was based (Lambert and Morgan, 2011). This set the pattern for constant reflection on relationships between communities, between countries and between cultures. It also led to the development of pedagogical approaches that enabled learners to examine and reassess their worldview, something that continued to develop through global education and which is still a live area of debate in ESD.

The extent to which the global perspective offered by DE to learners in the currently less affected countries of the North will lead to understanding and support for those affected by climate change in the South is yet to be determined. An indication of the link between education in the UK and support for a positive impact in other parts of the world is found in a Central Office of Information report published in 2012, which concluded that although it may be impossible to prove, there is a persuasive case that raising awareness of development issues in the UK has contributed to reducing poverty overseas (Lambert and Morgan, 2011).

One of the results of challenging an imperialistic worldview through DE has been the growing value attributed to indigenous knowledge. Responses to climate change will vary according to local contexts and DE can contribute to building support for adaptation initiatives through an understanding of those contexts. DE can also contribute to adaptation projects by combining a global perspective with indigenous knowledge. Egeru (2012) offers an example of indigenous knowledge being combined with modern methods of weather prediction in Eastern Uganda. The International Fund for Agricultural Development sees knowledge, innovation and advocacy being developed in partnerships between indigenous peoples and international organisations such as the International Institute for Environment and Development as part of its Climate Change Strategy (IFAD, 2010: 22).

DE has long recognised the important role of women in development and the importance of women's rights. Antonella Pyke argues that 'education directed towards women and the girl-child reaps benefits for the individual, the society and for development agendas at local, national and international levels' (Pyke, 2012: 267). This resonates closely with the IPCC's (2007b) *Climate Change 2007: Impacts, Adaptation and Vulnerability* report, which identified a focus on women in countries in the South as part of the strategy for bringing about adaptation to the impacts of climate change.

Mitigating future climate change involves influencing the activities which have led Paul Crutzen to determine we are living in the Anthropocene. These activities include the global production and consumption practices linked to the constant drive for economic growth, which is seen as a panacea within the dominant economic paradigm of neoliberalism (Haque, 1999). In Chapter 4 of this book Bourn sees the role of DE as contributing to an understanding of the relationship between development and global social change, and in Chapter 9 Selby and Kagawa assert that DE should be about challenging the dominant economic discourse. If education has a role to play in mitigating climate change, DE brings an appropriate and effective approach. Two linked aspects of DE that make it distinct from mainstream education in the formal sector are its inter-disciplinary nature and its holistic perspective that highlights connections (Parker, 2008).

As Jeffrey Sachs points out in his book *Common Wealth*, the global problems that we are facing 'just refuse to arrive in the neat categories of academic departments' (Sachs, 2008: 14). Climate change requires an approach to education that allows knowledge and skills from different disciplines to be applied to issues and challenges. Learners need the freedom to follow connections across subject boundaries to gain an understanding of the complex relationships and appreciate the systemic nature of the causes of climate change. The pedagogy which supports this approach to education, which accommodates uncertainty, and which allows for the emergence of knowledge and the reassessment of world views, has been central to DE and now appears in ESD. This demonstrates the influence DE has had on ESD over the last 20 years. The combined contributions of DE and ESD to addressing climate change are discussed in the next section.

DE and ESD in the context of addressing climate change

> In addition to its emergence in the political and public arena, climate change is an extremely complex epistemological phenomenon. Not only does it cover a range of issues that have been studied individually and by separate scientific disciplines, but the connections between these have given rise to a whole new architecture of inquiry and a set of challenges to conventional available knowledge (González-Gaudiano and Meira-Cartea, 2010: 13).

Unsurprisingly, because of the links between them, DE and ESD contribute to the overlapping epistemological and pedagogical debates and face similar challenges in bringing change to established education systems. The epistemological question raised in the quotation about climate change relates to a broader educational issue which is common to both DE and ESD. Learning and decision-making in relation to both development and sustainability are based on the best available knowledge. In DE and ESD learning takes place in the context of recognising that emerging knowledge may contradict current understanding at some point in the future. The formal sectors of education are resistant to incorporating the uncertainty inherent in this epistemological perspective, particularly where syllabi are linked to qualification frameworks that are influential and rigid. The knowledge relating to climate change is recognised as being limited, leaving gaps in our understanding and a lack of precision in predictions as discussed by Lynas (2007) in the Introduction to *Six Degrees*. This uncertainty provides an opening for the criticism of those like Goreham (2012), who are sceptical of the IPCC stance.

Gayford notes, learning which 'simply develops knowledge, understanding and skills is not enough' (Gayford, 2010: 6), and goes on to emphasise the importance of the values learners attach to knowledge and the attitudes linked to applying skills. The participatory methods found in DE and ESD engage learners in critically reviewing their values and worldviews as well as promoting active citizenship that can effect change at different levels. This approach to education has greater potential for creating agency for change in the human contexts that are causing climate change than the more established approaches in mainstream education which tend to reinforce existing political and economic structures.

This chapter has emphasised the importance of recognising connections in understanding climate change. Adopting a holistic perspective and applying systems thinking to make sense of a complex whole is something that DE and ESD bring to the understanding of issues like climate change. Figure 10.2 is based on a diagram from the *Climate Change 2007: Synthesis Report* (IPCC, 2007a), and shows the systemic connections between major areas of natural and human systems linked to climate change. A closer look at Figure 10.2 reveals the involvement of a wide range of sub-systems such as governance systems, trading systems, hydrological systems and food systems that are all connected at various levels. Understanding the connections within systems and between systems helps learners to analyse and make sense of their world (Strachan, 2009). From an ESD perspective Sterling (2009) argues that systems thinking alone does not necessarily lead to sustainable

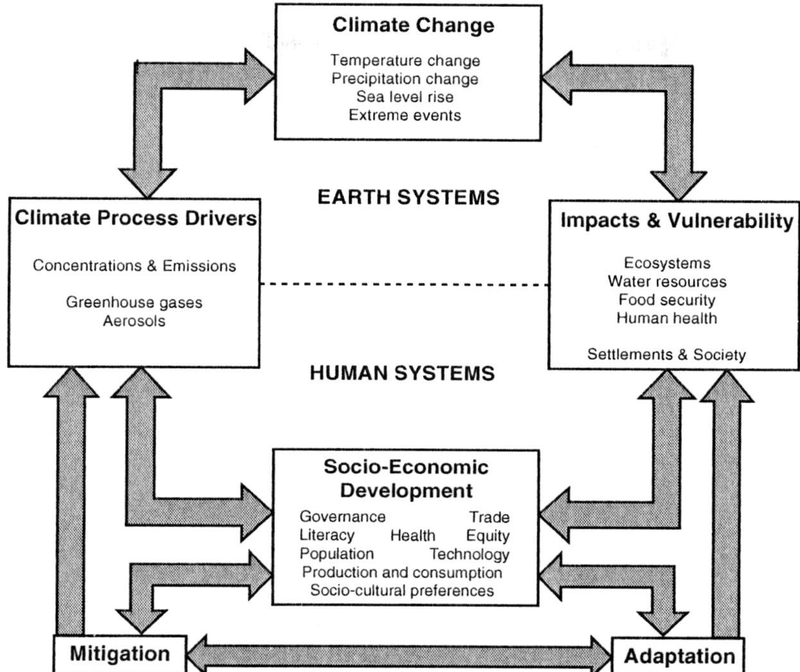

Figure 10.2 Schematic framework of anthropogenic climate change drivers, impacts and responses
Source: Adapted from IPCC, 2007a: 26, Fig 1.1.

solutions, there is a need to apply ecological thinking to achieve purposeful outcomes. Sterling does not use the word ecological simply to refer to the science of ecology, but as an ontological metaphor, as a way of seeing the world from a relational ecological perspective.

The wide range of systems operating at different levels and the processes operating between the systems in Figure 10.2 emphasise the complexity and the diversity of the challenge posed by climate change. From an educational viewpoint it is important to retain the holistic perspective on climate change, but its diversity does allow for a variety of 'entry points' for learners including earth sciences, ecology and health education. In Figure 10.2 the box labelled 'Socio-Economic Development' is placed at a key junction in terms of responding to climate change via mitigation and adaptation. The issues raised in this box have long been the concern of DE, which places DE in a particularly strong position to intervene in critically significant areas in relation to climate change.

For education to engage in addressing climate change and other major issues of inequality and unsustainability there is a need for a radical shift in, or reorienting of, education as identified by Sterling (2001). In Chapter 9 of this book Selby and Kagawa examine the extent to which DE and ESD retain their radical edge and challenge the top down global hegemony. If education is to be effective in challenging the root causes of climate change (and related issues of unsustainability) then DE and ESD need to increase the pressure for significant change to the dominant approaches to education, change akin to the paradigm shift outlined by Sterling (2001) and Kagawa and Selby (2010).

Conclusion

> The word 'learning' undoubtedly denotes *change* of some kind (*sic*, Bateson, 1972: 283).

Figure 10.2 summarises the relationships between earth systems and human systems and it is the influence of the human activities on earth systems which have led to the notion that we are living in the Anthropocene. This places climate change in a larger context, it reveals the links to its causes and impacts and it demonstrates the need for a holistic approach to achieve credible responses to mitigations and adaptation.

Education alone will not address the issue of climate change, but as the quotation above from Bateson points out, learning and change are closely linked and there is a role for education to play in both adaptation and mitigation. ESD draws in the environmental science which contributes to the understanding of the climatic systems that are changing, and it highlights the connections between the environment and the activities of people. DE has always looked in depth at economic, social and cultural activities and many of these activities are now linked to both the causes and impacts of climate change. The most significant contribution of DE and ESD is that they offer particular approaches to education that challenge the established practices that have led to climate change. The urgency inherent in the reports from the IPCC to adapt to the changes that will inevitably result from greenhouse gases already emitted, and to mitigate against future changes will require a radical shift in practices. DE and ESD must continue to act as catalysts for change by continuing the debates around the types of pedagogy that can transform worldviews and drive understanding forward in relation to the best way to educate people for a secure and sustainable future.

References

Bateson, G (1972) *Steps to an Ecology of Mind*, Chicago: University of Chicago Press.

CIEH (2008) *Climate Change, Public Health and Health Inequalities: A Resource for Environmental Health Practitioners*, London: Chartered Institute of Environmental Health.

Das, P K (2010) *Climate Change and Education: Maldives*, London: DFID.

Department of Environmental Affairs and Tourism (DEAT) (2004) *South Africa Climate Change Response Strategy*, Pretoria: Department of Environmental Affairs and Tourism.

Egeru, A (2012) 'Role of indigenous knowledge in climate change adaptation: A case study of the Teso sub-region of Eastern Uganda', *Indian Journal of Traditional Knowledge*, 11(2), April 2012, pp. 217–224.

Gayford, C (2010) *Learning for Sustainability in Schools: Effective Pedagogy*, WWF-UK: Godalming.

González-Gaudiano, E and Meira-Cartea, P (2010) 'Climate change education and communication: A critical perspective on obstacles and resistances', chapter 1 in F Kagawa and D Selby (eds) *Education and Climate Change: Living and Learning in Interesting Times*, London: Routledge, pp. 13–34.

Goreham, S (2012) *The Mad Mad Mad World of Climatism: Mankind and Climate Change Mania*, Illinois: New Lenox Books.

Griswold, E (2013) 'Islam is not the real issue we are facing in Africa', *The Guardian*, 8 February 2013.

Haque, M S (1999) 'The fate of sustainable development under neoliberal regimes in developing countries', *International Political Science Review*, 20(2), London and New Delhi: Sage Publications, pp. 197–218.

Hertwich, E G and Peters, G P (2009) 'Carbon footprinting of nations', in *Environmental Science and Technology*, Vol. 43, Issue 5, Washington DC: ACS, pp. 1239–1654.

International Fund for Agricultural Development (IFAD) (2010) *Climate Change Strategy*, Rome: IFAD.

Intergovernmental Panel on Climate Change (IPCC) (2007a) *Climate Change 2007: Synthesis Report*, Contribution of Working Groups I, II & III to the Fourth Assessment Report of the Intergovernmental Panel on Climate Change, Geneva: IPCC.

Intergovernmental Panel on Climate Change (IPCC) (2007b) *Climate Change 2007: Impacts, Adaptation and Vulnerability*, Contribution of Working Group II to the Fourth Assessment Report of the Intergovernmental Panel on Climate Change, Cambridge: Cambridge University Press.

Kagawa, F and Selby, D (2010) 'Introduction', in F Kagawa and D Selby (eds) *Education and Climate Change: Living and Learning in Interesting Times*, London: Routledge, pp. 1–11.

Kolbert, E (2007) *Field Notes from a Catastrophe: A Frontline Report on Climate Change*, London: Bloomsbury.

Lambert, D and Morgan, J (2011) *Geography and Development: Development Education in Schools and the Part Played by Geography Teachers*, Research Paper No. 3, Development Education Research Centre, London: Institute of Education.

Lynas, M (2007) *Six Degrees: Our Future on a Hotter Planet*, London: Harper Perennial.

Meadows, D H et al. (1972) *The Limits to Growth*, London: Pan Books.

NASA (National Aeronautics and Space Administration), available: http://climate.nasa.gov/scientific-consensus (accessed 26 April 2013).

National Research Council (2011) *Climate Stabilization Targets: Emissions, Concentrations and Impacts over Decades to Millennia*, Washington: National Academies Press.

Parker, J (2008) 'It's life Jim – but not as we know it: The unique contribution of development education to "Big Picture" sustainability education with a focus on climate change', *Policy and Practice: A Development Education Review*, Vol. 6, Issue 6, Spring 2008, pp. 95–100.

Pyke, A (2012) 'Understanding and invoking rights: Education and development', chapter 15 in C Regan (ed.) *80:20: Development in an Unequal World*, 6th edition, Bray, Ireland: 80:20 Education for a Better World, pp. 267–280.

Regan, C (ed.) (2012) *80:20: Development in an Unequal World*, 6th edition, Bray, Ireland: 80:20 Education for a Better World, Bray.

Sachs, J (2008) *Common Wealth: Economics for a Crowded Planet*, London: Allen Lane.

Steffan, W et al. (2005) *Global Change and Earth System: A Planet Under Pressure*, Heidelberg: Springer.

Sterling, S (2001) *Sustainable Education: Re-visioning Learning and Change*, Devon, UK: Schumacher Briefing No. 6, Green Books.

Sterling, S (2009) *Ecological Intelligence*, chapter 10 in A Stibbe (ed.) *The Handbook of Sustainability Literacy: Skills for a Changing World*, Devon, UK: Green Books.

Strachan, G (2009) *Systems Thinking*, chapter 11 in A Stibbe (ed.) *The Handbook of Sustainability Literacy: Skills for a Changing World*, Devon, UK: Green Books.

The Heartland Institute, www.heartland.org (accessed 26 April 2013).

UK Climate Change and Migration Coalition (UKCCMC) (2012) *Communicating Climate Change and Migration: A report by the UK Climate Change and Migration Coalition*, Oxford: UKCCMC.

World Bank, available: http://climatechange.worldbank.org/overview (accessed 26 April 2013).

Part IV

New Development Paradigms: Lessons for Development Education

11

Groping towards a New Future: Education for Paradigm Change

Peadar Kirby

> We are experiencing now I believe an intellectual crisis that is far more serious than the economic one which fills the papers, dominates the programmes in our media. Such a crisis has arisen before at times of grave crisis or impending change and it has drawn a response from intellectuals as they were forced to react to the collapse of the prevailing assumptions and they engaged with the need for a new paradigm of life and politics.
>
> (Michael D. Higgins, President of Ireland, in a lecture in the London School of Economics, 21st February 2012)

We live in an era, very likely already at an end, in which our basic assumptions about change are evolutionary and optimistic: our horizon of expectation is that standards of material comfort and quality of life are going to improve for ourselves and for our children. When, as is currently the case, many face a decline in income and opportunity, there seems a generalised instinct to treat this as temporary and a presumption that things are going to return to a state of continuing improvement before too long. Indeed, many of the fundamental disagreements in public debate about today's crisis relate to how soon this is likely to happen and what means are most likely to bring it about. Development discourse, whether it relates to development theory and practice or to development education, is particularly prone to these evolutionary and optimistic assumptions, reflecting the optimism of the post-war era in which the development project was born.

This chapter takes issue with such assumptions through examining the challenges for social change raised by the contemporary financial crisis, both nationally (in my own country, Ireland) and internationally. It begins by drawing attention to some of the deeper features of the crisis, features often hidden in mainstream analyses. In doing this, it draws attention to the nature of the paradigm change to which this crisis challenges us, as identified by President Michael D. Higgins in the quote with which this chapter opens. In its second section, the chapter examines the role of education in addressing this challenge, asking how adequate are our forms of education for the transition to a new paradigm of society. Section three turns to Latin America where new left governments are leading action for paradigm change; examining the process that led to the emergence of the new left, the role of education is highlighted. However, this section also points to the tensions and contradictions that are increasingly evident as political leaders seek to lay the foundations of what some of them call '21st century socialism'. These tensions and contradictions, it is argued, raise questions about the nature of this new paradigm and, indeed, about our dominant notions of development. The final section focuses on the larger challenges of paradigm change that now confront us.

Crisis, what crisis?

The general reading of our contemporary crisis is that its origins lie in the financial sector which, due to the deregulation of the Reagan and Thatcher era, was incentivised to indulge in ever more risky and complex speculative practices. The many bubbles through which it created wealth eventually exploded with severe effects on the wider productive economy, resulting in high levels of debt both public and private, high unemployment, austerity politics and economic recession. This was worst in those countries that went furthest in deregulating their financial sectors, Ireland being one of the very worst both in terms of the reckless behaviour of the banking sector (rivaled only by the actions of the banks in Iceland) and the extent of the reliance of the national economy on the housing sector.

This account, however, avoids the deeper structural issues that the crisis reveals, instead putting the blame on the excessive greed of bankers and the inaction of regulators. It therefore leads to the impression that with a tighter regulation of the financial sector, action to return the banks to a sustainable business model and a period of austerity to ensure the debt crisis is brought under control, society can soon return to growth and prosperity. This impression has become widely accepted thereby deflecting attention from the deeper systemic causes of the crisis. In a deeper probing, the founding chairman of the UK's Financial Services Authority (FSA) and former director of the London School of Economics (LSE), Howard Davies, identified 38 distinct causes of the financial crisis, among them the deep-seated inequality of contemporary capitalism and the unsustainable levels of personal indebtedness built up by many households as they tried to maintain high levels of consumption while real incomes were declining over time. As Davies put it, 'the rich get richer – the poor borrow'. He also draws attention to the weaknesses of the political system, unwilling to impose stricter conditions on financial practices as politicians were captive to a naïve belief in the benefits for society of extreme market freedom (Davies, 2010). This analysis therefore focuses on inherent features of today's dominant form of capitalism – the profound inequalities being generated by a free market system and the ways in which political authority has become deferential to the power of these markets (namely powerful economic corporations). Nothing in the reform agendas being implemented in Europe and North America promises to address these features; indeed, as the evolution of the euro crisis illustrates only too clearly, the needs of markets are taking precedence more and more over the needs of society.

Just a few years after the crisis struck, therefore, it is difficult not to conclude that the bulk of the reform effort is designed to salvage the very model of speculative financial capitalism that caused the crisis in the first place. This form of capitalism that became dominant from the 1970s onwards is based on a financial system that is to a large extent decoupled from the productive economy and, instead of making its money from productive investments that create jobs, goods and services, makes its money from highly complex financial instruments such as derivatives (which include futures, options and swaps) traded by an array of new and often unregulated actors such as hedge funds and investment banks. It has been estimated that 90 percent of global financial transactions are now speculative and have nothing to do with productive investment (Castells, 2001). This has been made possible due to the application of the microchip to financial transactions, allowing instantaneous and real-time transfer of limitless amounts of money to anywhere in the world at virtually no cost. But also implicated, of course, are the political authorities who liberalised their financial systems, often under severe pressure from the International Monetary Fund (IMF), so as to facilitate these operations.

The other major feature of the crisis that is generally overlooked means that if attempts to salvage the model of speculative financial capitalism are successful, they are likely to result in a future crisis the magnitude of which will dwarf what we are now living through. Few analysts of the crisis have examined the role of energy, either in creating the model of financial and highly indebted capitalism or in sparking the present crisis. The sociologist John Urry links inflation in the price of United States (US) housing in the 1990s to the declining price of oil and claims that house price inflation, which was around 2.5 times greater than increases in per capita income at the time, was linked to the fact that the real price of oil was falling. This meant that households could afford to spend more on housing since they were saving on fuel costs. However, as petrol prices began dramatically to increase in the mid 2000s it brought the US housing boom to a shuddering halt as it 'tipped financially weak households over the brink' (Urry, 2011: 84). As Urry writes:

> The house price reductions in far-flung suburbs were most marked where there were no alternatives to the car and hence there was the greatest dependence upon the price *and* the availability of petrol. Households were spending up to 30 per cent of their income on travel. House prices in commuter belts dropped very steeply, so much so that some suburbs came to be known as 'ghostburgs', full of 'For sale' signs. This generated a more general reduction in consumer spending, similar to 1990–1 during the first Gulf War, and it led to the escalating collapse of especially investment banks in the US and then around the world, as this house of financial cards came tumbling down (Urry, 2011: 85; emphasis in original).

As Urry concludes, 'the probable peaking of oil has *already* had major economic and social consequences that could be a harbinger of future catastrophes' (Ibid.: 82; emphasis in original).

There are therefore deep links between the energy crisis and the financial crisis; rather than being two separate crises, each is a sign of the breakdown of a development paradigm based upon a constant expansion of the production of goods and services made possible by abundant sources of energy derived from oil, and the decoupling of money from any link to the biophysical world (as it had when linked to gold or silver). As environmental economist, Herman E. Daly put it, 'the financial world is built around debt and expectations of future growth in wealth to redeem the debt pyramid built by expansion of fiat money' [paper]. He added that 'peak oil will disrupt the physical basis of those growth expectations and lead to a financial crash resulting in levels of real production that are even below physical possibility, as happened in the Great Depression' (Daly, 2007: 122).

Richard Douthwaite's work shows how most developed countries have resorted to debt as a way of paying for their energy needs; for example, during its Celtic Tiger boom Ireland's debt tripled over five years and it had the worst external debt per $1,000 of Gross Domestic Product (GDP) among a range of OECD (Organisation for Economic Co-operation and Development) countries in 2006. For Ireland, fuel costs rose from 2.26 percent of Gross National Product (GNP) in 2001 to 4.17 percent in 2008 thus draining more and more of the country's foreign exchange (Douthwaite, 2010: 82). The double blow of high levels of debt coupled with fast rising energy prices as oil grows scarce and becomes more expensive to extract, poses a profound question mark over our economic future.

Even so mainstream an economist as Ashoka Mody, former IMF mission chief for Ireland and Germany, in discussing the constant downgrading of growth forecasts since the current recession began in 2008, cautions that 'faith in renewed growth is an ill-advised policy strategy. At its core the global economic crisis is a growth crisis' and he concludes that: 'It may simply be time to learn how to live with less' (Mody, 2013). For an economy and society premised on endless growth, these simple words underline the challenge of paradigm change facing us. Our future as a global society depends on recognising that it is our central paradigm of development that is in deep crisis and on moving in an ordered way to a new paradigm before collapse sets in. It is this challenge that brings the role of education to the fore.

Challenges for education

A central role for education has always been to socialise people into the dominant culture and development model, making these appear 'normal' and inculcating the disciplines to allow people to live within their constraints. Development education focused on socialisation into the worldview of the project of international development that emerged as a successor to the system of European colonialism after the end of the Second World War. This was essentially a project that purported to be attempting to help the majority of countries in Asia, Africa, the Caribbean, Latin America and the Pacific to 'catch up' with those countries that had developed more industrial economies and, based on this, societies that were deemed more 'modern'. In its more progressive versions, development education brought issues of economic, social and cultural inequality to the fore and sought to ensure that processes of development benefited disadvantaged groups in society. However, both mainstream and progressive versions presumed a model of evolutionary economic growth that would eventually lift the majority out of poverty and offer a better standard of living to them.

Yet, education has never been wholly subservient to the society it served. It has always produced challenges to the dominant orthodoxies and been a space for inculcating alternatives to the 'common sense' of the era. Different eras have therefore posed different and varied challenges for educators. At a time when religious institutions dominated society, education was the space in which new ideas emerged often at great personal cost to those developing and teaching them. Similarly, it was educators who pioneered the methods of scientific enquiry that came to challenge the dominance of speculative philosophical approaches to the generation of knowledge. In more recent decades, educators have developed new social scientific approaches that have greatly deepened our knowledge of society and of processes of social change. All of these developments, though they emerged from the educational sector, went on to exercise major influence over public thinking and policy development. Education, therefore, as well as socialising people into dominant paradigms, is the space in which these paradigms have been challenged and new paradigms emerged. We can say that educators, being closely attuned to the intuitions and aspirations of emerging generations, are often the first to pick these up, deepen and systematise them, and seek to respond to them. And, of course, this is always done in an active and often very vibrant interchange between educators and their students. Education must always be essentially dialogical.

Paulo Freire is a towering example of such an educator. When I interviewed him in his apartment in São Paulo in the summer of 1980, he emphasised that many of those who purported to use his theories completely misunderstood them because they failed to realise that the objective was people's liberation rather than the correct implementation of Freirean theories as outlined in the books he wrote. 'I sometimes come across a praxis with the name "conscientisation" but which is really very manipulative', he told me. 'What I'm referring to are very paternalistic types of teaching activity. They might be called "conscientisation" but really they have nothing to do with it. They imply, despite how well-meaning those who use them might be, the preservation of the status quo, divorcing so-called poor people from the process of liberating themselves' (Kirby, 1988: 59). This is an essential insight which can be applied to all education: what matters is nurturing people's curiosity and critical insight so that they become powerful and wise change makers in their own right, not the 'correct' communication of some previously defined body of knowledge. The former leads to paradigm change whereas the latter reinforces dominant paradigms.

Another major educator of the same generation as Freire is Thomas Berry. His analysis of education focuses on wider horizons than that of Freire but is similarly critical of its destructive effects. Education, for Berry, 'became more an external conditioning than an interior discipline, more a training in manipulative techniques' and functional to the imperatives of our scientific-technological age. 'The creators of the scientific-technological age had only minimal awareness of what they were doing. The industrial civilization that came to dominate this period has required some centuries of functioning before its creative and destructive aspects could be revealed in any effective manner' (Berry, 1988: 94). We are now facing a transition from this manipulative age to establishing a new and more sustainable relationship with the biosphere on which our survival depends. This is the challenge for education today: 'Education must be a pervasive life experience. Yet formal education must be transformed so that it can provide an integrating context for the total life functioning', he writes, enabling people to understand 'the immense story of the universe' and especially their role in the next phase of that story (Ibid.: 96–97). For Berry, therefore, the paradigm change that education has to assist, is a fundamental transition away from a narrow scientific-technological civilisation that is destroying the planet towards a wholly new and mutually nurturing relationship between the human venture and the rest of the biosphere. And, as he tellingly puts it: 'At such moments of cultural transformation, the educational process must go through a period of groping toward its new formal expression' (Ibid.: 96).

If education is the space in which dominant paradigms are challenged and new ones nurtured, then the acute social, economic and cultural crisis through which we are passing raises central questions for educators. Where, in our extensive forms of organised education from the formal to the informal sector, do we find examples of emancipatory education that challenge the dominant paradigm of change and create the conditions for exploring a new paradigm? For many working in the formal state sector, it is acutely depressing that, at the very time when education needs to explore new possibilities, it has been battered into complete subservience to the dominant neoliberal, commercial paradigm that is the fundamental cause of the crisis. As Berry puts it, 'the university may be one of the principal supports of the pathology that is so ruinous to the planet' (Berry, 1999: 76). And, it appears, the more acute the crisis gets the more determined policy-makers and educational managers are to ensure that education serves no ends other than equipping students to succeed within this paradigm. The great fear is that we are educating young people for a world that is fast disappearing and failing to equip them with the critical thinking, informed imaginations and practical skills to prepare them for a world of acute crisis and fundamental change.

Predictably, in a technology obsessed society, our instinct is to seek solutions in technology while neglecting the social structures in which such technology is embedded; one obvious reason for this is that we would like to think we can adjust to the challenges we face without the wrenching change in values, lifestyle practices and social structures that will profoundly impact all our lives. It is very revealing that, though we like to think we live in a scientific age in which we make decisions, both private and public, on the best of evidence, when that evidence is screaming at us that we cannot go on living as we have done we bury our heads in the sand and live as if the evidence of peak oil and climate change did not exist. This predominant social response indicates the failure of education to provide the spaces in which these challenges can be discussed, their implications for how we organise our economies and societies critically and thoroughly examined, and responses generated. Yet, this is only being done on the margins and superficially; by and large, our forms of education are failing society as they remain far too subservient to the dominant paradigm and therefore are unable to provide the critical space to begin incubating a new social paradigm.

Lessons from Latin America

The one region of the world where paradigm change does seem to be taking place is Latin America. Contradicting all the presumptions of neoliberal thinking, country after country began electing left-wing governments from the late 1990s onwards so that some ten countries are now ruled by the left, and countries like Venezuela, Bolivia and Ecuador are experimenting with what their presidents call a '21st century socialism'. While major debates are taking place among social scientists about how significant are the changes taking place in the region, a consensus is beginning to emerge that this is not just a minor modification of the neoliberal model that has been dominant in the region for three decades but that a fundamental change of model is taking place, even though the contours of the new emerging model are not yet clearly visible (Wylde, 2012).

What is important for the purposes of this chapter is to appreciate the process that resulted in governments coming to power committed to a change of paradigm and the role that education played in this process. Understanding the process draws attention to the importance of a mobilised citizenry, the emergence of which characterises Latin America like no other region in the world over recent decades. As political scientists Philip and Panizza acknowledge in their book on the new left, as the power of the military has waned, 'the importance of mass protests in shaping the outcome of institutional crisis has made mobilized civil society the new *moderating power* of Latin American politics' (Philip and Panizza, 2011: 41; emphasis in original). Yet, these authors fully appreciate that what is needed is far more than simply spontaneous protest in resistance to particular governmental actions; for civil society to be effective, it must be a permanent presence turning grievance into concrete and realisable political, economic and social demands that help to unite a wide cross-section of citizens. It is the ability of civil society to do this that marks out Latin America and explains the rise of the new left throughout the region:

> Underlying socio-economic factors and political opportunities are important but insufficient factors in explaining the resurgence of movements of mass protest. The social movements' new role cannot be properly understood without taking into consideration the collective action strategies, institutional environment and framing processes that made it possible for localized social movements to expand their political reach and to challenge the political order (Ibid.: 50).

Silva has offered the most detailed analysis of how this process happened over about two decades in Venezuela, Bolivia, Ecuador and Argentina, and why it did not succeed in Peru and Chile (though in both countries this now seems to be changing). This analysis focuses attention on what distinguishes these new movements from the labour movement, traditionally seen as the backbone of social protest: 'People come together around a shared identity of place (village, indigenous community, working-class neighbourhood or barrio) intertwined with shared cultural and material concerns. Equally novel is the fact that these organizations joined streams of national mobilization and that their contentious action has significance beyond the locality'. In doing this, he adds, they challenged 'theories that argue that their heterogeneity and precarious livelihood strategies absolutely prevent the development of their associational, not to mention collective, power' (Silva, 2009: 269). What is clear therefore is that new forms of empowered action have emerged from the grassroots which have been able to find common cause in identifying neoliberalism as their common enemy, across the many class, ethnic, gender and ideological issues that inevitably divide them. In doing this, they have not followed any pre-set blueprint, indeed they have defied the accepted wisdom that such forms of empowered common action could not emerge from such heterogeneous sources.

What none of these analysts examine is the contribution of the practices derived from the work and influence of Paulo Freire on creating the conditions, particularly the empowered and socially aware consciousness, that is a necessary precondition for these movements to emerge. Yet, for anyone who has experienced at first hand the widespread impact of these practices throughout Latin America, this is an obvious dimension requiring attention. For Freire's work is oriented precisely towards fostering a consciousness that probes social reality to identify fundamental causes, that develops the ability to respond in a creative and novel way to the injustices identified, that links people and groups to each other in a broad horizontal awareness of common cause, and that fundamentally inculcates a deep sense that people have power and through this power fundamental change is possible. All of these are precisely the dimensions that are identified by political scientists as the surprising and novel features of the contestatory social movements that have so dramatically changed the political landscape of Latin America and led the world in challenging the dominant neoliberal paradigm.

Yet, of course, these processes are also full of tensions as is inevitable in any process of contesting power. Central to these tensions in today's left-led countries in Latin America is just how far one goes in challenging the dominant neoliberal paradigm. Essentially, one can identify two competing alternatives emerging. All agree on the need for more state direction of the economy, more social investment and more recognition of multiple identities, especially in countries with large populations of indigenous origin. However, where real differences are emerging is in the balance to be struck between economic development and environmental protection. Recent examples from Ecuador and Bolivia have highlighted these. Examining Ecuador, de la Torre highlights the differences that have emerged between the left-wing government and indigenous and environmental groups over attitudes to mineral extraction: while the former sees this sector as providing jobs and economic development, the latters' commitment to create a new relationship between humans, nature and development lead them to oppose government plans (de la Torre, 2012). In Bolivia, while the left-wing government of Evo Morales has deep roots in the country's powerful indigenous movement, Schilling-Vacaflor and Vollrath conclude that 'the compatibility between extractivism and a *vivir bien* (living well) regime (including harmony between nature and society) has increasingly been questioned' and they give examples of standoffs between local communities and government agencies (Schilling-Vacaflor and Vollrath, 2012: 138). '*Vivir bien*' is defined in the country's new constitution to be the primary aim of the state. We therefore see emerging a more fundamental paradigm clash between those sectors of the left who espouse a more socially just version of modern technological society and those who promote a society based on a more balanced relationship between human activities and environmental sustainability.

Taking paradigm change seriously

In essence, therefore, we face a challenge not just of paradigm change but of disputing, at a most fundamental level, how far that change must go. Indeed, this is what makes our age so unique. Our human civilisation has passed through a number of very wrenching changes of paradigm, going back to the early settled societies of Mesopotamia, central and southern Mexico and the Andes, and China. Most recently, we have moved from feudalism to capitalism and, within the latter, from a largely agrarian capitalism to an industrial capitalism and now to a highly financialised form of capitalism. The principal challenge to the latter has come from the socialist tradition and, indeed, there was the claim for most of the 20th century that a new socialist paradigm was emerging in communist-ruled countries. The collapse of these countries and the promise that for some they embodied, resulted in the naïve belief that the era of paradigm change was at an end in Francis Fukuyama's famous 'end of history' claim.

But what is unique about the present moment is that our mental map of what kind of paradigm change is needed is in dispute. The socialist tradition continues to provide a very telling critique of the inequalities that are a systemic part of capitalism and thereby inform one set of principles to guide a transition to a new paradigm. Indeed, the collapse of 'real existing socialism' as it used to be called has given new life and creativity to that tradition, nowhere more evident than in Latin America. However, might such a new paradigm be enough? This is what is in dispute as some draw disquieting attention to the fundamental challenge to our industrial societies posed by peak oil and the ever more intensive emission of greenhouse gases that are changing our climate in ominous ways. For those who take this challenge seriously, what is urgently required is a far deeper paradigm change, to a degrowth economy using far lower levels of energy and achieving low-carbon ways of producing and consuming goods and services (Jackson, 2009; Garcia, 2012). As with any true paradigm change (such as, for example, the transition from the Roman Empire to the Middle Ages, or from subsistence agriculture to industrial society), the contours of the new society are only perceived in the faintest of ways.

What will be crucial in developing society's awareness of these options and what they entail, and in empowering society to act so as to move decisively towards paradigm change, will be the contribution of education. Development education is particularly challenged to rethink what development means in this new context and how to expand its horizons and become a space for debate and new thinking. Environmentalists are also challenged to move beyond what is often a narrow 'green' agenda to join debates about political economy models and how we can move to a new paradigm in a constructive way. Fundamentally, we all need to critically examine the often optimistic and evolutionary assumptions we have about social change and to realise that paradigm change is a process of very fundamental struggle which more often than not involves great upheaval, destruction and violence. What can make the difference between collapse and transition is education; perhaps never before have educators been more challenged to provide the spaces for society to grope towards a new future, to use Berry's telling and very accurate term.

References

Berry, T (1988) *The Dream of the Earth*, San Francisco: Sierra Club Books.

Berry, T (1999) *The Great Work: Our Way into the Future*, New York: Bell Tower.

Castells, M (2001) 'Information technology and global capitalism' in W Hutton and A Giddens (eds) *On the Edge: Living with Global Capitalism*, London: Vintage, pp. 52–74.

Daly, H E (2007) 'The steady-state economy and peak oil' in H E Daly (ed.) *Ecological Economics and Sustainable Development: Selected Essays of Herman Daly*, Cheltenham: Edward Elgar, pp. 117–124.

Davies, H (2010) *The Financial Crisis: Who is to Blame?*, Cambridge: Polity Press.

de la Torre, C (2012) 'Rafael Correa's government, social movements and civil society in Ecuador' in B Cannon and P Kirby (eds) *Civil Society and the State in Left-led Latin America: Challenges and Limitations to Democratisation*, London: Zed Books, pp. 63–77.

Douthwaite, R (2010) 'The supply of money in an energy-scarce world', in R Douthwaite and G Fallon (eds) *Fleeing Vesuvius: Overcoming the Risks of Economic and Environmental Collapse*, Dublin: Feasta, pp. 58–83.

Garcia, E (2012) 'Degrowth, the past, the future, and the human nature', *Futures*, Vol. 44, pp. 546–552.

Jackson, T (2009) *Prosperity Without Growth: Economics for a Finite Planet*, London: Earthscan.

Kirby, P (1988) *Has Ireland a Future?*, Cork: Mercier Press.

Mody, A (2013) 'We are treating the present as if bubbly growth from 2000 to 2007 will return', *The Irish Times*, 8 February 2013, *Business this Week* supplement, p. 1.

Philip, G and Panizza, F (2011) *The Triumph of Politics: The Return of the Left in Venezuela, Bolivia and Ecuador*, Cambridge: Polity Press.

Schilling-Vacaflor, A and Vollrath, D (2012) 'Contested development: Comparing indigenous and peasant participation in resource governance in Bolivia and Peru' in B Cannon and P Kirby (eds) *Civil Society and the State in Left-led Latin America: Challenges and Limitations to Democratisation*, London: Zed Books, pp. 126–140.

Silva, E (2009) *Challenging Neoliberalism in Latin America*, Cambridge: Cambridge University Press.

Urry, J (2011) *Climate Change and Society*, Cambridge: Polity.

Wylde, C (2012) *Latin America after Neoliberalism*, Basingstoke: Palgrave Macmillan.

12
New Paradigms for Social Transformation in Latin America

Ronaldo Munck

Introduction

Once again Latin America figures prominently in development studies and development education in the North representing for many commentators a new paradigm for social transformation. This chapter feeds into these debates from a critical Latin American perspective. The first section below traces the emergence of new paradigms in Latin America *From Dependencia to Sumak Kawsay (Buen Vivir)*. They are contextualised both intellectually and in the political era in which they arise. This is followed by a consideration of *Left Governments and Social Movements* in Latin America which is the point of entry for much international attention and publishing. It is also part of the context for the new paradigms for social transformation. Finally we turn to *Latin America in the North*, that is to say how the region's experiences and conceptual paradigms are received and reworked in the global North. In doing so the relevance of recent transformation in Latin America for development education is critically assessed.

From *Dependencia* to Sumak *Kawsay (Buen Vivir)*

Countering the hegemonic 'made in US' modernisation theory of the 1960s was Latin America's own indigenous development theory, known as the dependency approach or paradigm. While in its more grounded variants such as the F H Cardoso and Enzo Faletto classic *Dependency and Development in Latin America* (1969, 1979) it was a nuanced, structural and historical take on development and its relationship to social classes but also had a much cruder manifestation. The later trend, best exemplified by the work of Andre Gunder Frank

(1970) – elevated outside Latin America to *the* dependency theorist – often seemed to just reverse the modernisation discourse to create its binary opposite. Where one saw the diffusion of capital into backward areas as the key to development, the other saw it as simply developing underdevelopment. Diffusion of innovation would develop the traditional areas for one theory but simply create stagnation and decapitalisation for the other. Creating a mirror image of a theory is probably not the best way to move critical analysis forward.

The main issue was that modernisation and dependency theory both took for granted and saw as natural the nation-state framework. National economic development was the objective and the state would play a crucial role in that process. Inevitably the diversity of social interests – and the capital/wage-labour conflict in particular – was somewhat subsumed under this paradigm. A social transformation perspective on the development process in Latin America would stress, rather, the emergence and development of social classes and class conflict. From the colonial period onwards, different social groupings were vying for hegemony and to impose their particular interests as the general interest. Landowners, industrialists, urban workers, rural smallholders, artisans and others all had diverse social interests. It was the struggle for hegemony which set a particular development path and determined the modalities of social transformation in each country. National development choices were really the outcome of class development and struggle, not something emerging spontaneously.

Ultimately, the modernisation and simple dependency approaches shared a methodological nationalism that took the nation-state to be a natural and self-sufficient envelope for the development process. They also shared a strong economism which led them to ignore or at least downplay the political process, not to mention the cultural dimension. They were also equally teleological in assuming a given end-station for the development process. For modernisation theory the end of the journey was to be a consumer-based modernity *á la* United States (US) while for the dependency approach it was socialism *á la* Cuba, based on an ill-defined delinking from the global system. Both thus rejected the complexity of history, the contradictions of the accumulation process in a context of class struggle, and that the future is open to different outcomes and not present in some original DNA pattern of development or underdevelopment.

We could go further in relation to a critique of the dependency approach from a postcolonial stance. In a way, dependency shares with modernisation theory a strong attachment to modernity as an overarching perspective and a commitment to the *logos* of development. It is very much centered on the nation-state which it takes as the unproblematised unit of analysis and the sovereign subject of development as it were. But some authors have gone further and accused the dependency approach of ignoring culture and the politics of representation leading to a general ethnocentrism bordering on Orientalism (Kapoor, 2008: 10). Europe is still seen as the universal model against which development on the periphery is judged and deemed (in)adequate. For their part, the broad brush visions of capital accumulation on a world scale run the risk of submerging the local and creating a totalising narrative which itself may disable alternative accounts of and strategies for development. We should maybe direct ourselves instead to the more complex cultural and political boundaries which shape the subaltern consciousness in the majority world.

A post-dependency approach would need to break out of its binary opposition with regards to modernisation theory. We might still question, of course, whether the structures of domination located by the dependency theorists in Latin America have simply been superseded in the era of 'inter-dependent' globalisation. Few progressive or critical analysts would argue today that the problems of development, as conventionally defined, have been overcome in Latin America. What is being challenged is more to do with the totalising vision of dependency, one it shares with other modernist epistemologies. The challenge of a transformationalist approach would be to decolonise development knowledge and to adopt a more critical or deconstructionist approach towards the received terminology of development/dependency. We might thus consider more insecure forms of knowledge, a greater receptivity towards bottom-up or indigenous forms of knowledge and less assurance in presenting a polished alternative to the status quo developed solely at the level of social and political theory.

In recent years it is the concept of hybridity that has gained most purchase within Latin America as an analytical category seeking to explain its specificity. For Nestor García Canclini and others, the Manichean world of the dependency theorists – with its First and Third Worlds – misses out on the more flexible, hybrid world we now live in. For example, 'it does not explain the planetary functioning of an industrial, technological, financial, and cultural system whose headquarters is not in a single nation but in a dense network of economic and ideological structures' (García Canclini, 1995: 229). The transnational cultural political economy which holds sway today, the flows of migrants and money, and the dense network of images and information which shapes our understanding is not amenable to a simplistic explanation around geographical or political belonging to a 'Third World'.

Latin America since 2000 has lived through a political spring which is quite unprecedented in the depth and breadth of progressive social transformation. New paradigms of social change and political experimentation are arising which are, perhaps, of global significance. Just as the dependency approach was the overarching development paradigm of the 1970s, so today the concept of *Sumak Kawsay* (Buen Vivir) – only imperfectly rendered as 'Good Living' or 'Living Well' in English – captures the radical edge of current thinking. It essentially speaks to the extended reproduction of life rather than of capital. It advocates a different civilisational model to that of individualistic capital where community values and respect for nature take priority. It is a development paradigm now enshrined in the constitutions of Ecuador and Bolivia and causing ripples across the region.

Sumak Kawsay works on the premise that there are two transitions underway in Latin America: a relatively recent transition towards socialism barely 100 years old and a longer-term transition out of colonialism which goes back to the fifteenth century. An end to all forms of racism and greater self-determination form part of that longer-term struggle. It does not deny at all the relevance of Western forms of representative democracy but adds as well the need for participative and communal forms of democracy. While this new cosmovision does not simply rearticulate ancient indigenous practices and is characterised by a profound hybridity, it does represent a challenge to Eurocentrism. It articulates new principles of production and property, identity and subjectivity and, not least, a new way of understanding the world and producing knowledge about it.

The Amerindian past is very much part of the present especially in the Andean countries. As Bolivian left intellectual and Vice-President García Linera puts it, we are seeing the emergence of 'an alternative system, anchored in the world of indigenous experience marginalized by Bolivia's uneven modernization process, [which] is challenging the state's centuries long pretence at modernity' (Linera, 2011: 78). Collective aims and values from the Amerindian collective memory (revoked by contemporary political actors such as Linera) play a key role in the articulation of an alternative political paradigm in Latin America. The relevance of the Inca *ayllu* (a community unit) is set in the context of a party system where patrimonial politics have prevailed and the popular masses have been co-opted though clientelistic networks.

The contemporary indigenous perspective in Latin America provides a different logic to that dominant in the Western corridors of power. It is keenly attuned to bio-diversity and sustainability rather than the pursuit of private profit above all else. It values reciprocity and sharing rather than self-advancement and greed as indicators of a good life. Central to the current debates around a new indigenous politics of transformation is the question of autonomy. Like the term multiculturalism, it can be quite compatible with neoliberalism (Žižek, 1997) but it can also be a very positive value in promoting the autonomy of indigenous peoples. An affirmation of autonomy as a value does not resolve the concrete question of political alliances which the indigenous and other movements might enter into. The point is simply that there is no simple indigenous paradigm of social change at play here.

A critical assessment of *Sumak Kawsay* would need to engage with previous attempts to create an 'Andean utopia' through an invocation of the Incas to rethink colonialism and injustice since the Spanish conquest. One of the best known is Alberto Flores Galindo's *In Search of an Inca* (2010) which stresses the idealisation of the pre-colonial Inca past as a period of harmony and prosperity which could become a guide for the future. Galindo himself denied that he was promoting an Andean utopia as a blueprint for socialist or *neo-indigenista* political projects and acknowledged its authoritarian stands. However this work is a rich repository of ideas and social practices which can inform current debates around transformative alternatives. As Galindo puts it: 'For people without hope, the Andean utopia challenges a history that condemned them to the margins. Utopia denies...the illusion of development understood as westernization' (Galindo, 2010: 247–248).

In previous engagements between the socialist and indigenous paradigms for social transformation, it is Peruvian communist thinker and organiser José Carlos Mariátegui (1894–1930) who stands out. Having engaged with the thinking and politics of Antonio Gramsci while in exile in the early 1920s, he returned to Peru with a clear understanding that: 'Without the Indian no Peruvianness is Possible' (Vanden and Becker, 2011: 141). The self-activity of the Amerindian masses and their move from a regional to a national level of organisation would play a key role in that process. Thus the making of the nation, encapsulated in this slogan *Peruanicemos el Perú* (let us Peruvianise Peru), is inseparable from a recovery of the indigenous past of the 'hidden Peru' in which an indigenous non-market logic of reciprocity and communalism was core to the meaning of society.

Mariátegui was not, to be sure, nostalgic for a lost past nor did he romanticise Inca society. Peru in the 1920s was characterised by semi-feudal landownership patterns with severe forms of production so that the emancipation of the indigenous peoples was seen primarily as a land question. Given the centrality of land to Amerindian identity, Mariátegui was posing a fusion of indigenous and land revindications as part of the project of constructing a counter-hegemonic force to the ruling *gamanalismo* (boss or *cacique*). The Amerindian imaginary – including traditional cultivation and irrigation methods – served to promote a socially embedded form of social relation which countered the dominant land ownership and their legitimation through market ideologies. Contemporary socialism could only gain from an engagement with Inca communism/communalism and prefigurative social relations.

Left governments and social movements

Since 2000 most of Latin America – with the major exceptions of Mexico and Colombia – has been under left governments of one type or another. What we need to note at the start is how totally unprecedented those left governments are. Not since Jacobo Arbenz in Guatemala in the 1950s, Salvador Allende in Chile in the 1970s and the Sandinistas in Nicaragua in the 1990s has a self-declared left been in office in Latin America (except Cuba of course). Certainly also unprecedented is a swing of this type across a whole region. What is also significant in world historical terms is that this shift to the left (although what that means remains to be established) occurred only a decade after the fall of the Berlin wall and Fukuyama's declaration of the 'end of history'. We were supposedly moving with a smooth post-ideological world where the hegemony of neoliberal globalisation would be utterly hegemonic. To even have a president (Hugo Chávez) stand up and proclaim '21st century socialism' is not something anyone would have expected at the time.

There has been a huge amount of international interest in the rise of the left of centre governments in Latin America. However, much of the analysis has been somewhat driven by external political agencies and is often reduced to a 'good left' versus a 'bad left'. The first variety is deemed to have learned the economic lessons of the neoliberal phase and has a healthy respect for Western liberal democratic political norms. The latter are deemed economically irresponsible and politically authoritarian. In short, we are led to believe there is a democratic left versus a populist left. This is essentially a neocolonial perspective with its view of the good native who has learnt his lessons well and the rebellious, still part-savage, colonial who will revert to type, spend money he has not earned and make false promises to the people, all held together by a dubious non-rational non-European type of charisma. It is clear that international financial institutions would prefer not to deal with someone who might be unpredictably swayed by the will of the people. Nevertheless there are still distinctive strands in current Latin American left theory and practice which we need to analyse not least to assess the prospects of this new political order.

There is not one clearly defined single social democratic left, although Chilean socialists and F H Cardoso in Brazil are most often mentioned in this regard. Others may view these political figures as belonging to the centre-right. Be that as it may, they clearly aspire to a social democratic type of social order. The democratisation of the market economy, or at the very least its regulation or reorganisation to compensate for its inequalities, is a key belief. In political terms it preaches a reform of the state and a social policy based on empowerment and capacity building. Roberto Mangabeira Unger, the Brazilian philosopher and politician who might be seen as a maverick social democrat, argues clearly that: 'Empowerment, both educational and economic, of the individual worker and citizen, democratization of the market economy and the establishment of a social solidarity based on social responsibility requires a deepening of democracy...' (Mangabeira, Unger, 2011: 42). Democracy is at the core of this new Latin American political current and that is probably unique in a situation where democratic politics most often responded to an economic or military crisis in the past.

The populist left is not, of course, a self-proclaimed category but rather an epithet deployed against radical nationalists by observers at home and abroad. We could say that they take a different approach to democratising democracy to that of the more European social democratic discourses just mentioned above. At the heart of this 'populist' current lies a commitment to economic nationalism and a recovery of the category of people [*pueblo*]. Thus, for example, Nestor Kirchner, former President in Argentina 'set up a discursive dividing line' (Panizza, 2009: 245) between the previous anti-national neoliberalism of (ex-President Carlos) Menem and the military to frame his own economic and political project as the current manifestation of the national-popular politics of the 1940s and 1950s. Its economics mirrored the neodevelopmentalism being articulated by CEPAL (Comisión Económica para América Latina y el Caribe/the United Nations Economic Commission for Latin America and the Caribbean) and its politics was based on democracy plus personalism. Rather than read this 'populist left' in a purely negative anti-democratic sense it would be better to conceive of this emerging current as national-popular governments which represent a twenty-first century national popular politics, rebalancing globalisation in favour of the nation-state.

From an international left networked perspective the main progressive alternative is the grassroots or autonomist left in Latin America symbolised most clearly through the Zapatistas. Certainly many myths have circulated about the Zapatistas and their autonomism that have never really been theorised, although John Holloway's *Change the World Without Taking Power* comes close to an unauthorised version. For Holloway 'the starting point of theoretical reflection is opposition, negativity, struggle. It is from rage that thought is born...' (Holloway, 2002: 1). Given that capitalist relations are everywhere, even embedded in the state, seizing power through reformist or revolutionary means is futile. Thus, for Holloway, 'The struggle to liberate power is not the struggle to construct a counter-power, but rather an anti-power...' (Holloway, 2002: 184). This strategy is based on a rebuttal of the state, of power, of the party form – it is ultimately negative. The autonomism of the Zapatistas is not the only form – and other Amerindian groups in Mexico and elsewhere conceive it differently – but it has come to symbolise a politics which has not really made any significant advances 20 years since the Zapatistas shook up international politics in 1994.

Not surprisingly, a plethora of interpretations have emerged to theorise and deconstruct the new left governments. What seems clear from the evidence so far is that this turn is not due to a massive shift to the left in terms of public opinion. It would be complacent of us to see the leftist parties in government as a result of a great swing to the left by the masses, now totally disenchanted with neoliberalism. Marco Morales is right to argue that 'the more plausible story is that the leftist parties that won elections were skilled at broadening their appeal beyond those that identify with the left' (Morales, 2008: 37). That is most clearly the case in Brazil, Chile and Uruguay. Over and above that we can argue that this shift at government level does reflect a growing disenchantment with a 'made in U.S.' economic model and a deep desire to explore more nationalist and regionalist approaches to development. The 2008–2009 global crisis, with its clear roots in the US economic system, deepened the feeling that a more indigenous response to the crisis was called for.

The rise of the new left governments since 2000 has been interlinked with the emergence of a series of novel and influential social movements. Those have ranged from traditional trade union-based mobilisations (Mexico, Brazil and the Southern Cone countries for example), new peasant-based uprisings (Chiapas and the Movimento dos Trabalhadores Rurais Sêm Terra [MST]/Landless Workers Movement in Brazil for example), ongoing road blockages by the unemployed (the *piqueteros* in Argentina), mobilisations against privatisation (the Water Wars in Bolivia), the emergence of indigenous social movements and parties (most notably in the Andean countries) and the ongoing movements of women and environmentalists which trace their roots back to the 1970s. This diverse range of social movements do not have a unifying point of reference as they once might have had, be it revolution, dependency or imperialism.

Those social movements may be called 'new' but they also reflect a long history of contestation in Latin America. What is significant to us, for the purposes of this chapter, is to examine, the broad parameters of how these social movements impact on and are impacted by the new wave of left governments that have prevailed in the region since 2000. We could argue with some evidence that it was the mass mobilisations of the 1990s and early 2000s which brought the left governments to power. Sometimes this happened dramatically or with the semi-insurrectionary situation in Argentina following the collapse of neo-liberalism at the end of 2001, start of 2002. In Brazil the Workers' Party was helped into government, at least indirectly, by the workers mobilisations which created the Workers Party in the first place. In the Andean countries, there were many mass mobilisations prior to the left governments but in Venezuela that was not so clearly the case.

Once the left governments were in power there was no necessary symbiosis between them and the progressive social movements. Already in the 1980s and 1990s we had seen how many thriving human rights and women's movements had been co-opted once the dictatorships were displaced, as in post-democratic Chile for example. In this new situation of self-declared left governments in power there were several questions that needed to be asked. As Gary Prevost and co-authors put it: 'Once in power, does the progressive government view the country's social movements as partners in government to be consulted or, as is frequently the case, to be held at arm's length as continuing opponents?' (Prevost et al., 2012: 14). Conversely the social movements will consider to what extent the government in power is 'their' government and thus it might be allowed some latitude or not. This last question has been particularly pressing in Brazil.

This is, effectively a research programme which could be undertaken by a development education course. It certainly cannot be answered here with limited space. What we can say is that an analysis based on categorising 'good' governments and movements on the one hand and 'bad' governments and movements on the other is unlikely to lead to a nuanced, relevant and grounded answer. Thus mainstream commentators distinguish between a 'good' responsible left as in Chile from a bad 'populist' one such as Chávez in Venezuela (e.g. Castañeda and Morales, 2008). From the left we also have many commentators who bemoan the 'selling out' of the once radical *piqueteros* in Argentina to the Kirchner government or the MST in Brazil not being forceful enough in opposing the administration of former President Lula (Luiz Inácio Lula da Silva) in Brazil. Chávez, for his part, has given rise to a mini industry of literature for and against him that adds little to our critical understanding.

Critical perspectives

What I propose now is a cursory examination of some of the arguments around the left government and the social movements in Bolivia by way of example of how we might approach analysis from a critical perspective. Internationally, the prestigious *New Left Review* publishes the President of Ecuador and Vice President of Bolivia as spokespersons of the left (see Correa, 2012 and Linera, 2006). Trotskyist analysts subscribe to the think tank *Comuna* (associated with Linera) arguing that it overcame all the errors of the traditional left in Bolivia since 1952, best understood the neoliberal era, and most clearly saw the need for a new historical subject and the need for marrying the Evo Morales leadership with the indigenous movement as the essential historical protagonist of the current period (Sader, 2009: 119). Now, the achievements of the Evo Morales government are considerable and the rise of the indigenous movement is simply remarkable, but this view does seem somewhat uncritical.

Bolivia's Vice President Garcia Linera has produced an extraordinary amount of critical analysis as well as policy development. It reflects a thinking which is both bold and unbound by left tradition. He has, for example, articulated a theory of 'Andean-Amazonian capitalism' as a stage in the transition to socialism (Linera, 2006). In theory a strong state would regulate industrial expansion and transfer the surplus to the community sector to empower self-organisation and a broader development process. But it can also be seen as standard free market orthodoxy dressed up in indigenous clothing which might become a vehicle for corruption. More broadly we need to consider the pessimistic verdict of Jeffrey Webber who finds a considerable degree of continuity with the inherited neoliberal model in terms of the Morales government's commitment to fiscal austerity, low inflation growth and its mining, agricultural and labour market policies (Webber, 2009: 165).

If we were to pursue this analysis beyond the polemical level, and of course in Bolivia those polemics are about power, then we might want to take a longer view. We might argue that when Che Guevara landed in Bolivia in 1967 to start a guerrilla war his 'sociological analysis' was flawed insofar as he ignored the critical weight of the workers movement. The miners and peasant led revolution of 1952 had created a very different country from pure, revolutionary Cuba. Now the mines are closed and the miners have gone back to the land, many cultivating the profitable coca leaf. The working class had become more flexible, mobile and complex as elsewhere. The miners were no longer hegemonic in the counter-hegemonic movement. This is the context in which Morales came to power. As Hardt and Negri note: 'This shift, however, signals no farewell to the working class or even a decline of worker struggle but rather an increasing multiplicity of the proletariat and a new physiognomy of struggle' (Hardt and Negri, 2011: 110).

Latin America in the North

Latin America plays an important role in development education courses in the global North. The influence of Brazilian popular educator Paulo Freire can still be felt in the ethos of development education. Freire's dialectical theory of knowledge, despite the criticisms by orthodox Marxists concerning his idealism, marked a new phase in critical pedagogy theory and practice. The social production of knowledge and the rejection of education as a one-way transmission process are now part of the common sense in popular education in general and development education in particular. Liam Kane (2001) in his review of popular education in Latin America shows a very good understanding of a 'situated' Paulo Freire (including his conceptual fuzziness and eclecticism) which is relevant to how we, and development education, might take up 'the lessons' of current social transformations in Latin America.

I think it is important to situate 'Latin America' quite critically as an object of analysis and teaching in the Northern academy which includes development education. Previous paradigms for social transformation have been received and reworked in the global North in particular ways. The reception of the Latin American dependency approach in the 1970s is a case in point. On the one hand, radical writers such as Andre Gunder Frank popularised a version of dependency which lost its original subtlety in terms of method and its open politics. On the other hand its Northern critics reduced a historical-structural method of enquiry into a bland and generic statement about 'dependency' which could then easily be disproved. F H Cardoso, one of its earlier Latin American promoters notes in this regard that 'instead of demanding an empirico-analytical effort of reconstructing a "concrete whole" dependency came to be consumed as a "theory" implying a corpus of formal and testable propositions' (Cardoso, 1977: 19).

More recently we have seen the cause of the Mexican Zapatistas championed globally through the Internet. Judith Hellman noted how 'virtual Chiapas holds a seductive attraction for disenchanted and discouraged people on the left that is fundamentally different from the appeal of the struggles underway in the real Chiapas' (Hellman, 2000: 175). On the grounds that not everyone is a 'Zapatista', there are divisions and weaknesses and *realpolitik* does not always reflect the seductive political rhetoric of sub comandante Marcos online. 'Civil society' is not such a homogeneous and progressive milieu as the international supporters of Zapatismo might believe. Certainly there are romanticised, essentialised views of indigenous peoples permeating international online Zapatismo. We can also argue that vicarious participation through transnational solidarity might hinder the development of grassroots activism through its celebratory acritical tone.

So, in terms of the new *Sumak Kawsay* (Buen Vivir) paradigm what can we say about its reception in the North? There is a good chance that it will be absorbed and domesticated by the Northern academy as have the postcolonial literature and subaltern studies strands of thinking in the past. It answers questions about 'what next?' after the global crisis of 2008 and onwards and the collapse of neoliberal hegemony at least as a belief system. But an enchantment with *Pachamama* (Mother Earth) does not help us understand the complexity of the Latin American indigenous movements and their political or ideological expressions. And, much like Debray's *Revolution in the Revolution* (1967) for a different political era there is a danger of generalising what might be applicable in one sub-region (Cuba then, the Andean countries now) to the thriving urban and industrial economies of Brazil, Mexico and Argentina.

I am not arguing here for a pure Latin American essence that becomes corrupted when it travels North. Latin American hybridity – in economic, social and cultural terms – should warn us against any form of essentialism. But, all knowledge needs to be situated and grounded in the situation from which it emerges. We saw how dependency went from being a critical method of analysis to an empty rhetorical theory. Torn from its context it is 'consumed' elsewhere for very different purposes than it was intended for. This is not an argument that theory cannot travel and can only be consumed locally as some argue for tropical fruit. It is, rather, a plea for situated knowledge, one rich with social and political mediations and not a simplistic 'lessons of' type reading of Zapatismo, Chávez, the MST in Brazil, Morales and the next leading force.

What I would articulate as my own position is that we need to 'bring politics back in'. To a large extent the postcolonial critique and an emphasis on *interculturalidad* as in the Andean countries now dominate counter-hegemonic discourses about Latin America. However, through a closer reading and deeper understanding of the varied impact of colonialism and imperialism across Latin America we might understand the limits of a 'coloniality of power' (Quijano, 2000) approach. I would argue, for example, that the trajectory and current dilemmas faced by Brazil, Mexico and Argentina, cannot be grasped by a lens dominated by the colonial experience. It is capitalism – in its particular manifestation of uneven development – which has shaped Latin American history and political struggles over the last 50 years. An understanding of Latin America's capitalist development and its contradictions is vital today as global neoliberalism loses effectiveness as a development paradigm.

As Ilan Kapoor argues in a critical assessment of the postcolonial politics of development: 'While many may consider dependency old-fashioned today, put into conversation with postcolonial theory, it regains relevance and contemporaneity' (Kapoor, 2008: 18). In the 1970s the dependency approach very much mirrored modernisation theory in its methodological nationalism and its Eurocentric understanding of development. The coloniality of power approach has been a useful corrective. Conversely the postcolonial approach has often stressed cultural and representational issues to the neglect of poverty and class politics. The emphasis of the local and the authenticity has sometimes diverted attention from the global conditioning situation which dependency so clearly articulated. It is precisely this type of rich dialogue that Northern development education might profitably engage on with an open and critical mind.

Further reading

Burbach, R, Fox, M and Fuentes, F (2013) *Latin America's Turbulent Transitions, The Future of Twenty First Century Socialism*, London: Zed Books.

Munck, R (2013) *Rethinking Latin America: Development, Hegemony and Social Transformation*, New York: Palgrave.

Prevost, G, Campos, C O and Vanden, H (eds) (2012) *Social Movements and Leftist Governments in Latin America. Confrontation or Cooptation?* London: Zed Books.

Webber, J (2013) *Red October: Left Indigenous Struggles in Modern Bolivia*, New York: Haymarket Books.

References

Cardoso, F H (1977) 'The consumption of dependency theory in the United States', *Latin American Research Review*, 12(3), pp. 7–24.

Cardoso, F H and Faletto, E (1969, 1979) *Dependency and Development in Latin America*, California: University of California Press.

Castañeda, J and Morales, M (2008) (eds) *Leftovers: Tales of the Latin American Left*, London: Routledge.

Correa, R (2012) 'Ecuador's path', *New Left Review*, 77 (Sept/Oct).

Debray, R (1967) *Revolution in the Revolution*, New York: Monthly Review Press.

Frank, A G (1970) *Lumpenbourgeoisie: Lumpendevelopment – Dependence, Class and Politics in Latin America*, New York: Monthly Review Press.

Galindo, A F (2010) *In Search of an Inca: Identity and Utopia in the Andes*, Cambridge: Cambridge University Press.

García Canclini, N (1995) *Hybrid Cultures: Strategies for Entering and Leaving Modernity*, Minnesota: University of Minnesota Press.

Hardt, N and Negri, A (2011) *Commonwealth*, Cambridge, Mass: Harvard University Press.

Hellman, J (2000) 'Real and virtual Chiapas, magical realism and the Left', *Socialist Register*, Vol. 36.

Holloway, J (2002) *Change the World Without Taking Power: The Meaning of Revolution Today*, London: Pluto.

Kane, L (2001) *Popular Education and Social Change in Latin America*, London: LAB.

Kapoor, I (2008) *The Postcolonial Politics of Development*, London: Routledge.

Linera, A G (2006) 'State crisis and popular power', *New Left Review*, January–February, Vol. 37, pp. 73–85.

Mangabeira Unger, R (2011) *La alternative de izquierda*, México: Fondo de Cultura Económica.

Morales, M (2008) 'Have Latin American turned left?' in J Castañeda and M Morales (eds) *Leftovers: Tales of the Latin American Left*, London: Routledge.

Panizza, R (2009) *Contemporary Latin America: Development and Democracy Beyond the Washington Consensus*, London: Zed Books.

Prevost, G, Campos, C O and Vanden, H (eds) (2012) *Social Movements and Leftist Governments in Latin America: Confrontation of Co-optation?* London: Zed Books.

Quijano, A (2000) 'The coloniality of power: Eurocentrism and Latin America', *Nepantla*, 1(3), pp. 538–580.

Sader, E (2009) *El Nuevo Topo: los caminos de la izquerda latinoamericana*, Buenos Aires: Siglo XXI.

Vanden, H and Becker, M (eds) (2011) *José Carlos Mariátegui: An Anthology*, New York: Monthly Review Press.

Webber, J R (2009) 'From naked barbarism to barbarism with benefits: Neoliberal capitalism, natural gas policy, and the government of Evo Morales in Bolivia' in A Ruckert and L Macdonald (eds) *Post-Neoliberalism in the Americas*, New York, NY: Palgrave Macmillan.

Žižek, S (1997) 'Multiculturalism, or, the cultural logic of multinational capitalism', *New Left Review*, Vol. 220, pp. 28–51.

13

Political Society[1] and Subaltern[2] Social Movements (SSM) in India: Implications for Development/Global Education

Dip Kapoor

> Peasant movements like Chipko (northern India) and peasant protests reveal how policies of 'economic development' or 'modernization' formulated at the top levels of states, corporations and international financial institutions are often experienced by peasants, rural women, and laborers – as exploitation. In the strategies of economic development, indigenous peoples, landless peasants, and women are expected to bear the brunt of industrialization; disease, social unrest, food security and land hunger testify to the impact of this process (Guha, 1990: 195–196).

Introduction

This chapter suggests that development education (DE) [also when discussed in relation to Global/Citizenship Education (G/CE)] in Canada and potentially in the 'First World' (imperial societies), could benefit from radical democratisation in terms of the potential range of relevant source(s) of knowledge(s), experience(s), analyses and teleological/political possibilities that DE has strenuously avoided, ignored or remained suspiciously oblivious of, to date (e.g. from indigenous and development-displaced/dispossessed people's rural movements referenced here as Subaltern Social Movements [SSMs] – see Table 13.1 for a network of rural movements or the Lok Adhikar Manch [LAM] in the east-coast state of Orissa, India). DE needs to consider the possibilities of a critical dialectical approach which engages/exposes various contradictions unleashed by the Euro-American development project,

Table 13.1 Lok Adhikar Manch (LAM)

Movement participant (year established)	Location/operational area	Social groups engaged	Key issues being addressed
1. Kalinga Matchyajivi Sangathana (Kalinga fisher people's organisation) (early 1980s)	Gopalpur-on-sea (centre) including coastal Orissa, from Gopalpur in Ganjam district to Chandrabhaga and Astaranga coast in Puri district	Fisher people (mainly Dalits) originally from the state of Andhra Pradesh called Nolias and Orissa state fisher people or Keuta/Kaivartas	• Trawler fishing, fish stock depletion and enforcement of coastal regulations/zones (Trans/national Corporate – TNC – investments) • Occupation of coastal land by defense installations (e.g. missile bases) • Hotel/tourism industry developments along coast (TNC investment) • Special economic zones (SEZ) and major port projects for mining exports (TNC investment) • Pollution of beaches and oceans • Displacement of fisher communities related to such developments
2. Prakritik Sampad Suraksha Parishad (PSSP) (late 1980s)	Kashipur, Lakhimpur, Dasmantpur and adjacent blocks in Rayagada district of Orissa Approximately 200 movement villages	Adivasis including Jhodias, Kondhs and Parajas and Pano/Domb Dalits	• Bauxite mining (alumina) (TNC investments) • Industrialisation, deforestation and land alienation/ displacement • Peoples' rights over 'their own ways and systems'

Table 13.1 Lok Adhikar Manch (LAM) – *continued*

Movement participant (year established)	Location/operational area	Social groups engaged	Key issues being addressed
3. Jana Suraksha Manch (2007)	Adava region of Mohana block, Gajapati district including 60 or more villages	Saura and Kondh Adivasis and Panos (Dalits)	• Government/local corruption • Police brutality/atrocities • Deforestation and plantation agriculture (NC investment)
4. Adivasi Dalit Adhikar Sangathan (2000)	Jaleswar, Bhograi and Bosta blocks in Balasore district and Boisinga and Rasagovindpur blocks in Mayurbhanj including over 100 villages	Dalits, Adivasis, fisher people and Other Backward Castes (OBCs)	• Dalit and Adivasi land rights and land alienation • Industrialisation, port development and displacement of traditional fisher people (TNC investment)
5. Adivasi-Dalit Ekta Abhiyan (2000)	20 panchayats in Gajapati and Kandhmal districts including 200 plus villages (population of about 50,000)	Kondh and Saura Adivasis, Panos (Dalits) and OBCs	• Land and forest rights • Food • Sovereignty/plantation agriculture (NC investment) • Industrialisation, modernisation and protection of indigenous ways and systems • Communal harmony • Development of people's coalitions/forums (no state, NGO, corporate, 'outsider', upper/middle castes participants)

Table 13.1 Lok Adhikar Manch (LAM) – *continued*

Movement participant (year established)	Location/operational area	Social groups engaged	Key issues being addressed
6. Indravati Vistapita Lokmanch (late 1990s)	30 villages in the district of Nabarangapur	Several Adivasi, Dalit and OBC communities	• Dam displacement (Indravati irrigation and hydroelectric project) (NC investment) • Land and forest rights • Resettlement, rehabilitation and compensation for development displaced peoples (DDPs) • Industrialisation and modern development and protection of peoples' ways
7. Orissa Adivasi Manch (1993 to 1994)	State level forum with an all Orissa presence (all districts) with regional units in Keonjhar and Rayagada districts and district level units in each district	Well over 40 different Adivasi communities	• Adivasi rights in the state • Tribal self rule, forest and and rights and industrialisation (SEZs) (TNC investments)
8. Anchalik Janasuraksha Sangathan (2008)	Kidting, Mohana block of Gajapati district including some 20 villages	Kondh and Saura Adivasis and Panos (Dalits)	• Land and forest rights • Conflict resolution and communal harmony between Adivasis and Dalits over land and forest issues

Table 13.1 Lok Adhikar Manch (LAM) – *continued*

Movement participant (year established)	Location/operational area	Social groups engaged	Key issues being addressed
9. Dalit Adivasi Bahujana Initiatives (DABI) (2000)	Five blocks in the Kandhmal district with ten participating local movements (networks)	Kondh Adivasis, Panos (Dalits) and OBCs	• Land and forest rights • Food sovereignty and livelihood issues • Communal harmony
10. Uppara Kolab Basachyuta Mahasangh (late 1990s)	Umerkote block, Koraput district (includes a 30 village population base displaced by the upper Kolab hydroelectric and irrigation reservoir)	Paraja Adivasis, Panos and Malis Dalits and OBCs	• Displacement due to the upper Kolab hydro-electricity and irrigation reservoir (NC investment) • Compensation, rehabilitation and basic amenities for DDPs • Land and forest rights
11. Jeevan Jivika Suraksha Sangathan (2006)	Three panchayats in the border areas of Kandhmal and Gajapati districts including 50 or more villages with a population of 12,000 people	Kondhs and Saura Adivasis and Panos (Dalits) and OBCs	• Land and forest rights/issues • Communal harmony • Food sovereignty and livelihood issues

Table 13.1 Lok Adhikar Manch (LAM) – *continued*

Movement participant (year established)	Location/operational area	Social groups engaged	Key issues being addressed
12. Adivasi Pachua Dalit Adhikar Manch (APDAM) (2000)	Kalinga Nagar industrial belt in Jajpur district (25 or more villages, along with several participants in the Kalinganagar township area)	Adivasis, Dalits and OBCs	• Industrialisation and displacement (TNC investment) • Land and forest rights • Compensation and rehabilitation • Police atrocities/brutality • Protection of Adivasi-Dalit ways and forest-based cultures and community
13. Janajati Yuva Sangathan (2008)	Baliapal and Chandanesar block in Balasore district including 32 coastal villages being affected by mega port development (part of SEZ scheme).	Dalit fisher communities and OBCs	• SEZs (TNC investments) • Industrialisation and displacement • Land alienation and marine rights of traditional fisher communities

Source: Kapoor, 2011a: 132–134.

Note: In addition to the above LAM movements, leaders from two other movements were also included in the research, both of which have expressed an interest in joining LAM. These include: (i) the *Niyamgiri Bachao Andolan* (NBA), a Dongria and Kutia Kondh (Adivasi) movement against Vedanta/Sterlite (UK) bauxite mine/refinery in Lanjigarh, and the (ii) anti-POSCO (Wall Street/South Korea) movement, Santal Adivasi wing from the Khandadhar region and the parent *POSCO Pratirodh Manch or POSCO Pratirodh Sangram Samiti (PPSS)* which include several wings including small and medium farmers (e.g. Betel leaf farmers), Adivasi, Dalits and fisherfolk affected (or potentially affected) at the plant site or due to port development (Jatadhar river basin area; this includes the Paradip Port Trust which would have to handle iron ore exports) and water-affected areas/groups in the Cuttack district as water for irrigation and drinking in these areas is channeled through a proposed canal (going through five districts) to the POSCO plant.

including the imbrication of the development project in the continued exercise of a coloniality of power (Quijano, 2000). This would require problematising the Euro-uni-versal conception of development by engaging pluri-versal conceptions (and what lies in-between), as is often forwarded by anti-colonial/capitalist SSMs (Kapoor, 2011a, 2013a) in different time-space and onto-epistemic locations (Zibechi, 2005; Meyer and Alvarado, 2010; Zibechi and Ramon, 2012).

The insights and propositions advanced in this chapter regarding the implications of a political society-based SSM anti-colonial/capitalist praxis for DE are based on: (a) the author's association with Adivasi, Dalit and landless/development-displaced peoples in the state of Orissa, India since the early 1990s; (b) a Social Sciences and Humanities Research Council (SSHRC) of Canada funded participatory action research (PAR) (Kapoor, 2009a) initiative between 2006–2010 contributing towards and simultaneously developing knowledge about social movement learning in SSMs in south Orissa; and (c) specific research assignments (e.g. examining development non-governmental organisation (DNGO)-SSM political relations) conducted by the Center for Research and Development Solidarity (CRDS), a rural people's organisation that was established with the help of SSHRC funds in 2005–2006. More specifically, the insights developed here are based primarily on LAM's critical analysis of modern capitalist (colonial) development. LAM is a nascent 'trans-local alliance' (Da Costa, 2007: 315) of 15 development-displacement related SSM groups or a state-based network in rural Orissa that is an emergent and growing formation since the lead movements (e.g. ADEA) initiated the process in the late 1990s.

Development/global education in Canada: Preliminary critical interjections

DE and/or G/CE in Canada is formally undertaken by the Canadian International Development Agency (CIDA) and is generally informed by United Nations (UN)-centric conceptions of development such as the Millennium Development Goal (MDG) approach to development popularised at the turn of the twenty-first century. DNGOs, the other dominant DE and G/CE actor, have increasingly come to rely on CIDA for their funding (see Barry-Shaw and Jay, 2012: 60) and are subsequently and predictably wedded to a UN-MDG-CIDA developmental*ism* or development *project* (McMichael, 2012) that is for the most part, uncritically self-referential. This approach to DE relies on an unproblematic promulgation of Euro-American versions of capitalist-development (especially since the globalisation of capitalism post 1980s) as being the *solution* to, as opposed to the possible *cause* of, impoverishment, marginalisation, exclusion and underdevelopment which *such development* purportedly sets out to address.

A case in point, the Alberta Council for Global Cooperation's 'Development in a Box' DE effort aimed at schools in the province depicts hunger and poverty as original conditions faced by rural families in African, Asian and Latin American countries subsequently requiring individualised asset-based micro-entrepreneurial development interventions from outside (inputs to address deficits), going along with the preferred analysis and small c=capitalist antidote proffered by the Canadian Hunger Foundation, the authors of this unit. This ahistorical and partial approach obscures the past/current complicity of a colonial and/or modern capitalist transnational corporation (TNC)-led agro-industrial development model in perpetuating and causing persistent hunger and poverty in these regions (GRAIN, 2012). This is evident, for example, in colonial land/labour control systems or current land grabbing scenarios or debt-driven cotton farmer suicides in western India – now some 250,000 plus deaths over the recent decade. The agro-industrial development model thus impoverishes people over 'there' to provide cheaper food for consumption by families/children over 'here' in metropolitan/imperial centres, including the children/students being engaged in these blatantly ideological and politically myopic if not morally disabling CIDA-NGO developed DE materials.

Writing at the turn of the century, prominent development educators in Canada (Goldstein and Selby, 2000) continued to press for inclusion *in the development project* and for participation and peace with an associated notion of social justice as inclusive justice (or shared/equitable-development within the existing model). At the same time, they ignored the potential links (or even some consideration of a dialectical relationship) between what was being touted as inclusive/participatory development and postcolonial colonisations or colonial capitalist development. Inclusive or not, participatory or not, peaceful or not, as LAM's/SSM's analysis suggests, DE misses the elephant(s) in the room by failing to focus on colonial capitalist development as being the cause for problems it's advocates purport to seek to address. This is development that is predicated upon the logic of endless capitalist accumulation, and *rational* individual self-interest is by definition predatory, marginalising/exclusionary, colonising (of land, ecology and racialised-labour) and dependent upon the active creation of inequality to ensure a readily available surplus supply of (cheap) labour.

Development educators who have either worked for CIDA or CIDA-funded DNGOs or may have no such experience but rely on these sources of information, analysis and political-teleological positioning to inform their pedagogical work in schools for instance, tend to reproduce the sponsored approach to DE and G/CE for the most part. Critique and/or variations and debates pertaining to the CIDA/UN-centric approaches to DE or G/CE seldom stray too far from these dominant institutional perspectives. When entertained they rarely amount to more than domestic in-fighting between liberals including liberally-oriented *critical pedagogues* and/or *transformationalists* or *transcendentalists*, seeking to avoid the material violence or uncomfortable implications of a conflict-ridden colonial and capitalist history and present, and the related and wrenching demands of contemporary structural change. Liberal transformational-transcendentalist versions of globalism exercise this avoidance through recourse to an educational ideology informed by the notion that education and/or cognitive justice will fix all, including as it is perhaps presumed, material/political-economic injustices like hunger/poverty. These versions of globalism are heavily imbued with a cathartic and euphoric rhetoric of love, hope and normative pleas for a desired global unity/society to purportedly *address* a colonial-capitalist inspired conflict-ridden *structural* and *material reality* typically characterised by resource/class wars, poverty/inequality/hunger/exploitation, ecological destruction etc.

Whatever the arguments between liberals across this spectrum, there is a general commitment to the non-recognition of colonialism or capitalism in their versions of *critical pedagogical/transformational/transcendentalist* analyses. Academic prognostications of this ilk continue to, for instance, debate the de/merits of the *globally aware* versus the *globally active* approaches to global education (O'Sullivan and Smaller, 2013) while glossing over vexing questions around the controlling hegemonic political-economic, cultural and historical commitments of these approaches to either *awareness* raising and/or *action*, i.e., *awareness* about what and why and *action* for/towards what and why and for whom? Or neo/liberal DE and G/CE scholars and pedagogues engage in protracted debates positioned some where between the neoliberal end of the spectrum influenced primarily by World Bank/Organisation for Economic Co-operation and Development (OECD) initiated priorities in G/CE grounded in human capital economic (capitalist) imperatives on the one hand and UNESCO/International Non-Governmental Organisation (INGO)-led progressive education social justice formulations (read as: capitalism with a human face) of DE and G/CE on the other.

The latter approach finds expression in the UN's Cyberschoolbus online initiative introduced in 1996 to demonstrate the ability of Information and Communication Technologies (ICTs) to help people learning about the world or the UN-Sesame Street-Merrill Lynch-William J. Clinton Foundation partnership culminating in the likes of the Panwapa online learning game (available in five languages) inspiring young people in over 120 countries to become responsible global citizens (Spring, 2009). Regardless of the basis of contention between these so-called neo/liberal polarities, such versions of DE and G/CE steer clear of any critical historical and contemporary analysis of the exploitative forces unleashed by capitalism and colonialism. They also fail to acknowledge the continued complicity of neo/liberal development in relying upon and extending these racialised political-economic and socio-cultural vectors.

Other relatively recent DE and/or G/CE scholarship in Canada (Mundy et al., 2007; Mundy and Manion, 2008; Larsen and Faden, 2008) continues to perpetuate this silence by focusing on resource concerns and the potential for DE given existing student/teacher dispositions and inclinations. When and if content and pedagogical approaches are considered, this scholarship uncritically embraces the CIDA/UN-centric development canon on DE and G/CE (e.g. see Reimer and McLean, 2009 and their use of Mundy et al.'s 2007 Euro-centric development rubric). The scholarship does not adequately historicise and politicise development except to reproduce the dominant discourse, with a nod towards culture and sustainability incorporated in to, rather than problematising, development as defined. It also fails to challenge development, westernisation and modernisation as possible causes of immiseration, impoverishment, control, inequality and persisting colonisation. DE and G/CE scholarship and pedagogy in Canada remains unabashedly apolitical (hegemonic) and ahistorical and is largely impervious to the historical and political-economic and socio-cultural/educational links between colonialism, development and post-colonial colonialisms characterised by ongoing projects of racialisation (Heron, 2007; Kothari, 2006; White, 2002; Wilson, 2012) embedded in development processes of political-economic exploitation of non/pre-capitalist modes of production (Hall, 1980); knowledge/cultural colonisations and discursive representations of the post/colonised other (Abdi, 2006, 2009; Barua, 2009; Chana, 2011).

More egregiously perhaps, dominant approaches to DE and G/CE in Canada have reduced global *awareness* and *action* to a charitable, moralistic and normative spectacle focused on individual humanitarian need/mission to do good for 'Third World Others'. These approaches are rooted in an explicitly *ethical* orientation based on individual choice to do good that remains blatantly oblivious to historical and contemporary colonial injustices. These injustices continue to simultaneously connect privilege (those being asked to *consider* doing good) and marginalisation (those being exploited to ensure the choice/privilege of the former) in a rapidly globalising capitalist system. For an example of such a spectacle, consider the 'We Day Event/Campaign of Free the Children' (see: http://www.freethechildren.com/domestic-programming/our-model-we-day/) which is also touted as the NGO-model exemplar for DE and G/CE materials by CIDA, DNGOs and Canadian university-based academics for schools in Ontario; a model/approach that has also been endorsed by Goldstein and Selby (2000: 375).

Another case in point is the CIDA-funded 'Active Citizens Today (Act): Citizenship for Local Schools', a collaborative initiative between the University of Western Ontario's Faculty of Education, the Thames Valley District school board and Free the Children. As Fanon (1963: 76) has pointed out, and these DE and/or G/CE initiatives continue to fail to take in to consideration, 'Europe is literally the creation of the Third World...an opulence that has been fuelled by the dead bodies of Negroes, Arabs, Indians and the yellow races'. Others have demonstrated how the economies of the colonised were restructured to produce the requisite imbalance necessary for the growth of European industry and capitalism; a unique characteristic of modern European capitalism/colonialism as distinguished from earlier pre-capitalist colonialisms (Alavi, 1972; Galeano, 1972; Rodney, 1982; Sankaran, 2009). With no regard for these *historical, political* and the *social structural* elements of the role of exploitative colonial and capitalist relations, such DNGO and university-led activities indulge in emotional/cathartic display substitutes for having *done* something to address a *Third World* concern (Webber, 2012).

These activities are often tied to fundraising and reproduce colonial and racialised relations by substituting hard-nosed critical political-economic and socio-cultural analysis and critically-informed organised action, with what Ugandan-American writer Teju Cole refers to as the

'White Savior Industrial Complex' (WSIC) sentimentalist approach. Critiquing the KONI 2012 Campaign initiated by the non-profit Invisible Children, Cole is worth quoting here on this point: 'I deeply respect American sentimentality, the way one respects a wounded hippo. You must keep an eye on it, for you know it is deadly' and in relation to WSIC, 'The White Savior Industrial Complex is not about justice. It is about having one big emotional experience that validates privilege' (see: http://urchinmovement.com/2012/03/28/teju-cole-on-kony-2012-and-the-white-savior-industrial-complex/).

CIDA/UN/DNGO-led DE or G/CE continues to fail to address the *seed of development* that is *colonialism* (including postcolonial variations exposed by LAM/SSM analysis) and the project of *racialisation* (an analysis which also eludes global justice activism in Canada – see Choudry, 2009). They have historically and continue to be imbricated in the globalisation of capitalism and development as externally-imposed modernisation. Given recent attempts to profit from potential synergies between international aid and foreign affairs (CIDA has recently been merged in to foreign affairs by the current Conservative government in Ottawa) in terms of global trade and economic development and current geo-political military priorities and directives (prompting some to reference this as the 'militarisation of aid' – see Duffield, 2001), CIDA/DNGO-led and constructed DE is compromised by and is often a product of this relationship. It remains to be seen if being un-tethered from CIDA/state support (as CIDA undergoes fiscal restructuring and political redirecting in the current environment) and being cut adrift to rely even more on funds from corporates, foundations and public donations will prompt critical revisitations in terms of NGO-led DE. Meanwhile, DE would do well to engage with and learn from social groups and processes currently under-represented in the DE lexicon with the view to democratise the knowledge/political space within its current ambit and to listen to those in whose name development often claims to find its justification in the first instance.

SSMs, political society and critical perspectives on colonial-capitalist development: Emergent implications for development/global education in Canada and beyond

Contrary to Marxist prognostications about the 'death of the peasantry' (Hobsbawm, 1994), peasant and rural resistance/political alternatives remain resolute as demonstrated by, for instance, the establishment of Via Campesina (www.viacampesina.org) or 'the peasant way' on the global stage in 1993 (one year before Hobsbawm's book), offering an alternative paradigm of agricultural development to the corporate agro-industrial model called 'food sovereignty' (Bello, 2009). Similarly, rural classes and social groups/communities facing development-related displacement and dispossession caused by mining, dams, roadways, military bases, tourist/conservation resorts etc. in the rural regions of an emerging global economy like India with its growing contradictions (Sanyal, 2010; Kohli, 2012) are also being contested (along with related perspectives and critiques of the dominant development model) by various social struggles and movements (Baviskar, 2005; Menon and Nigam, 2007; McMichael, 2010; Oliver-Smith, 2010; Shah, 2010). These struggles include what are being referenced here as SSMs (Kapoor, 2011a) such as the various movements that have come together as LAM and advanced the following critique of (colonial-capitalist) development.

1. *Terra Nullius*, eminent domain and colonial-capitalist development dispossession of place, community and meaning: Growing development-contestations in the rural belt

According to LAM's Manifesto:

> At this crucial juncture, we resolve to work together to protect ourselves, our interests, our natural bases [*prakrutik adhar*] and fight against any unjust appropriation of our natural habitations by commercial and state development interests. The manner in which industrialization is taking place [especially mining and dam projects], displacing the sons and daughters of the soil, destroying our resource and life base, we collectively oppose it and resolve to stand together to oppose it in the future. We have nothing to gain from liberalization [*mukto bojaro*], privatization [*ghoroi korono*] and globalization [*jagothi korono*], which are talked about today. We want to live the way we know how to live among our forests, streams, hills and mountains and water bodies with our culture, traditions and whatever that is good in our society intact. We want to define change and development for ourselves (*amo unathi abom parivarthano songhya ame nirupuno koribako chaho*). We are nature's friends (*prakruthi bandhu*), so our main concern is preserving nature and enhancing its influence in our lives (LAM statement, field notes, April 2009).

Colonial development has always adopted a stance of *terra nullius* (empty space or land of no one) towards territory inhabited by people whose social or political organisation is not recognised as *civilised* (or is considered backward or primitive), such as Adivasi and subalterns located in remote rural regions of the country. This is also true of the postcolonial/independent development era where attempts to compensate and/or resettle and rehabilitate the development-displaced peoples (DDPs) has an abysmal record to date – according to one estimate 75 percent of DDPs are yet to be accommodated (Bharati, 1999: 20).

The state's power of eminent domain (Mehta, 2009) is used to justify such internal colonisations in the name of a national and public modern developmental interest that does not recognise (despite legal and human rights stipulations to the contrary – see Kapoor, 2012) the claims of Adivasi and subaltern rural political-economies and socio-cultural histories. Whitehead (2003: 4229) notes for instance, 'that most of the maps of the areas surrounding the Sardar Sarovar Dam development (western India) do not contain the names of villages that hold historical importance for the Tadvi, Vassawa, Bhils and Bhilalas (Adivasis), even ones they consider centres of their cultural histories'. This act of erasure, expressed and acknowledged by LAM in the Orissa context was referenced in several ways, including: examples of state officials taking measurements of land in pre-displacement villages (for mining development) without explanation nor permission, 'walking through their square/mandap or even through people's hutments going about their business as if there was nobody there' as if 'we are nothing to them, so that they think they don't need to ask before taking and going ahead' (Kondh woman leader, Kapoor, 2009b: 19).

The concept of abstract space (as opposed to local place-based histories referenced by LAM constituents), emerged with the rise of colonial capital and the Enlightenment, wherein space was conceived of (drawing from Newton, Descartes and Galileo) as homogenous, isometric and infinitely extended (Lefebvre, 1990). The colonial conception of space, i.e., primitive accumulation or accumulation by dispossession (Harvey, 2003):

> is usually accompanied by erasure, or at least a denigration of preexisting ways of relating to such resources, which are often defined as nomadic, unsettled, uncivilized etc...it involves the rearrangement of space since it constitutes an annihilation of pre-existing property and of customary ways of relating landscapes and waterscapes

> which now become emptied of people, history, entitlements, myth and magic (Whitehead, 2003: 4229).

The ensuing material and cultural violence of such development or the 'dispossession of meaning' (Da Costa, 2007: 292) is not lost on Adivasi and rural subalterns:

> After displacement we stand to lose our traditions, our culture and own historical civilization...from known communities we become scattered unknown people thrown in to the darkness to wander about in an unknown world of uncertainty and insecurity (Adivasi Leader, field notes, April 2009).

Unsurprisingly, the Dilip Singh Bhuria Commission's Report (2000–2001) concluded that the state which is supposed to protect tribal interests (as established by Nehruvian paternalism at the time of independence), has contributed to their exploitation through the location of industries and other development projects in tribal areas which are rich in natural resources, estimating that 40 percent of related displacement of 9–20 million people is accounted for by Adivasi alone (Munshi, 2012: 4). Despite Constitutional provisions in the 5th and 6th Schedules that recognise tribal ownership rights over land and forests in Scheduled/Protected Areas (reaffirmed in the Forest Rights Act, 2006), 'people do not have the right to question the decision of the government on forceable evictions' (ACHR, 2005: 9). According to other estimates, dams, mining, industries and parks have displaced 21.3 million people between 1951–1990 (prior to the neoliberal turn and the establishment of Special Economic Zones, or SEZs, that have accelerated this process), of which 40 percent were Adivasi and 20 percent Dalit (Scheduled Caste) peoples (Nag, 2001). Rural development dispossession compels migration to already dense urban centres, leading to the proliferation of a 'planet of slums' (Davis, 2006) where subalterns are again compelled to take on urban-based struggles for space and livelihood (Harvey, 2009).

Despite these repeated postcolonial capitalist development colonisations, SSM assertions 'continue to exist vigorously and even develop new forms' (Ludden, 2005: 100). SSM struggles in India today clearly continue to proliferate (Rajagopal, 2003; Baviskar, 2005; Menon and Nigam, 2007; Da Costa, 2007, 2009; Hussain, 2008; McMichael, 2010; Oliver-Smith, 2010; Padel and Das, 2010) in conjunction with the penetrations of a colonial trans/national capitalist development both agricultural and industrial. Relatively well publicised political society SSMs and resistance to dispossession in the eastern regions include Singur (Bengal), Nandigram (Bengal), Lalgarh (Bengal), Kashipur (Orissa), Lanjigarh (Orissa), Kalinganagar (Orissa), Earasama/Dhinkia (Orissa), Keonjhar (Orissa), Jagdalpur (Chattisgarh) and several lesser known or documented subaltern resistances which are scaling up their actions through a trans-local coalitional politics such as LAM. These movements are challenging a growing number of state-corporate trans/national industrial ventures involving various partners at different points in time including TATAs, Jindals, Birlas, Ambanis, Mittals, Vedanta, POSCO, Salim, Norsk Hydro, ALCAN etc.:

> If the government continues to control lands, forest and water that we have depended on since our ancestors came, then...we will be compelled to engage in a collective struggle (*ame samohiko bhabe, sangram kariba pahi badhyo hebu*)...and building a movement (andolan) among us from village to panchayat to federation levels ...we have been creating a political education around land, forest and water issues and debating courses of action. We are expanding in terms of participation... (Saora Adivasi Leader, field notes, Kapoor, 2009b: 26).

2. Development violence, human rights equivocation and NGO (civil society) politics in zones of development dispossession

LAM's analysis questions the myth that human rights (based development) is an anti-state discourse or an unambiguous avenue for Adivasi resistance to neoliberal state-market-led displacement, dispossession and continued colonisation (Kapoor, 2012, 2013a), i.e., what Jack Donnelly (1989: 188) has referenced as 'development repression' of Adivasi and other subaltern classes and social groups. For instance, as Balakrishnan Rajagopal (2003: 195) notes, the mass eviction of 33 million development refugees from their homes due to development projects such as dams in India is simply seen as a social cost (if at all) of development, thereby exposing human rights discourse as a 'discourse concerning justified violence' (p. 174).

> There were at least 5,000 of us when they fired. I too was one of 12 injured (points to scar on the thigh) but I never spoke up for fear of police retaliation. I have endured my lot in poverty and silence and could not get treated even but we will never back down...even in Chilika, after Tatas got shut down by the Supreme Court decision

> because they violated the Coastal Regulation Zone with their aquaculture project, their mafias came and destroyed people's fishing boats...it seems we act non-violently and use the law and the courts but they always respond with customary violence and break their own laws...signatures of 'consent' for the project (in Kashipur – bauxite mining) were some times taken at gun point and under heavy police presence and after 'consenting' we were forcibly fed meat and liquor (Focus group notes, February 2008).

Such selective blindness around certain forms of violence can be explained by the pathological link between human rights and models of the state in the economy that are derived/embedded in the dominant development discourse, that is:

> ...human rights discourse remains aloof from the 'private' violence of the market on individuals and communities. This tendency has become more pronounced in an era of globalization and privatization wherein the march of the market is celebrated unreservedly... In essence, economic violence – that is violence caused by the market, is treated as out of bounds of human rights law, even as it attempts to assert itself as the sole liberatory discourse in the Third World (Rajagopal, 2003: 196).

> We have people here from Maikanch who know how the state police always act for the industrialists and their friends in government who want to see bauxite mines go forward in Kashipur against our wishes, even if it meant shooting three of our brothers; we have people here from Kalinganagar where Dalits and Adivasis are opposing the Tata steel plant and there too, 13 of us were gunned down by police...many people have been killed by the state and industrialist mafias (Field notes, April 2009).

Frantz Fanon's (1963) theorisation of violence is instructive here in relation to subaltern political responses to persistent market and colonial developmental violence and the related blindness of an estatised-human rights recourse to the same, while simultaneously advocating for civility and non-violence as the axiomatic principles for any response considered by aggrieved groups, i.e., the colonial burden is once again placed on those being colonised and violated by the development project (Williams, 2010: xxviii). Fanon recognised the totalising nature of colonial violence as do Adivasi/subalterns engaged in

LAM; forms of violence that are the *sine qua non* of imperialism and colonialism and which provoke confrontation and the absolute violence of decolonisation.

> We all know that our problems today are because of colonialism (*samrajyobad*) and capitalism (*punjibad*) and these MNCs (multinational corporations), NGOs, DFID (Department for International Development, UK) and the government are its forces (L, Niyamgiri Bachao Andolan/NBA activist, Interview notes, February 2011).

> They are fighting against those who have everything and nothing to lose. We will persist and as long as they keep breaking their own laws – this only makes it easier for us. That is why even after the police firing in Maikanch in 2000, over 10,000 of us showed up to oppose the UAIL project the very next month (Focus group notes, February 2008).

Given that there are some 8,000 NGOs (Padel and Das, 2010) operating in the state of Orissa, NGOs are significant players in Adivasi/Dalit and rural subaltern contexts and are often promoted as agents of the people and champions of human-rights-based development, including in contexts of development dispossession. While a majority of NGOs follow a state-prescribed and circumscribed role predominantly in terms of service provision in areas where there are development-displaced-peoples (DDPs), a few NGOs do claim to support, if not represent social movement activism directed at mining/industrial development interventions in the rural areas. LAM, however, views the majority of these NGOs as subordinate partners in the state-corporate nexus, undermining SSMs by engaging in political obscurantism and in active attempts to demobilise and immobilise movements opposed to these projects by derailing, obstructing, diverting and depoliticising through numerous avenues including: corporate espionage; sowing seeds of division in displacement-affected communities; persuasion as corporate propaganda merchants and projectising dissent; disrupting movements with a staged politics; and disappearing when movements are engaged in direct action (Kapoor, 2013b: 54–65). In KJ's words (an APDAM/LAM activist), 'education, health, SHGs have no relevance at the moment where we are in the process of losing everything (*ame shobu haraiba avosthare ehi prokaro kamoro kaunasi artha nahi*)' (Kapoor, 2013b: 59).

> In Baliapal we fought against the missile testing range against the government during my youth. Here I learnt that NGOs are slaves of the system – they bring people on to the roads for small issues, within the system issues and not system-challenging issues like what we are talking about here today... . Ours is collective action from the people's identified issues and problems – our action is from outside the institutions and NGO action is institutional action (C, Adivasi Dalit Adhikar Sangathan activist, Focus group notes, April 2009).

> NGOs often try to derail the people's movement by forcing them into Constitutional and legal frameworks and by relying on the slow pace of legal avenues to make it seem like they are working in solidarity with the people but all the while using this delaying tactic to help UAIL...they make us in to program managers and statisticians concerned with funding accountability and the management of our people for the NGOs...what they fail to realize is that we are engaged in an Andolan (movement struggle) and not donor funded programs (ADEA activist, Focus group notes, February 2008).

SSMs continue to view NGOs with suspicion when it comes to the politics of development dispossession of rural peoples and NGO-social movement relations.

> People's movements of the traditional communities (*parompariko goshthi*) fighting for the protection of their natural resource base need to be more cautious about the role NGOs play. We all know that the government is pushing for not only mineral based industries but also for creating SEZ (Special Economic Zones) for thermal and hydro-electric power and primarily in Dali-Adivasi-fisher people's areas. With this in mind, the business and state/political interests have already put up their own NGO fronts to work on this directive to fool the people through charity and free services until displacement goals are met and they disappear (KJ, Kalinganagar movement activist, Focus group notes, April 2009).

It should be evident from this critical analysis that LAM formations are primarily located outside and against the state-market-civil society developmentalist nexus; a nexus – despite competing visions within capitalist/other versions of Euro-American modernity and commitments to a post/industrial society – that constructs and strategically deploys laws and institutions to 'legalise' and 'normalise' displacement and dispossession (colonise). The state market nexus also encourages post-displacement disciplining into welfare, resettlement and rehabilitation and related market schemes (Swamy, 2013) or subjects Adivasi/Dalits and other rural subalterns to abject poverty in urban slums and constant migration in search of precarious and exploitative work (recolonise) (Kapoor, 2011b). Given these elements of LAM's critique of colonial capitalist development, SSMs involved with LAM continue to make a conspicuous case for pluri-nationalism (and pluri-modalities of production and power) by exposing and resisting the machinations of trans/national colonial-capitalist dispossession in forest and rural spaces where 80 percent or more of Orissa's 36 million people reside in some 55,000 villages. DE needs to embrace this on a context-specific basis and highlight these struggles with/against colonial capitalist development while applying a critical dialectic to developmental*ism*.

Political society SSMs and LAM formations inform DE in relation to some of the following possibilities that DE in Canada (and elsewhere) need to consider in the interests of developing a more complete understanding of the 'development project' (McMichael, 2012) and what is being accomplished in its wake:

(1) the need to embrace burgeoning indigenist and critical colonial literatures and theoretical perspectives (including development and racism accounts) in order to introduce a dialectical appreciation of the dominant capitalist development project and related colonial excesses/point of germination – to expose the links between capitalism, colonialism and contemporary capitalist-development and globalisation;
(2) elaborating on pluri-versal projects of subaltern, rural and indigenous peoples as pre/existing versions of cultural, political-economic and socio-educational forms of development and ways of being/living and the ongoing capitalist/modernist colonisations and social movement resistances/responses to the same;
(3) moving from a DE politics of individuated emotionalism, moralism, charity and racialisation (the WSIC sentimental approach) and contrived notions of consensus/peace and social justice embedded in privilege, towards a politics of conflict which exposes fundamental historical and current colonial-capitalist political-economic and socio-cultural relations and projects of domination, while emphasising avenues for collective mobilisation to address

national colonial/capitalist development policies and practices which continue to perpetuate conflict (e.g. critiquing and advocating for changes to Canadian mining policy and the associated state-corporate mining development displacement/dispossession of subaltern/rural and indigenous peoples in Canada, Africa, Asia and Latin America);

(4) critically evaluating and understanding various options for possible *political* collaboration and solidarity opportunities with social movements/resistances to colonial capitalist developments at home and around the globe (e.g. how might DE consider linking Canadian students with the efforts of Via Campesina globally or the Lubicon Cree struggle, Idle No More, Mining Watch and others here in Canada?); and

(5) developing a critical awareness, disposition and active engagement with efforts to address the links between capitalism and poverty/inequality/class formations, racialisation and racism, gender-exploitation, ecological destruction (including genetic colonisations, e.g., of seeds and life forms), resource wars/ conflict/arms trade, social-psychological pathology and fragmentation of societies (atomisation of the individual), colonial relations (racism) with non-capitalist/other societies/cultures, moral/spiritual dislocations prompted by an unbridled materialism and capitalist philanthropy/solutions (versions of *doing good*) to address capitalist problems (e.g. market-based solutions to ecological destruction or consumer justice and labour/ecological exploitation – see Mahrouse, 2010).

While this is not intended as an exhaustive laundry list for DE, it provides a possible direction emergent from political society SSM analysis for a more critical and dialectical approach to DE in imperial societies.

Concluding reflections

Having taught DE and GE in BEd programmes for over a decade at McGill University and then at the University of Alberta in Canada, it has become apparent that students will wrestle with the contradictions of these involvements and engage the critique despite hegemonic (common/dominant sense) conceptions reproduced by CIDA-UN-DNGO defined DE or G/CE. This chapter makes the case for democratising (widening) approaches to DE and G/CE in Canada and beyond in the interests of including critical anti-colonial/capitalist analyses of development shared by the likes of SSM formations facing the brunt of development dispossession in eastern India and elsewhere. Such an approach would also point in new directions for active engagements stimulated by DE and GE which could include political solidarity with social action/movements in near and distant locations and for the need to build recognition and acceptance for pluri-versal conceptions of development and ways of being (multiple modes of production, meaning making and being) while continuing to make conspicuous the colonial and exploitative implications of a globalising capitalism undeterred by ecological, social, cultural and moral boundaries. SSM articulations make it clear that DE needs to embrace a more overtly political-pedagogy which problematises the very roots of the development project in terms of its ontological, epistemic and axiological assumptions and historical-political trajectory, including its class/sectoral interests.

Ashis Nandy (2002) makes the case for such consideration in DE in quite compelling terms when articulating a distinction between poverty and destitution which he suggests is not a mere aberration of modern capitalist development but is rather intrinsic to its very logic. He notes (pp. 117–118):

> Destitution usually means zero income in a fully modern, contractual political economy. In an impersonal situation where individualism reigns, in the absence of money income, one can no longer depend or fall back upon the global commons, either because it is exhausted or depleted, or because it has been taken over by the ubiquitous global market. Neither can you live off the forest and the land nor can you depend on the magnanimity of your relatives and neighbors. The neighbors are no longer neighbors; you discover that they have become individualized fellow citizens, who neither expect nor give any quarter to anyone, often not even to their own families.

Notes

1 According to Partha Chatterjee (2001), contrary to Gramsci's usage in relation to political parties/formal politics, *political society* refers to local spaces outside normal *civil society* and is constituted by populations (taxonomised/enumerated in state Schedules for instance) that are not bodies of citizens belonging to the lawfully constituted *civil society* but are populations in need and deserving of welfare and who are not proper citizens under the law, consequently having to make collective demands on the state founded

on a violation of the law, or who survive by side-stepping the law. It is being suggested here that anti-colonial SSMs constitute and take root in *political society* as movements that are primarily located outside and against the state-market-civil society nexus and outside the laws and institutions constructed and strategically deployed by this nexus to reproduce their political-economic and social interests (Kapoor, 2011b).

2 A term first coined by Antonio Gramsci (1971: 55, 325–326) to refer to peasants and labouring poor/common people and a 'subaltern consciousness' (a possible basis for a unifying peasant consciousness) in Italy, the term is being used here interchangeably with 'people' (and 'subaltern classes' where industrial/agrarian capitalism has *classed* subalterns), in keeping with Guha (1997) who acknowledges the historical specificity of this empirical judgment, wherein subaltern is loosely defined in the Indian context with all its ambiguities to refer to landless poor (migrant un/der employed labour), poor (small) peasants, pastoralists/nomads, Adivasis (original dwellers or Scheduled tribes in state parlance), Dalits ('untouchable castes' or Scheduled Castes), Other Backward Castes (OBCs) and development displaced peoples (DDPs) specifically from these former categories, including women in any of these groupings. Subalternity is also understood as a social location and in terms of the dialectics of super-ordination and subordination in global and national hierarchical social relations of exploitation (including but not restricted to those that reproduce capitalist property relations).

References

Abdi, A (2006) 'Culture of education, social development, and globalization: Historical and current analyses of Africa' in A Abdi, K Puplampu and G Dei (eds) *African Education and Globalization: Critical Perspectives*, NY: Rowman and Littlefield, pp. 13–30.

Abdi, A (2009) 'Oral societies and colonial experiences: Sub-Saharan Africa and the de-facto power of the written word' in D Kapoor (ed.) *Education, Decolonization and Development: Perspectives from Asia, Africa and the Americas*, Rotterdam: Sense Publishers, pp. 39–56.

Alavi, H (1972) 'The state in post-colonial societies: Pakistan and Bangladesh', *New Left Review*, Vol. 74, pp. 59–81.

Asian Center for Human Rights [ACHR] (2005) *Promising Picture or Broken Future? Commentary and recommendations on the Draft National Policy on Tribals of the Government of India*, New Delhi: ACHR.

Barry-Shaw, N and Jay, D (2012) *Paved with Good Intentions: Canada's Development NGOs from Idealism to Imperialism*, Halifax and Winnipeg, Canada: Fernwood Publishing.

Barua, B (2009) 'Colonial education and non-violent activism of rural Buddhist communities in Bangladesh' in D Kapoor (ed.) *Education, Decolonization and Development: Perspectives from Asia, Africa and the Americas*, Rotterdam: Sense Publishers, pp. 57–74.

Baviskar, A (2005) 'Red in tooth and claw? Looking for class struggles over nature' in R Ray and M Katzenstein (eds) *Social movements in India: Poverty, Power and Politics*, Lanham, MD: Rowman and Littlefield, pp. 161–178.

Bello, W (2009) *The Food Wars*, London: Verso.

Bharati, S (1999) 'Human rights and development projects in India', *The PRP Journal of Human Rights*, 3(4), p. 20.

Chana, T (2011) *Colonial Reproductions and Anti-Colonial Pedagogical Propositions for Educating about "the Global" in Urban Schools in India*, Unpublished Ph.D. Diss., University of Alberta.

Chatterjee, P (2001) 'On civil and political society in post-colonial democracies' in S Kaviraj and S Khilnani (eds) *Civil Society: History and Possibilities*, Cambridge: Cambridge University Press, pp. 165–178.

Choudry, A (2009) 'Challenging colonial amnesia in global justice activism' in D Kapoor (ed.) *Education, Decolonization and Development: Perspectives from Asia, Africa and the Americas*, Rotterdam: Sense Publishers, pp. 95–110.

Da Costa, D (2007) 'Tensions of neoliberal-development: State discourse and dramatic oppositions in West Bengal', *Contributions to Indian Sociology*, 41(3), pp. 287–320.

Da Costa, D (2009) *Development Drama: Reimagining Rural Political Action in Eastern India*, New Delhi: Routledge.

Davis, M (2006) *Planet of Slums*, London: Verso.

Donnelly, J (1989) *Universal Human Rights in Theory and Practice*, Ithaca, NY: Cornell University Press.

Duffield, M (2001) *Global Governance and the New Wars: The Merging of Development and Security*, London: Zed.

Fanon, F (1963) *Wretched of the Earth*, Boston: Grove Press.

Galeano, E (1972) *Open Veins of Latin America: Five Centuries of the Pillage of a Continent*, New York: Monthly Review Press.

Goldstein, T and Selby, D (eds) (2000) *Weaving Connections: Educating for Peace, Social and Environmental Justice*, Toronto: Sumach Press.

GRAIN (2012) *The Great Food Robbery: How Corporations Control Food, Grab Land and Destroy the Climate*, Cape Town, SA: Pambazuka Press.

Gramsci, A (1971) *Selections from the Prison Notebooks*, London: Lawrence & Wishart.

Guha, R (1990) *The Unquiet Woods*, Berkeley, CA: University of California Press.

Guha, R (1997) *Dominance Without Hegemony: History and Power in Colonial India*, New York: Harvard University Press.

Hall, S (1980) 'Race, articulation and societies structured in dominance', *Sociological Theories, Race and Colonialism*, Paris: UNESCO, pp. 305–345.

Harvey, D (2003) *The New Imperialism*, Oxford: Oxford University Press.

Harvey, D (2009) *Social Justice and the City*, Athens, GA: University of Georgia Press.

Heron, B (2007) *Desire for Development: Whiteness, Gender and the Helping Imperative*, Waterloo, Canada: Wilfred Laurier University Press.

Hobsbawm, E (1994) *The Age of Extremes: The Short Twentieth Century*, London: Abacus.

Hussain, M (2008) *Interrogating Development: State, Displacement and Popular Resistance in North Eastern India*, New Delhi: Sage Publications.

Kapoor, D (2009a) 'Participatory academic research (par) and People's Participatory Action Research (PAR): Research, politicization, and subaltern social movements in India' in D Kapoor and S Jordan (eds) *Education, Participatory Action Research and Social Change*, NY: Palgrave Macmillan, pp. 29–44.

Kapoor, D (2009b) 'Subaltern social movement learning: Adivasi (original dwellers) and the decolonization of space in India' in D Kapoor (ed.) *Education, Decolonization and Development: Perspectives from Asia, Africa and the Americas*, Rotterdam: Sense Publishers.

Kapoor, D (2011a) 'Subaltern social movement (SSM) post-mortems of development in India: Locating trans-local activism and radicalism', *Journal of Asian and African Studies*, 46(2), pp. 130–148.

Kapoor, D (2011b) 'Adult learning in political (un-civil) society: Anti-colonial subaltern social movement (SSM) pedagogies of place', *Studies in the Education of Adults*, 43(2), pp. 128–146.

Kapoor, D (2012) 'Human rights as paradox and equivocation in contexts of Adivasi (original dweller) dispossession in India', *Journal of Asian and African Studies*, 47(4), pp. 404–420.

Kapoor, D (2013a) 'Trans-local rural solidarity and an anti-colonial politics of place: Contesting colonial capital and the neoliberal state in India', *Interface: A Journal for and about Social Movements*, 5(1), pp. 14–39.

Kapoor, D (2013b) 'Social action and NGOization in contexts of development dispossession in rural India: Explorations in to the un-civility of civil society' in A Choudry and D Kapoor (eds) *NGOization: Complicity, Contradictions and Prospects*, London: Zed, pp. 46–74.

Kohli, A (2012) *Poverty amidst Plenty in the New India*, Cambridge: Cambridge University Press.

Kothari, U (2006) 'Critiquing "race" and racism in development discourse and practice', *Progress in Development Studies*, 6(1), pp. 9–23.

Larsen, M and Faden, L (2008) 'Supporting the growth of global citizenship educators', *Brock Education*, Vol. 17, pp. 71–86.

Lefebvre, H (1990) *The Production of Space*, Oxford: Blackwell.

Ludden, D (ed.) (2005) *Reading Subaltern Studies: Critical History, Contested Meaning and the Globalization of South Asia*, New Delhi: Pauls Press.

Mahrouse, G (2010) 'Questioning efforts that seek to "do good": Insights from transnational solidarity activism and socially responsible tourism' in S Razack, M Smith and S Thobani (eds) *States of Race: Critical Race Feminism for the 21st Century*, Toronto: Between the Lines, pp. 169–190.

McMichael, P (ed.) (2010) *Contesting Development: Critical Struggles for Social Change*, New York: Routledge.

McMichael, P (2012) *Development and Social Change: A Global Perspective*, Thousand Oaks, CA: Pine Forge Press.

Mehta, L (ed.) (2009) *Displaced by Development: Confronting Marginalization and Gender Injustice*, New Delhi: Sage.

Menon, N and Nigam, A (2007) *Power and Contestation: India since 1989*, London: Zed Books.

Meyer, L and Alvarado, M (eds) (2010) *New World of Indigenous Resistance: Noam Chomsky and Voices from North, South and Central America*, San Francisco, CA: City Light Books.

Mundy, K, Manion, C, Masemann, V and Haggerty, M (2007) *Charting Global Education in Canada's Elementary Schools: Provincial, District and School Level Perspectives*, Toronto: UNICEF Canada.

Mundy, K and Manion, C (2008) 'Global education in Canadian elementary schools: An exploratory study', *Canadian Journal of Education*, 31(4), pp. 941–974.

Munshi, I (ed.) (2012) *The Adivasi Question: Issues of Land, Forest and Livelihood*, New Delhi: Orient Blackswan.

Nag, S (1 March 2001) 'Nationhood and displacement in the Indian subcontinent', *Economic and Political Weekly* (Kolkata), 36(51), pp. 4753–4760.

Nandy, A (2002) 'The beautiful expanding future of poverty: Popular economics as a psychological defense', *International Studies Review*, 4(2), pp. 115–122.

Oliver-Smith, A (2010) *Defying Displacement: Grassroots Resistance and the Critique of Development*, Austin: University of Texas Press.

O'Sullivan, M and Smaller, H (2013) 'Challenging problematic dichotomies: Bridging the gap between critical pedagogy and liberal academic approaches to global education', *Canadian and International Education*, 42(1), Article 4.

Padel, F and Das, S (2010) *Out of this Earth: East India Adivasis and the Aluminium Cartel*, New Delhi: Orient Blackswan.

Quijano, A (2000) 'Coloniality of power and eurocentrism in Latin America', *International Sociology*, 15(2), pp. 215–232.

Rajagopal, B (2003) *International Law from Below: Development, Social Movements and Third World Resistance*, Cambridge: Cambridge University Press.

Reimer, K and McLean, L (2009) 'Conceptual clarity and connections: Global education and teacher candidates', *Canadian Journal of Education*, 32(4), pp. 903–926.

Rodney, W (1982) *How Europe Underdeveloped Africa*, Washington DC: Howard University Press.

Sankaran, K (2009) *Globalization and Postcolonialism: Hegemony and Resistance in the 21st Century*, Lanham, MD: Rowman & Littlefield.

Sanyal, K (2010) *Rethinking Capitalist Development: Primitive Accumulation, Governmentality and Post-Colonial Capitalism*, New Delhi: Routledge.

Shah, A (2010) *In the Shadows of the State: Indigenous Politics, Environmentalism, and Insurgency in Jharkhand, India*, Durham, NC: Duke University Press.

Spring, J (2009) *Globalization of Education: An Introduction*, NY: Routledge.

Swamy, R (2013) 'Disaster relief, NGO-led humanitarianism and the reconfiguration of spatial relations in Tamil Nadu' in A Choudry and D Kapoor (eds) *NGOization: Complicity, Contradiction and Prospects*, London: Zed.

Webber, M (2012) *I laughed, I cried: Gada Mahrouse's Keynote Address for the Nongovernmental Impulse Symposium*, available: http://unitcrit.blogspot.ca/2012/04/i-laughed-i-cried-gada-mahrouses.html, accessed 20 March 2013.

White, S (2002) 'Thinking race, thinking development', *Third World Quarterly*, 23(3), pp. 407–419.

Whitehead, J (2003) 'Space, place and primitive accumulation in Narmada valley and beyond', *Economic and Political Weekly*, October 4, pp. 4224–4230.

Williams, R (2010) *The Divided World: Human Rights and Its Violence*, Minneapolis, MN: University of Minnesota Press.

Wilson, K (2012) *Race, Racism and Development: Interrogating History, Discourse and Practice*, London: Zed.

Zibechi, R (2005) 'Subterranean echoes: Resistance and politics "desde el sotano"', *Socialism and Democracy*, 19(3), pp. 13–39.

Zibechi, R and Ramon, R (2012) *Territories in Resistance: Cartography of Latin American Social Movements*, Oakland, CA: AK Press.

14
The Deglobalisation Paradigm: A Critical Discourse on Alternatives

Dorothy Grace Guerrero

Introduction

The continuing and intensifying global economic crisis that started in the eurozone and the United States (US), and has reverberated in India, China and other developing countries, is a concrete manifestation of the depth reached by globalisation. The world has experienced a number of financial crises before. However, the combination of the economic and ecological crises, the impacts of drastic reforms being put in place to respond to the crises, as well as the magnitude of globalisation have made the challenges more daunting than previously experienced in history.

This chapter will discuss the link between deepening neoliberal globalisation, the role played by international financial institutions (IFIs) and transnational corporations (TNCs) as agents of globalisation, as well as how the global trade and investment regime that they influence produced the global climate and environmental crises that is threatening our very survival now. The resistance against neoliberal globalisation and the movements created by such resistance have pointed to the limits and downside of such globalisation. Many are promoting the strategy of deglobalisation, an alternative to neoliberalism, and are working for the realisation of social, economic, gender and climate justice. Development and political education, known in the global South as conscientisation or popular education, organisation and networking are crucial elements in building collective and transformative efforts and solutions needed to respond to the challenges that the world is now facing.

The Washington Consensus

Neoliberal policies also known as the 'Washington Consensus', are a set of economic policy prescriptions that constitute a 'standard' reform package prescribed for countries deemed to be in crisis by Washington DC-based institutions notably the International Monetary Fund (IMF), the World Bank and the US Treasury Department (Williamson, 1989; Stiglitz, 2002) which started the dismantling of social protection in the US and Europe. At the same time, neoliberal policies put developing countries under structural adjustment programmes to systematically squeeze resources from them to feed the global economy dominated by the IFIs since the 1980s. Former US President Ronald Reagan and former UK Prime Minister Margaret Thatcher were the major architects of such policies. Like Thatcher and Reagan, the supporters of neoliberalism occupy influential positions in the sectors of education, the media, corporations and financial institutions, government institutions, as well as international institutions that regulate global trade and finance (see Albo, 2005; Harvey, 2005; and Altvater, 2009).

Recent neoliberal policies and reform measures, packaged as austerity programmes to address the lingering crisis, were set to do the demolition job to the remaining thread of social protection. The attack on hard-fought rights and entitlements that were born out of long struggles by social movements in the global North, which have produced the safety nets that many in developing countries are still fighting to achieve, are eroding and as a result, breaking people's sense of security and dignity.

Globally, and especially in developing countries where biodiversity is rich and vital to people's livelihood and survival, the increasing assaults on the lands, forests and waters by transnational corporations and local businesses are severely threatening nature and ecosystems (Guttal and Manahan, 2011). Excessive and devastating extraction of minerals and resources, indiscriminate logging and fishing, and massive conversion of productive farmlands and forests to huge plantations, golf courses and industrial parks are altering nature and destroying its carrying capacity to sustain life on the planet. These unsustainable and damaging economic activities conducted in the blind pursuit of economic growth without regard to the limits of nature by big capital are causing climate change, which has now become the greatest challenge faced by humanity (Guerrero, 2012).

Despite the vast amount of wealth produced by the globalisation process and the rise of emerging economies like the BRICS countries composed of Brazil, Russia, India, China and South Africa, it has become more concentrated in fewer hands as poverty and inequality continue to grow and deepen across the world (UNDP, 2013). Injustice is also widening as states increasingly lose their power to regulate society and protect people and the environment (Bello, 2009). The increasing impacts of climate change, which is producing extreme weather changes, out-of-season super storms that are causing floods, longer droughts, colder winters, rising oceans and the melting of the ice in the polar regions are affecting the poor more, notwithstanding the fact that they have made the least contribution to climate change (Solon and Bello, 2012).

Globalisation and deglobalisation

More than a decade ago Walden Bello proposed his alternatives to the dominant economic growth paradigm in his book *Deglobalisation*. Bello defined deglobalisation as a comprehensive paradigm to replace neoliberal globalisation (Bello, 2002). In 2003, Focus on the Global South elaborated the strategy of deglobalisation as the guiding paradigm for its programmatic work in response to the growing clamour for alternatives to the current system of global economic governance. Many movements and groups saw the logic of the strategy and adopted it as a principle guiding their collective actions of resistance against the global system of trade and financial governance. It was used in education and mobilising work in the pursuit of building social and economic justice groups.

Considering the magnitude of the problems created by neoliberalism, the lingering dominance of actors and institutions that are reproducing disempowerment and the emergence of new concepts like the *Green Economy*, carbon trading, etc., that are promoting an even more destructive and disempowering version of the old development model, deglobalisation, together with other empowering concepts like *buen vivir* are tools for building resistance. Deglobalisation addresses the world-wide climate crisis, militarisation, globalisation, human rights violations and other increasing assaults to social justice and democratic principles. As an alternative it strengthens resistance to the oppressing system and structures of neoliberalism to build unity, hope and reciprocal solidarity.

Globalisation has made it possible for science to realise the leap and bounds in scientific and technological breakthroughs that advanced understanding of our world. Medical research and experiments are now yielding promising results that could lead to a significant breakthrough in diseases formerly considered incurable. What we only used to imagine and see in science fiction documentaries and films are now features of the gadgets we use in our daily lives. The advancements in communication are simply spectacular and the now widespread use of the Internet has made it possible to learn in an instant what is happening everywhere in the globe and to keep in touch with faraway relatives and friends. Even global organisation and networking are aided by modern communication infrastructures and services and are becoming increasingly creative through various forms of social media. The caveat though is the increasing level of incursion into people's privacy and how personal information is sometimes used without our knowledge and consent. The use and manipulation of data is more Orwellian than we may be aware.

There is a growing understanding now that the majority is not benefiting from neoliberal globalisation and is being harmed by the political economy it has produced. The first World Summit on Sustainable Development (WSSD) or Earth Summit, which was held in Rio de Janeiro, Brazil in 1992, produced a set of principles called Agenda 21 that acknowledged society's need to balance the pursuit of development and protection of the environment to achieve sustainable development. In 2002, the Rio+10 summit was held in Johannesburg, South Africa, at which social movement activists and representatives from various non-governmental organisations (NGOs) from inside Africa and beyond drew attention to worrying trends that were already emerging from the globalisation process, particularly the acceleration of neoliberalism.

Neoliberalism and global dissent against globalisation

Neoliberalism is a set of political economic practices supported by institutional frameworks that favour strong private property rights, free markets and free trade, which have become widespread in the last 40 years or so. 'Liberalism' can refer to political, economic, or even religious ideas while the prefix 'neo' means we are talking about a new kind of liberalism. Neoliberalism is a set of rules and mechanisms that encourages total freedom of movement for capital, goods and services by: eliminating barriers to encourage economic openness of international trade and investments; cutting social expenditure for social services; reducing government regulations that could diminish profits especially profits of transnational corporations; and privatisation of state-owned enterprises, goods and services to private investors. Supporters of the neoliberal way occupy influential positions in government, business and society, many of whom attend the World Economic Forum (WEF) in Davos, Switzerland 'to shape global, regional and industry agendas' (www.weforum.org).

These gatherings of key proponents of neoliberalism such as the WEF, the ministerial meetings of the World Trade Organisation (WTO), and the Group of Eight (G8) leading industrialised countries have been mirrored by the increasing mobilisation in civil society of social movements and non-governmental organisations. These movements have emphasised that neoliberal globalisation has caused increased poverty, conflicts, human insecurity, unsustainable patterns of production and consumption, dispossession, de-industrialisation of many developing countries and an increasing abandonment by governments of their responsibilities to provide even basic services to their people because of privatisation and deregulation (see for example the World Social Forum Statement of the Climate Space, 2013). Civil society organisations have regularly gathered at international conferences like Rio+10 in South Africa and Rio+20 People's Summit in Brazil, World Social Forums and other global events to organise parallel conferences and debate alternatives to neoliberalism. They have challenged the entrenchment of neoliberal policies, especially the global trade regime implemented by the WTO which was compared by Ha Joon-Chang to the act of 'kicking the ladder' away from underdeveloping countries to prevent them from growing their industries and achieving development (Chang, 2002).

The increasing capture by large transnational corporations (TNCs) of various policy spaces and decision-making processes posed big challenges to democracy in both developing and developed countries alike. Before the opening of the Rio+20 Summit, representatives of big transnational corporations that participated at the business meeting claimed that the said meeting, which was attended by chief executive officers (CEOs) of global companies, was the *real event* where decisions were made, while the Rio+20 discussions by government representatives were in reality the side event! In UN summit parlance, side events were spaces for the sharing of information, analysis and opportunities for education where no decisions of importance are made or followed.

It was no secret that the Brazilian president Dilma Rouseff had brought the draft text of the Rio+20 Agreement to the G20 meeting in Mexico before resolutions were reached in Rio. During a public debate held on 16 June at the People's Summit between the director of the UN

Environment Programme Dr. Achim Steiner and Mr. Pablo Solon, executive director of Focus on the Global South, the latter argued that the decisions for the future of the planet in Rio+20 were made not in the UN meeting but at the G20 in Mexico. The 20 richest and most powerful countries had decided on humanity's future. 'An outcome that makes nobody happy' (Brooks, 2012) was how Sha Zukang of China described the results of Rio+20 – and he was the Rio+20 Secretary-General.

The December 2013 ministerial meeting of the World Trade Organisation (WTO), held in Bali, Indonesia concluded with an agreement described as the Bali Trade Agreement (Bali Package). The package included increased support for Least Developed Countries (LDCs), and deals aimed at improving trade facilitation and agriculture. In his assessment of the deal the *Guardian*'s economic editor Larry Elliot suggested that the Bali meeting was successful 'only in the way that Dunkirk was a triumph for Britain in 1940' (6 December 2013). The WTO avoided 'calamity' but after 12 years of haggling during the Doha Development Round of talks very little had been achieved. Elliot argues that the 'threat of WTO marginalisation remains' (Ibid.).

This marginalisation has resulted, at least in part, from ambitious and comprehensive bilateral free trade agreements (FTAs) that have been pushed aggressively by dominant economies in parallel to the WTO process despite strong resistance from civil society movements in the global South. For example, in India and Thailand, civil society groups have been resisting EU–India and EU–Thailand FTAs. In both negotiations, the EU has been pushing for more comprehensive and stronger provisions on intellectual property rights, especially on the manufacture of medicines, compared to the WTO provisions (FTA Watch Thailand, 2013). Protestors in India and Thailand are concerned that, if implemented, these agreements will result in people losing access to cheaper medicines being produced by local companies and could ultimately mean the closure of local pharmaceutical companies.

What the global movements against FTAs and International Investment Agreement (IIA) treaties are concerned about is that despite the economic crisis, which has been caused by the current laissez faire system of wealth accumulation, more of the same export-led and resource extractive growth patterns are being pushed by new and stronger treaties. The new agreements also give increased powers to TNCs and strengthen further the already debilitating culture of impunity that takes away possibilities for governments to use their powers to regulate industries and use policy measures to protect local economies, people and the environment from abuses of business. The investment provisions of new and ongoing Free Trade Agreement negotiations (for example EU-India, EU-Singapore, EU-Thailand, EU-Philippines, etc.) are giving increased powers to corporations in the State-Company Disputes Settlement wherein corporations can sue governments in special courts under WTO and the World Bank rules if they deem that government actions will curtail their operations.

When the interests of people to protect their lands, water, forests, livelihoods, culture, social and economic rights clash with corporate interests, people normally lose because their governments are generally not supportive of their causes. Even if there is inclination to do so, government powers are already curtailed by the commitments they have agreed to under FTAs and investment treaties. They can no longer implement their existing laws and social standards legislation against corporations. International financial institutions and regional development banks, share a capacity to enforce agreements and contracts and punish governments in the event that the latter deviate from these contracts.

Moreover, the increasing and systematic violation of human and labour rights and what can be considered as economic and environmental crimes by corporations go unabated (Bassey, 2012). In many cases, TNCs are directly or indirectly involved in assassinations, persecutions and threats against trade unions, community and indigenous people's leaders that are resisting their actions and operations (Middleton and Pritchard, 2013). In the context of the global financial and environmental crises, this violence has intensified through the complicity of states and their role in the design and implementation of trade and investment agreements, as well as land and forest laws.

New global power relations: New actors, old play?

It is commonly said that the world is entering a multipolar phase in global governance with the 'rise of the South' or the growing powers of emerging economies, notably the BRICS and the strengthening of their relations as seen in the annual BRICS Summits since 2009. Many believe too that with the economic stagnation in the eurozone and the US, BRICS countries are gaining more wealth, expertise, consumption power and the political clout to influence and rearrange the global system to their advantage. The lingering economic crisis in the US is also seen as a signal of the beginning of the end of US hegemony and that among the new powers, many consider China to be the most likely challenger to US dominance (Ikenberry, 2008).

The results of recent attempts to reform global institutions (e.g. addressing the balance of voting powers in the World Bank and elect a non-American president of the Bank), however, prove that the North will resist efforts by the BRICS to assume a leadership role in global governance. It is still to be seen whether the new actors actually intend and have the capacity to provide alternative leadership. It is becoming increasingly clear however that the BRICS are advancing a similarly unsustainable and unjust development paradigm that facilitates accumulation of wealth by a few while resulting in the dispossession and pauperisation of the already marginalised and powerless (Bidwai, 2003; Globalreboot, 2013).

China and the other new actors have yet to present a new and better model of development and, importantly, a more equitable partnership paradigm with other developing countries. What is more troubling as observed by activist academics, is that they are gravitating toward 'sub-imperialism' that is offering similar or even more intense practices of exploitation and extraction of natural resources from poorer countries to enrich themselves. Patrick Bond defines sub-imperialism, as new powers, such as the BRICS, playing deputy-sheriff to advance rather than challenge the current system while controlling their own angry populaces as well as their hinterlands (Bond, 2004). The continuation of the 'maldevelopment' model throughout the BRICS works very well for corporate profits. Movements and concerned groups within the five countries started discussions and information sharing about their respective resistances, and found opportunities to start solidarities among themselves and others in various activities during the recent 'BRICS from Below People's Summit' held in Durban, South Africa on 25 and 26 March 2013.

The climate change challenge

Global warming, which was predicted by scientists in the 1960s and 1970s as a consequence of increasing Greenhouse Gas (GHG) concentrations, produced by human activities in the earth's atmosphere, is advancing at a rate of 0.16 degrees centigrade per decade according to the 2007 Fourth Assessment Report of the UN Inter-government Panel on Climate Change (IPCC) and the Potsdam Institute for Climate Impact Research. What is also disturbing is that the actual impacts of climate change are happening at rates that are faster than the IPCC forecasts. New studies show that the rise in sea level is 60 percent faster than previous predictions with an increase averaging at 3.2 millimetres per year instead of 2 millimetres per year (Hanna, 2012). At this rate, we can expect the sea level to rise by 3.25 feet at the end of the century. Given that 80 percent of the world's population lives within 200 miles of the coast, the prospect of seeing hundreds of millions of people becoming climate refugees as the sea envelops the land is a stark possibility.

The dismal outcomes of the negotiations of the 18th Conference of Parties (COP) under the UN Framework Convention on Climate Change (UNFCCC) held in Doha in 2012 do not match the urgency of the situation. The reluctance of Annex I countries (composed of 37 industrialised countries and in addition the European Union) to commit to deep cuts in their emission levels and agree on appropriate financial and technology transfer to developing countries to help the latter bear and adapt to the impacts of climate change, caused the world to pass up a significant opportunity to address the climate change issue. Results of negotiations in Copenhagen in 2009, Cancun in 2010, Durban in 2011 and Doha in 2012 resulted in a diluted Kyoto Protocol and a laissez faire regime wherein only 'voluntary pledges' for emissions reductions would happen only in 2020 (Solon and Bello, 2012). Likewise, the BRICS countries also want to avoid discussions that will bind them to commitments despite the fact that some of them are already major polluters. Worse still is the fact that a number of countries like Japan and Russia have withdrawn their commitment to the Kyoto Protocol altogether.

We are in an accelerating and deepening ecological crisis as a consequence of the growth-at-all-cost economic approach, promoted by IFIs and trade treaties, and due to human activities that have no regard for the carrying capacity of the environment and for the rights of people. The International Energy Agency has already added its voice to those that are saying that failure to reduce fossil fuel consumption would put the world on a path toward at least 6 degrees centigrade of global warming (IEA, 2012). The Asian Development Bank Report for 2011 attributed the current widespread poverty to severe environmental degradation affecting the livelihood of people who depended on the environment (ADB, 2012). Likewise, the World Bank also published the report 'Turn Down the Heat' that warned of projected climate impacts of a 4 degrees centigrade average temperature increase (World Bank, 2012).

The most intense discussions in the preparatory process for Rio+20 were around the 'Green Economy' agenda promoted by the United

Nations Environment Programme (UNEP). Green Economy is a concept that is likely to supplant 'sustainable development' as the dominant theme in future climate change discourse. In February 2011, UNEP launched a 631-page 'Green Economy' report which argued that the environment could be saved if people saw the value of environmental services by putting a price to them. It also said that faster growth would be achieved if governments cut environmentally damaging subsidies to fossil fuels and fisheries, etc. and used these funds to invest in new technologies as a response to climate change. Massive investment could then enable the transition from the 'brown' to the 'green' economy, according to the report (UNEP, 2011). The UN estimates that investments in infrastructure and technology to mitigate the effects of climate change will total as much as $130 billion a year by 2030.

Despite the many attractive ideas that are included in the 'Green Economy' concept like the need to recycle and use renewable energies, climate and environmental non-governmental organisations and social movements heavily criticised the report. Those who are criticising and opposing it understand that the real purpose of the Green Economy is to set a new stage in the reconfiguration of capitalism by treating nature as capital. This kind of solution to the climate crisis is a denial of the essential and deeper causes of the ecological problem (Focus on the Global South, 2012). The commodification of the services of nature in a reconfiguration of capitalism is likely to result in a more imperiled and exploited natural environment.

The Green Economy is premised on the idea that it represents a way to grow sustainably without destroying the environment and that this can be achieved through technology and market-based approaches. The prominence given to market-based approaches is not surprising given the background of the Special Adviser and Head of UNEP's Green Economy Initiative, Pavan Sukdhev, lead author of the UNEP report 'Towards a Green Economy'. Sukdhev spent over 20 years as a senior banker with ANZ and Deutsche Bank, one of the biggest derivative traders in the world. Green Economy promoters rationalise that nature must have monetary value. By putting a price to nature, good environmental policies can be implemented effectively through the more 'efficient' ways of the market. The ideological battle is expected to intensify with this framework, as it moves beyond 'business as usual' to represent a reconfiguration of capitalism. The ethical, political and economic arguments against commodification of nature's services show however that it could even be worse than the growth model since the power to manage, use, allocate and decide on the use of nature will heavily favour the business sector. In the past, solving the climate crisis meant reducing emissions, today discussions are concentrated on how to involve the market in the process. Investors are therefore putting money into businesses that will create profits as the planet gets hotter.

Globalisation of resistance and the task to change the system

An ideological battle has emerged on how to solve the crisis created by neoliberalism and unsustainable growth. On one side, the pro-market elite seeks a central role for corporations that will further erode the capacity of governments to regulate capital. On the other side are the growing movements that see the direct role of the dominant economic system in the creation of the crisis and are espousing alternatives to the system and the dominating structures of neoliberalism. The main contentions are in the treatment of capitalism: progressive social movements, NGOs and academics that are blaming it for the crisis and looking at counter-processes and practices vis-à-vis the elite that are pushing for business-as-usual and finding increasingly profitable market-based solutions.

The increasing condition of powerlessness brought about by the loss of rights and spaces to engage as political subjects in the ever-deepening phase of capitalism is producing intensifying social and political resistance across the world and in some instances bridging differences across many sections of societies (Mertes and Bello, 2004). The negative impacts of development projects in the global South and the brutal austerity plan in Europe and the US are bringing about massive and assertive initiatives to build a more just world and increase support for deglobalisation.

The last two decades of the last century saw extraordinary forms of collective action such as the People Power in the Philippines in 1986 and Velvet Revolution in the Czech Republic in 1989 among others. In the early part of this century, we witnessed global anti-war protests against the US actions in Iraq, and the Arab Spring which started in Tunisia and toppled dictators and governments in the Middle East and has spread to Egypt and other neighboring countries. The stream of collective actions has also echoed in the very heart of capitalism. Anti-capitalist and anti-system groups in the US such as the 'Occupy Wall Street' movement have protested against Washington's mismanagement of US financial and debt problems by bailing out banks and large financial corporations and cutting basic services like health and education. There have also been massive protests in southern Europe against governments and the so-called Troika (the European Union, the International Monetary Fund and the European Central Bank) that imposes austerity programmes to manage failing economies.

The huge economic problems and the failure of the system to address them show that we need an alternative development paradigm to neoliberalism. As long as this does not happen, economic and development planning will forever be at the service of growth, policies will be written to accommodate corporations, and governments will repress social movements and groups that question why poverty and inequality are rising and the planet threatened by climate change. More than a decade ago, Focus on the Global South proposed that global, regional and national movements and networks support the collective work of deglobalisation, which rests on two pillars or two logics that are in synergy: deconstruction and reconstruction or recreation. Both are mutually dependent on the other. Deconstruction refers to the dismantling, paralysis, or drastic reduction of the power of the current structures and institutions that support neoliberal global governance. This is an imperative in order to provide space for alternatives.

The powers of the WTO, the IFIs, the TNCs and other agents of finance capital must be confronted and their schemes continually exposed. Collective demands for change and people's empowerment must be creatively shaped through organising, political and development education and solidarity strengthened by campaigns based on goals that reflect existing political conditions, but at the same time are firm on the goal of putting life and the environment first in order to build an alternative world. The structure and institutions of neoliberal capitalism have perfected the art of sustaining the status quo and leadership of hegemonic powers, not only through their control of the policy process, but more importantly in presenting themselves as knowledge-bearers and experts on what is needed to resolve the economic crisis, poverty, climate change or uphold social and economic rights. The impressive protests in the Maghreb and the Middle East, the expression of collective indignation by the people of southern Europe and the act of occupying targets and spaces in the global South, be it in major financial centres, or rural barricades and roadblocks to resist projects that symbolise the capitalist growth model, such as environmentally destructive power plants or mines, have managed to link the crises/problems to the capitalist system up front.

The tasks of reconstruction or re-creation processes or the collective effort to articulate and popularise the need for alternative systems of national and global economic and political governance are more challenging, but at the same time a task we could and should not turn away from. The idea that responses and alternatives must also be diverse, like nature, is gaining support and acceptance. The concept that the law of nature and the processes of the ecosystem articulated as the 'rights of Mother Earth' (Cochabamba Declaration, 2010) must be respected as much as we respect the principles of our rights as humans, is also gaining ground. There have been good discussions and agreements by movements for alternatives on what constitutes the principle of living well or 'Buen Vivir' (Heinrich Boell Foundation, 2011).

The above principles, in order to be properly piloted and flourish, need an alternative system of local and national economic governance that respects the diversity of societies. What needs to be globalised is the principle of reciprocal solidarity, the struggle for decommodification and collective action against all the bad solutions being presented as a way out of the economic and ecological crises. This work requires consciousness-raising or conscientisation through political, development and popular education to reach the grassroots and various communities or collectives. Development and political education encourages collective action and organisation that will take back social, welfare, economic, labour, cultural and other basic rights, public services, as well as our governments.

A summary from Focus on the Global South's 2003 paper and 2012 Statement for the Rio+20 People's Summit outlines that in practice deglobalisation and the means to protect the planet means:

- Changing the framework of political economy by protecting and prioritising domestic economies and local needs. Instead of overproducing for export, reorient the economy and support small, local, peasant and indigenous community farming. Big agribusiness that deforests, destroy soils and indigenous crop species, heats the planet and pollute rivers and air must be dismantled. We should promote local production and consumption of products by reducing the free trade of goods that travel long distances and use millions of tonnes of carbon dioxide;
- Reduce asphyxiating Greenhouse Gases that are causing global warming by steep decreases of extractivism and end society's addiction to fossil fuels by leaving more than two-thirds of the fossil fuel reserves under the soil. The exploitation of tar sands, shale gas and coal must be stopped. We should develop safe, clean and sustainable

energy production through more subsidies to renewable energy development;
- Instead of geo-engineering and expensive technologies that are aimed at altering the natural course of sunrays, behaviour of oceans and changing the ecosystem, we should significantly increase and develop public transport systems and services to reduce and discourage the unsustainable dependence on cars;
- Wars are not just killing people, destroying civilisations and culture, they are also greatly contributing to emissions and environmental damage. Promote peace by pressing governments to avoid warfare and dismantle the military and war industry and infrastructure.

To realise these goals, there must be a fundamental transformation in the economy, democracy, the legal system, media, popular culture and habits, and so on. Development education plays an important role in the task of transformation. A growth-driven and market-dependent system is incompatible with the reality of a finite world and a life of dignity and rights. The need to rethink the way states and society values nature and how resources are allocated and managed must be done now and decided by those who believe in a meaningful and productive life.

There is no alternative but to resist the destructive grip of exploitative capitalism. It is a responsibility to educate oneself and be a conscious political subject, to organise, mobilise, forge unities and strike a blow to avoid further harm to the planet and all beings. Political and development education can play an important role in building a collective voice and sense of agency and this is the primary reason why non-governmental organisations and civil society groups such as Focus on the Global South stand with the poor and their movements. The work of questioning reality and concepts, asking the question who wins and who loses from economic and social arrangements, and what actors and institutions dominate and gain from injustice is a key component of the deglobalisation process. By means of organising local, national and cross-border workshops and conferences, Focus on the Global South has critiqued institutions and processes that perpetuate exploitation and injustice and, at the same time, helped to build common visions and strategies for a better world. It is a complex and challenging task that cannot be comfortably waged and requires the expansion and forging of new alliances beyond usual partnerships. We have our planet and our humanity to lose if this is not achieved.

References

Albo, G (2005) 'Contesting the "new capitalism"' in D Coates (ed.) *Varieties of Capitalism, Varieties of Approaches*, London: Palgrave, pp. 63–82.

Altvater, E (2009) 'Postneoliberalism or postcapitalism: The failure of neo-liberalism in the financial market crisis', *Development Dialogue*, No. 51, Rosa Luxemburg Foundation, January 2009.

Asian Development Bank (2012) 'Asian Development Bank outlook 2012: Confronting rising inequality in Asia', Manila: Asia Development Bank.

Bassey, N (2012) *To Cook a Continent: Destructive Extraction and the Climate Crisis in Africa*, Cape Town, Dakar, Nairobi and Oxford: Pambazuka Press.

Bello, W (2002) *Deglobalization: Ideas for a New World Economy*, London: Zed Books.

Bello, W (2009) 'The deadly triad: Climate change, free trade and capitalism' in U Brand, N Bullard, E Lander and T Mueller (eds) *Contours of Climate Justice: Ideas for Shaping New Climate and Energy Politics*, Dag Hammarskjöld Foundation: Uppsala.

Bidwai, P (2013) 'BRICS: A loosely held group with little sense of purpose', *Alternative Regionalisms*, Transnational Institute, Amsterdam: TNI.

Bond, P (2004) 'Bankrupt Africa: Imperialism, subimperialism and the politics of finance', *Historical Materialism*, 12(4), Leiden: Koninklijke Brill NV, pp. 145–172.

Brooks, B, 'Rio+20: the unhappy environmental summit', *The Guardian*, 23 June 2012, available: http://www.guardian.co.uk/world/feedarticle/10303144 (accessed 8 December 2012).

Chang, Ha-joon (2002) *Kicking Away the Ladder: Development Strategy in Historical Perspective*, London: Anthem Press.

Cochabamba: Documents of the World People's Conference on Climate Change and the Rights of Mother Earth, Bolivia: April 2010, available: http://readingfromtheleft.com/PDF/CochabambaDocuments.pdf (accessed 13 January 2014).

Elliot, L (2013) 'Bali trade agreement: WTO set the bar high but has achieved little', *Guardian*, 6 December.

Focus on the Global South (2003) 'Programme Plan 2003–2005', Bangkok: Focus on the Global South.

Focus on the Global South (2012) 'Why the Green Economy is a wrong path to restore the equilibrium with nature and what alternatives do we have?', Statement on Rio+20, May 2012.

Friends of the Earth (2008) 'REDD myths: A critical review of proposed mechanisms to reduce emissions from deforestation and degradation in developing countries', *Primavera Quint*, Issue 114, Amsterdam.

FTA Watch Thailand (2013) 'Reasons of the civil society's campaign kick-off to scrutinize the Thailand-EU FTA negotiation', Bangkok, March 2013, http://www.focusweb.org

Globalreboot (2013) 'Latecomers: Why the BRICS party will soon be over', *Rethinking Development, Rethinking Governance*, 18 March 2013, available: www.globalreboot.org/2013/03/18/latecomers-why-the-brics-party-will-soon-be-over (accessed 30 April 2013).

Guerrero, D (2012) 'The ASEAN and the challenges of climate change: Is green economy the solution or is it business as usual', paper presented at the *Second*

International Conference on International Relations and Development, Regional Economic Integration, Environmental Changes and Transnational Justice Panel, held in Chiang Mai, Thailand on 26–27 July 2012.

Guttal, S and Manahan, M A (2011) 'In defense of the commons' in *Land Struggles*, LRAN Briefing Paper Series, 'Defending the Commons, Territories and the Right to Food and Water', August 2011.

Hanna, E (2012) 'Greenland plays a large role in the gloomy picture painted of probable future sea level rise', *Environmental Research Letters*, 7(4), October–December, available: http://iopscience.iop.org/1748-9326/7/4 (accessed December 2012).

Harvey, D (2005) *A Brief History of Neoliberalism*, Oxford: Oxford University Press.

Heinrich Boell Foundation (2011) 'Buen Vivir: Latin America's new concepts for the good life and the rights of nature', *Ecology*, Vol. 17, July 2011, Berlin: Heinrich Boell Foundation.

Ikenberry, G J (2008) 'The rise of China and the future of the West: Can the liberal system survive?, *Foreign Affairs*, 87(1), January/February, pp. 23–37.

Inter-government Panel on Climate Change (2007) Fourth Assessment Report on Climate Change, available: http://www.ipcc.ch/ipccreports/ar4-syr.htm (accessed 9 June 2013).

International Energy Agency (2012) 'Energy Technology Perspectives 2012 – How to secure a clean energy future?', available: http://www.iea.org (accessed 3 April 2013).

Mertes, T and Bello, W (2004) *A Movement of Movements: Is Another World Really Possible?* London: Verso.

Middleton, C and Pritchard, A (2013) *Corporate Accountability in ASEAN: A Rights-based Approach: A Report for the Solidarity for Asian People's Advocacy*, Bangkok: Forum Asia.

Pachauri, R K and Reisinger, A (eds) (2007) 'Climate Change 2007: Fourth Assessment Report of Inter-government Panel on Climate Change', IPCC Geneva.

Solon, P and Bello, W (2012) 'Why are climate negotiations locked in a stale-mate?', *Bangkok Post*, 4 September 2012.

Stiglitz, J (2002) *Globalization and its Discontents*, New York and London: W.W. Norton, p. 53.

The Cochabamba Declaration (2010) 'People's Agreement during the World People's Conference on Climate Change and the Rights of Mother Earth', 22 April 2010, Cochabamba, Bolivia.

UNDP, *Human Development Report 2013 – The Rise of the South: Human Progress in a Diverse World*, United Nations Development Program, available: hdr.undp.org/en/reports/global/hdr2013/ (accessed 15 April 2013).

UNEP (2011) 'Towards a Green Economy: Pathways to Sustainable Development and Poverty Eradication 2011', available: http://www.unep.org/greeneconomy/Portals/88/documents/ger/ger_final_dec_2011/Green%20EconomyReport_Final_Dec2011.pdf (accessed 11 April 2013).

United Nations Framework Convention on Climate Change (UNFCCC), available: http://unfccc.int/2860.php (accessed 11 April 2013).

Williamson, J (1989) 'What Washington means by policy reform' in J Williamson (ed.) *Latin American Readjustment: How Much has Happened*, Washington Institute for International Economics.
World Bank (2012) 'Turn down the heat: Why a 4°C warmer world must be avoided', Washington DC: World Bank.
World Economic Forum (WEF) see www.weforum.org
World Social Forum (2013) 'World Social Forum Climate Space Declaration: To reclaim our future we must change the past', Tunis, Tunisia: April 2013, available: http://ggjalliance.org/climatespacedeclaration (accessed 13 January 2014).

Part V

Development Education's Shifting Policy Landscape

15
Development Education in a European Context

Gerard McCann

Introduction

Agreement on the importance of Development Education (DE) within the institutions of the European Union (EU) has been evolving from as far back as 2001 when the Council of Europe requested a greater understanding of what it termed 'global interdependence'. Since then there has been dialogue around the nature of DE across the member states and a series of substantial moves to create a DE framework which would operate at a transnational level, yet could be supported through European Commission resources in Brussels. This dialogue culminated in the Commission's working document of December 2012 under the title 'Development Education and Awareness Raising (DEAR) in Europe'. As protocol would have it within the policy-making structures of the EU, it has taken ten years for the Council resolution on DEAR to reach its policy implementation stage. DE has also been subjected to the general policy framework and indeed the ebb and flow of the broader European integration process.

With the Lisbon Treaty carrying member states into uncharted scenarios globally through the rapid reaction force, diplomatic expansion and the precedence of the High Representative's office, the EU has become a global actor in a manner that could not have been foreseen a decade ago. This has all impacted on the EU's perception of the strategic role of DE in international cooperation. While DEAR is implicit to development, humanitarian and external policies, this new context is a challenging environment for DE practitioners and theorists across Europe. This article will look at the emergence of a DEAR strategy and survey the manner in which DE has consolidated its position within EU education and development policy. It will survey policy adaptation and explore the ways in which DE has altered with the evolution of the EU as a global leader. Finally, it will assess the ways in which DE as a discipline will need to reconfigure in order to capitalise on the potentials of a transnational institution such as the EU that is – at this point – sympathetic to the principles of the sector.

The milestones for DE

The integration of DE into mainstream policy across the EU has been a long drawn out process, originating in the 1970s when non-governmental development organisations (NGDOs) set out to lobby governments at a regional level for recognition of the need to promote development issues through formal and non-formal education sectors. The debate reflected a general disconnection between the activities of the various government agencies working in the field of Official Development Assistance (ODA) and the operations of the development agencies which had a concern about how the global South was being represented in Europe. DE was also subject to a highly volatile funding environment. It was recognised at an early stage by the NGDOs that DE could be utilised as an educational method of informing people about key issues affecting the global South, and to engage the public in actions that would help address the causes of poverty and injustice. The multilateral nature of the European Community made it difficult to coordinate activities around DE, resulting in the emergence of disparate agencies and initiatives with often differing approaches to the promotion of development issues. The most notable differentiation came with the prioritisation of remarkably diverse, region specific agendas (such as human rights, the environment, arms control etc.), where member state governments and indigenous NGDOs worked on their own national concerns. There was also tension around development education's perceived role by national governments, some of whom regarded DE as a means of promoting their aid programmes rather than educating the public about development issues.

With increased coordination between NGDOs, the advent of the Internet and networking between organisations, common agendas were becoming the norm. Furthermore, the emergence of the European Parliament as a major political force in the EU provided NGDOs with a forum to promote DE beyond the local and regional contexts. The influence extended to the other institutions. The awkwardly titled 'Council Resolution on development education and raising European public awareness of development cooperation' in 2001 was the first significant statement from the EU on the need for DE provision. This principle of intent caught both the mood at the time and the vision under which DE agencies were operating:

> Given the global interdependence of our society; the raising of awareness by development education and by information contributes to strengthening the feeling of international solidarity, and also helps to create an environment which fosters the establishment of an intercultural society in Europe. Heightening awareness also contributes toward the changing of lifestyles in favour of a model of sustainable development for all (EC, 2001: 2).

The links between DE and international cooperation were topical and predated the more security sensitive dispensation of the late 2000s and the recessionary period. There was also an awareness of the connection between multiculturalism and global development – although as a principle this was also later to be questioned by member state leaders. The influence of the DE lobby can be recognised in the approach taken by the Council and Parliament, where formative and substantial policy areas such as development and international cooperation were in need of being presented at a transnational level. Lobbying on DE interests was largely undertaken by DARE (Development Awareness Raising and Education), a forum of CONCORD (the European NGO Confederation for Relief and Development) and associated national agencies. A programme called Developing Europeans' Engagement for the Eradication of Global Poverty (DEEEP) was established to advance the work of the DARE Forum by contributing to 'the creation of a global civil society through citizens' empowerment for change in order to achieve global justice and the eradication of poverty' (DEEEP website, 2013). DEEEP was created as a mechanism for building capacity and strengthening practice in development education across the EU through the participation of national networks from each of the member states. It promoted joint action in the EU and targeted systemic changes in recognition of the need to pursue international goals as well as target the causes of poverty. Conversely some were to note that it was also constrained by political sensitivities within the matrix of the EU. Limitations to its work have been noted in its lack of engagement with economic issues and analysis of neoliberalism (see Chapter 9).

The adaptation of sustainable development (SD) in its broadest sense further enhanced the credentials of the DE sector, presenting a case for a broader long-term strategy which would include issues such as water and food security. It also tied in with the growing discourse on climate change and definitions of sustainable development that were encompassing a raft of DE issues. Sustainable development as a complement to DE was initially flagged up in *Our Common Future*, a report by the World Commission on Environment and Development as far back as 1987. This report presented what is now considered to be the 'classic' definition of sustainable development – that is 'development which meets the needs of the present without compromising the ability of future generations to meet their own needs' (UN, 2010: 2). The United Nations General Assembly accepted this definition as the starting point for dialogue on the topic leading to the principles of sustainable development at the United Nations Conference on Environment and Development in Rio de Janeiro, Brazil, in 1992. From that point onward DE and SD were linked for the purposes of policy design.

The 2001 Council resolution led through to the next major intervention by the EU on a DE strategy and that was the Global Education Congress which was coordinated by the North-South Centre of the Council of Europe. Held in Maastricht, dialogue took place on the potential of a global education framework and brought with it the commitment to strategise on a long-term basis dependent on the involvement of DE agencies from across the EU. This enabled the sector to introduce agreed transnational themes and issues which could provide benchmarking for provision within formal and informal education. The report that emerged from the Congress was to become a template in defining DE within the European policy arena. It recommended and anticipated the evolution of DE as an integral aspect of development work and encompassed the breadth of NGDO activity. While innovating, this intervention was restricted in its influence for one major reason, as Rilli Lappalainen pointed out in *DEAR Matters: Strategic Approaches to Development Education in Europe*: 'While still being an important reference document and commitment by representatives of a broad range of state- and non-state actors, this paper was not politically binding and seriously lacked systematic implementation...' (DEEEP/Concord, 2011: 9). The upshot of this was that there was, at this point, a substantial lobby for DE enhancement across the EU and an urgent need for the embedding of a DE strategy within the development and education policies of member states.

The May 2005 European Consensus on Development gave a window of opportunity to further build the case for DE in that it included an awareness raising clause. Significantly this call came from within the institutions of the EU itself, through the auspices of the Council. The

Consensus was also a marker in acknowledging the importance of the link between civil society and policy implementation. It served to bring the work of the NGDOs together with community wide initiatives to carry DE into development policy as defined in the seminal articles 177 and 181 of the Treaty of the European Community itself. 'The EU will enhance its support for building capacity of non-state actors in order to strengthen their voice in the development process and to advance political, social and economic dialogue' (EC, 2006: 18). This was definitive in that for the first time DE was recognised as instrumental in delivering awareness raising on a range of development issues. It also provided a platform for the facilitation of transnational agencies working to strengthen DE as a sector, including CONCORD (the umbrella body for development NGOs based in Brussels) operating at the heart of EU decision-making.

Along with projects such as DEEEP, sustained efforts were made to group the sector for the maximisation of influence and to communicate common positions on concerns pertinent to the various DE and Education for Sustainable Development (ESD) actors across the continent. For the first time there was also a coordinated voice on DE within the EU and the opportunity to cross reference different interpretations of the core principles of DE. In Belgium for example the sector's ACODEV (Fédération des ONG de coopération au développement) defined DE as: 'a process which seeks to generate changes in values and attitudes both at the individual and collective level, with an eye to a fairer world in which resources are fairly shared in a spirit of respect for human dignity'; in Germany VENRO (Verband Entwicklungspolitik Deutscher Nichtregierungs-Organisationen) sees DE as: 'the strengthening of self-organisation and self-competencies as a prerequisite of human development...' focusing on '...subject areas of social and economic development, related to ecological, political, and cultural aspects as well as interactions between local and global realities'; the DARE forum based in Brussels endorsed DE as 'an active learning process, founded on values of solidarity, equality, inclusion and co-operation. It enables people to move from basic awareness of international development priorities and sustainable human development, through understanding of the causes and effects of global issues to personal involvement and informed actions' (DEEEP 'DEAR definitions', 2013: 1). Across the European Union, operating from different educational contexts and vastly diverse international involvement, a notion of learning for global development was moving towards a more standardised vision. While national schools' curricula differed throughout the member states and education policy remained a reserved (national) policy, similar DE activities were emerging across the board.

Some member states, such as the UK or Germany, had long standing and government supported sectors while others, such as the post-2004 accession states, were only beginning to envisage a global role for their societies. This discourse fed into consultation and lobbying, leading to a more informed understanding of the link between knowledge of global issues, agency and policy initiation. Other factors and policies contributed to a shift in reference to DE. The Cotonou Agreement – between the EU and most global South countries (2000–2020) – placed this network of 89 countries and their development issues within the legal competence of EU development policy. Implicit to this was a need to explain what was actually going on with the EU globally and a need to justify how it was attempting to enhance the development potential of many former colonies. In addition, the United Nation's Millennium Development Goals (MDGs) provided another transnational influence on changing attitudes to DE and the sector – as did the Make Poverty History campaign of 2005. By the mid-2000s there was a formidable policy structure in place and DE was in a unique position to provide an informational hub for the promotion and justification of EU involvement in development issues.

The European Development Education Consensus was launched in Lisbon in 2007 by Louis Michel, the Commissioner for the Directorate General for Development. The sector was influential in drafting the Consensus and a direct result of the work undertaken at the Helsinki Development Education Conference held from 3–4 July 2006. The Consensus was to become the focal point for the promotion of the discipline across the continent, leading to adaptation and convergence of DE policy and practice. This document, formally titled *The European Consensus on Development: The Contribution of Development Education and Awareness Raising*, outlined the challenges for DE and set out a series of targeted recommendations which should be applied by the sector, civil society and governmental agencies to maximise its potential (EC, 2007: 2). Crucially, the Consensus profiled the role of DE in enhancing development strategies through awareness raising, social and political activities and life skills education. It also specifically name checked educational sectors as a component part of public awareness:

> At the same time a diverse range of organisations, institutions and educators has been designing and implementing school and out-of-school curriculum programmes and projects. Known by various

> names – and not always called 'development education', these initiatives all provide an educational response to the issues and challenges of development, helping learners and educators alike in obtaining a critical understanding, skills, values and attitudes through investigations of a wide range of global development issues (EC, 2007: 3).

The DE Consensus introduced exploratory principles such as solidarity and moral responsibilities, principles that had not been currency in the lexicon of EU policy since the Youndé negotiations of the 1960s. With input from civil society and member state departmental experts the challenges were defined and opportunities outlined. The Consensus committed the EU to enhancing the status of awareness raising within the public domain. Its focus was on what it defined as 'the South', a NGDO term that highlighted what the document termed 'shared experiences and common humanity' (EC, 2007: 4). The Consensus was a staging post in the sense that it was not legally binding for member states but it nonetheless represented a significant advancement in shaping the parameters of DE as an agent of social change within the EU.

There was an acceptance within the evolving policy-making bodies working on DE and awareness raising that much had been done already, but that there was a need to reengage with the methodology of how to encourage European society to view global development in terms of *interdependence*. This clarification of intentions would have to operate from local through to transnational levels. There was also an acceptance that public perceptions of international development were often challenging (security and migration focused) and that there was an obligation by the EU to increase understanding through educating the general public about the importance of various key issues. Furthermore, and with reference to the diverse nature of national education systems, the Consensus emphasised: 'The need to integrate development education and awareness raising efforts in the mainstream of existing formal and informal education and information systems and processes, making full use of appropriate and pedagogical approaches to reach the European public' (EC, 2007: 4). This suggested a move towards strategically including DE within policy implementation at a number of points in the EU system; particularly humanitarian, development and generic education policies. The Consensus anticipated a framework for the expansion of the work already being undertaken by civil society organisations and member state governments alike. Importantly, it acknowledged the potential impact of linking transnational networks of DE agencies and the possibility of drawing new actors into the process.

The recommendations that were put forward in the Consensus, notably launched at one of the European Development Days (EDD), were very telling when it came to the authors' intentions for the future of DE. The financial needs of a future DE strategy demanded a definitive commitment to the sector at Council level through a strategy and enhanced provision of related practice-driven programmes. Recommendations included a commitment to create dialogue between various agencies – state, civil society and the media – to promote DEAR; investing in existing practice and facilitating new initiatives; enhancing the transnational features of DE and development cooperation in general; encouraging more interaction between the EU educational institutions, DE organisations and the global South; and finally profiling the importance of global development across the EU (Lappalainen, 2008: 103). What was interesting about the strategic framework was the innovative linking of sectors and state actors not only within the remit of EU boundaries, but towards organisations in the global South. It conveyed an appreciation of the practical forms of interdependence through educational linkage and cross-learning methodologies. It also sent out the right signals to the member state governments in regards to awareness rising of global issues. The impact could be seen almost immediately with a shift in attitudes at policy-making level across the EU. Crucially, innovative examples of engagement by governments (such as Sweden, Finland, Denmark and Ireland) in DE activities were given a profile which had not been seen previously. With tools for comparative analysis good practice could be highlighted across the continent.

The first opportunity the sector had to absorb the content and implications of the DE Consensus was at the 'Intercultural Dialogue in Development Education' conference held in Ljubljana, Slovenia from 9–10 June 2008. This gathering of the sector brought together various practitioners, policy-makers and specialists with an overarching organisational role for CONCORD, the Slovene Ministry for Foreign Affairs and SLOGA, a Slovene umbrella development organisation. The discussion focused on applying the Consensus recommendations, discerning a pan-European methodology for DE, locating research potential and presenting best practice in collaboration. At this stage the intelligent lobbying by organisations such as CONCORD within the institutions of the EU was paying dividends. This could be seen very clearly with the European Parliament's resolution of 6 May 2009 which stated quite explicitly that it wanted to see 'the inclusion of Global/Development Education within all education' across the education systems of the member states of the Community (DEEEP/CONCORD, 2011: 10). Within the relevant Directorate Generals of the Commission DE was – at this stage – accepted as a component feature of development cooperation, recognising DEAR not only as a means of communicating the purpose of the EU in international affairs, but valuing it as an important contributor to multiculturalism and interdependence.

This growing acceptance at institutional level of the value of DE concepts carried with it the potential of greater financial security for the sector and its activities. In this the Consensus had become a catalyst for strategic synergy on a transnational and inter-sectoral basis. Hesitancy by the European Council, however, in finalising a policy and putting in place a formal strategy for the member states of the Union did cause some frustration within the sector and the two other institutions, the Parliament and the Commission, in progressing from consensus building on the topic to strategy. The launch by the Commission of the *DEAR Study* on 24 November 2010 in Brussels brought a mapping exercise to the dialogue on a strategy. Subtitled 'Study on the experience and actions of the main European actors active in the field of Development and Awareness Raising' it covered the scale and involvement of the sector across the EU by analysing 268 EU-funded projects delivered between the years 2005 and 2009. It was able to take stock of the breadth and depth of activities and brought into focus the practical role that the EU had played in supporting DEAR (EC, 2010: 4–6). The strength and vibrancy of the sector was notable. It coincided also with the DEEEP/CONCORD survey of DE activities throughout the respective national schools' curricula in the EU member states. The survey results detailed 'the expanding range and currency of what are perceived as "global" issues influencing school curricula and linked to subject teaching in the classroom' (DEEEP/CONCORD, 2010: 6). However, they also point (in 70 different responses) to 'perceived weaknesses and problems in national education systems regarding effective integration, awareness raising and training, or recognition of the global dimension in school curriculum and whole school practice' (p. 6). Importantly though, the survey did not evaluate the depth or quality of education provision on the global dimension in schools. It concluded that there had been progress across the systems, but that the ubiquitous nature of the subject could be served by more interconnection across the continent.

Towards a DEAR strategy

At a DEEEP seminar in Brussels on 19 May 2011, which was convened to bring together organisations working at a national level to promote DEAR, the whole question of a specific transnational strategy for development education was tabled. It was agreed that the main focus of the drive to establish DE across the EU should be a 'multi-stakeholder process'. It was found that the DE sector in some countries was doing outstanding work, despite the absence of a national DE government strategy. In countries such as Norway, Portugal, Poland and the Czech Republic work was being undertaken in the field that was meaningful and innovative without governmental strategic involvement (DEEEP, 2011: 4). Indeed, there was a fear that government intervention in the DE sector could prove to be shallow without sufficient input from the existing DE sectors and the accommodation of the sector's work into state-driven initiatives. Thus any genuine strategy should entail a multistakeholder/agency dimension, transparency and with clearly agreed targets. Of this process-based approach to DEAR, Tobias Troll from DEEEP commented:

> The intended outcome is a strategic framework document, which will contain a descriptive (where are we?) and more forward looking part (where do we want to go?)... Such an internal clarification seems to be particularly promising in order to strengthen DEAR within the NGO sector first, before starting a strategic reflection in a broader multi-stakeholder frame (DEEEP, 2011: 7).

This also revealed a more cautionary position by the DE sector fearing the dominance and influence of government departments in the outworking of any defined strategy. It also brought to the table for the first time sensitivities from the sector regarding shifts in practice across the EU, notably from NGO specialists about government education departments. In effect the DE sector needed to have a defining role. Evidence from across the continent showed that these were based on real, although not insurmountable, concerns. For example, in the Czech Republic the NGDO FoRS (Českého fóra pro rozvojovou spolupráci) contributed significantly to the production of a national strategy; in the Republic of Ireland Irish Aid and the DE sector had worked successfully together to roll out a comprehensive programme for DE provision; and in Poland, a country without a DE tradition, the government had listened carefully and acted where possible on the advice and guidance provided by the NGDO platform (Grupa Zagranica and PAH). In the latter case it was the drive and determination of the sector which brought DE provision into the country from disparate foundations a decade ago to the point of a formal signing of a Ministry of Foreign Affairs and Ministry of National Education 'Agreement on Global Education' in Warsaw on 26 May 2011. The Polish NGDOs adapted what the sector perceived to be good practice in other EU states for a bespoke strategy that would be appropriate to the Polish educational system. What has been noticeable across the continent since the formation of a more coordinated lobby around the Consensus has been the level of professionalism and confidence conveyed by the sector in engaging with governments, driving the process towards a transnational strategy while not compromising on the integrity of the core principles of development education. As a downside however, the global financial crisis has reduced some national funding streams across the EU and threatened to undermine some of the capacity and good practice supported by the EU and national governments. Funding cuts have also strained relations between governments and NGO partners as the latter have had to adjust to ongoing austerity measures.

It has been generally accepted within the auspices of the EU institutions that DEAR is an important feature of both development and education policies for member states. The ubiquitous manner in which it has evolved across the regions has meant that a coordinated framework approach for its promotion has been difficult. This could explain the extended time line for the development of an agreed strategy. Each country has adapted in different ways to the needs and demands of their own respective systems for a better understanding of global issues and their own distinctive roles in global development. For example, France would have a different perception of international cooperation and how to communicate this to their population with a long history of colonial involvement than Cyprus or Denmark would have. Working towards a strategy, while taking into consideration a web of differing approaches to global development, has meant that actions could only be based on approximations and general principles. The process itself has been immensely important in creating a transnational dialogue which has opened space for the prioritisation of issues applicable to all, to profile DEAR within the evolution of the EU's education and development policies, and to facilitate synergies that could generate partnerships across the continent.

To these ends the Consensus has come to play a formative role in the creation of a strategy with its core recommendations carrying with them aims and objectives which are readily adaptable to a programme for DEAR in the EU. Rilli Lappalainen of CONCORD and the European Development Education Multi-Stakeholder Group, in 'Call to Action: A European Development Education Strategy', reasserted the proposals for a DEAR strategic framework:

- Quality and learning, including monitoring, organisational learning and knowledge management;
- Global perspectives, including involvement of non-European actors and global initiatives in DEAR;
- Grants and administration, including general EC grant management, the introduction of mini grants and structural support mechanisms;
- Management of DEAR within the EC, including staff roles and structures, role of grant assessors and information provision (Lappalainen, 2012: 78–79).

A major injection of energy for a DE strategy came within the institutions of the EU itself with a number of actions that have brought DEAR to a point of systemic integration within the programme scheduling of the EU. The Directorate General of Development and Cooperation has been advocating continually for a cross-policy role for DEAR, particularly between education and external affairs. Within education policy this recalibration of DE would invariably mean the mainstreaming of the sector and its work, and ultimately the establishment of a dedicated DE unit within the Commission itself.

A significant marker in the evolution of the DEAR strategy came on 5 July 2012 when the European Parliament – which was given additional policy-making and budgetary powers under the Lisbon Treaty – voted for an official declaration on development education and active global citizenship. The assertiveness of the declaration left all agencies involved in the sector with no doubt as to the seriousness of the institutional base of the EU in its intentions towards DE. While the Parliament acknowledged the funding role of the Union in DE provision, it also referred to the fact that there was no dedicated strategy. The Parliament's declaration: '1. Calls on the Commission and the Council to develop a long-term, cross-sectoral European strategy for development education, awareness-raising and active global citizenship; 2. Calls on the Member States to develop or strengthen national development education strategies' (European Parliament, 2012). This statement in effect brought the Parliament in line with a transnational commitment to the activities that were being undertaken by the DE sector for many years and was to be a 'milestone' in the position of DE within the policy mechanism of the EU itself. In practice it gave the authority, subject to a final proviso to come from the Council, to build DEAR into the Multiannual Financial Framework (MFF) for 2014–2020 and a dedicated budget line for DE. From here it was over to the Commission in Brussels to provide a case for a DE programme remit and the national governments to recognise the importance of the field in education and society in general.

The Commission's response to the DEAR community and the Parliament was enthusiastic working towards a formal and legal integration of DE into EU policy, specifically through the Civil Society and Local Authorities Thematic Programme for 2014–2020. The release of the Commission Staff Working Document 'On Development Education and Awareness Raising (DEAR) in Europe' on 20 December 2012 brought forward a comprehensive statement on the status of DE within the EU (EC, 2012: 1–21). The Commission's authors recognised instinctively the links between what it called the 'cornerstones of DEAR' and the founding principles of the EU itself, sharing keywords that resonate throughout Community treaties – such as interdependence, cohesion, integration, pluralism, justice and solidarity. The links are conveyed succinctly:

> Combating poverty and promoting sustainable development through development cooperation, as well as through consideration of transversal themes such as environmental protection and climate action, are affected by wider global and local economic, social, environmental and political changes and structures. Developing a better understanding of development challenges requires, inter alia, the development of analytical and critical skills. DEAR contributes to strengthening the critical understanding of European citizens with regard to the processes and structures of interdependence and development, enabling them to understand better complex and interconnected aspects of development (EC, 2012: 4).

The Commission also usefully looked at the budgetary aspects of DEAR provision across the EU, estimating total bilateral expenditure in 2010 alone to be €220 million. Projects funded directly by the EU between 2004 and 2012 amounted to 362 non state agencies and 43 local authorities being allocated €256 million covering a range of thematic issues (EC, 2012: 12). This commitment to the sector – including DEEEP, DARE, CONCORD, Development Days, Global Education Week and until recently a summer school – was also acknowledged as being integral to the outworking of a multilayered DEAR advocacy.

Conclusion

The DE sector across the continent has been immensely pro-active in lobbying the EU to formally integrate DEAR into the established educational and development policies of the EU. The tenacity and professionalism of the sector has proved to be instrumental in elevating the principles and methodology of their field to a point where, certainly within the Parliament and Commission, they have become synonymous with the basic values of the European integration process. This compatibility has benefited the sector significantly and is very noticeable in the emergence of the sector in regions such as Eastern Europe, while consolidating the position of the established sector in the West. The following objective by the Commission gives some sense of the position of DE and the sector within the 'conscience' of the EU:

> The overall objective that the European Commission has been pursuing with Development Education and Awareness Raising could be articulated as follows: *'To develop citizens' awareness and critical understanding of the interdependent world, of their role and responsibility in relation to a globalised society; and to support their active engagement with global attempts to eradicate poverty and promote justice, human rights and a sustainable social-economic development in partner countries'* (EC, 2012: 20).

While the debate over budget allocation continues and will continue for some time to come, at this point in the assimilation of DE into the formal policy framework of the EU, the status of the sector is secure. The context, however, is continually changing for DE within the EU. For the foreseeable future it will have to compete with other priority areas in domestic and development policies, areas such as the management of the euro crisis, the post-Millennium Development Goals development framework, security and migration issues. Threats do exist in light of the austerity regimes that have been put in place by a number of the member states and the growing security focus of the Council in its attempts to rebalance the EU on a global stage as a global leader vis-à-vis the United States (US). However, all these extraneous geo-political and economic circumstances should be seen as challenges for the sector and further validation of the necessity for a comprehensive DEAR strategy.

Key commitments in the EU policy framework for development education:

- The EU Council of Development Ministers, 'Resolution on Development Education' (2001)
- North-South Centre of the Council of Europe, 'Global Education in Europe to 2015 – Strategy, Policies, and Perspectives' (2002)
- The Brussels Conference on 'Public Awareness and Development Education for North-South Solidarity' (2005)
- 'The European Consensus on Development' (2005)
- The Helsinki Conference on 'European Development Education' (July 2006)
- The 18-month (2007–2008) programme on development policy of the EU Presidencies of Germany, Portugal and Slovenia
- European Union Multi-stakeholder Group on Development Education, *European Consensus on Development: The Contribution of Development Education and Awareness Raising*, European Development Education Consensus (2007)
- The Ljubljana Conference on 'Intercultural Dialogue in Development Education' (9–10 June 2008)
- European Parliament resolution on the draft Commission decision establishing the 2009 Annual Action Programme for Non-State Actors and Local Authorities in Development (6 May 2009)
- *Development Education and the School Curriculum in the European Union*, DEEEP/CONDORD (2010)
- *The DEAR Study. DEAR in Europe – Recommendations for Future Interventions by the EC: Final Report of the Development Education & Awareness Raising Study* (24 November 2010)
- The European Parliament's 'Written Declaration on Development Education and Active Global Citizenship' (5 July 2012)
- European Commission Staff Working Document 'On Development Education and Awareness Raising (DEAR) in Europe' (20 December 2012)

European organisations that have contributed directly to the EU's DE policy platform

CONCORD Development Education Forum
Council of European Municipalities and Regions
Development Centre Institute of International Relations – Czech Republic

European Commission DEV A4
European Parliament
European Youth Forum
Federal Ministry of Foreign Affairs, Trade and Development Cooperation – Belgium
Global Education Network in Europe (GENE)
InWEnt GmbH for Federal Ministry for Economic Cooperation and Development (BMZ) – Germany
Irish Aid, Department of Foreign Affairs – Ireland
Ministry of Foreign Affairs Direction de la Coopération au Développement – Luxembourg
Ministry of Foreign Affairs – Slovenia
North-South Centre of the Council of Europe
Organisation for Economic Co-operation and Development (OECD) Development Centre
Portuguese Development Agency (IPAD)
Slovak Agency for International Development Cooperation
Developing Europeans' Engagement in the Eradication of Poverty (DEEEP)

References

Developing Europeans' Engagement for the Eradication of Global Poverty (DEEEP), available: www.deeep.org (accessed 14 May 2013).

DEEEP/CONCORD (2010) *Development Education and the School Curriculum in the European Union: A Report on the Status and Impact of Development Education in the Formal Education Sector and School Curriculum in Member States of the European Union*, Brussels, available: http://www.deeep.org/schoolcurricula.html (accessed 1 May 2013).

DEEEP/Concord (August 2011) *DEAR Matters: Strategic Approaches to Development Education in Europe*, Brussels.

DEEEP 'DEAR definitions', available: hppt://www.deeep.org/dear-definitions.html (accessed 13 March 2013).

European Commission (EC) (2001) 'Council resolution on development education and raising European public awareness of development cooperation', Brussels: European Commission.

European Commission (EC) (2006) *The European Consensus on Development*, Official Journal of the European Union, Brussels, 2006/C 46/01.

European Commission (EC) (2007) *The European Consensus on Development: The Contribution of Development Education and Awareness Raising*, Brussels, available: http://ec.europa.eu/development/icenter/repository/DE_Consensus-eductation_temp_EN.pdf (accessed 8 September 2013).

European Commission (24 November 2010) *The DEAR Study. DEAR in Europe ~ Recommendations for Future Interventions by the EC: Final Report of the Development Education & Awareness Raising Study*, Brussels, available: https://webgate.ec.europa.eu/fpfis/mwikis/aidco/images/d/d4/Final_Report_DEAR_Study.pdf (accessed 12 December 2012).

European Commission (EC) Staff Working Document (20 December 2012) 'On Development Education and Awareness Raising (DEAR) in Europe', Brussels (SWD(2012) 457 final), available: http://ec.europa.eu/europeaid/how/finance/dci/documents/swd_2012_457_dear_en.pdf (accessed 4 January 2013).

European Parliament (5 July 2012) 'Declaration on development education and active global citizenship', Strasbourg (C 316 E/149), available: http://eur-lex.europa.eu/LexUriServ/LexUriServ.do?uri=OJ:C:2012:316E:0149:0182:EN:PDF (accessed 4 January 2013).

Lappalainen, R (2008) 'Consensus in development education in the European Union', *Policy and Practice: A Development Education Review*, Vol. 7, Autumn, pp. 102–105.

Lappalainen, R (2012) 'Call to action: A European development education strategy', *Policy and Practice: A Development Education Review*, Vol. 15, Autumn, pp. 74–82.

United Nations (September 2010) *Sustainable Development: From Brundtland to Rio 2012*, prepared by John Drexhage and Deborah Murphy, International Institute for Sustainable Development (IISD), New York.

16
Beyond the MDGs: Toward a New Development Framework

Mwangi Waituru

Introduction

This chapter is a contribution to the ongoing debate around the framing of a United Nations (UN) development framework after 2015 – the year targeted for the achievement of the Millennium Development Goals (MDGs). The chapter presents the author's perspectives based on lessons learnt from lead positions in civil society organisations (CSOs) including National Co-ordinator of the Global Campaign Against Poverty (GCAP) in Kenya and co-chair of the Beyond 2015 steering committee. These two positions have afforded me a central position at CSOs' discussion forums, and advocacy and lobbying activities at national, continental as well as international levels on the UN post-MDGs agenda. It has also meant a deep involvement in lobbying activities around the post-2015 UN process and most importantly, a lead role in ongoing participatory research processes with people living in poverty.

From a reflection on online advocacy work, position papers, workshop and seminar proceedings, and policy sessions with the UN High Level Panel of Eminent Persons (UN, 2012) set up to advise the UN Secretary-General on the global development framework beyond 2015, the chapter considers what kind of policy framework is needed post-2015 taking into account new global realities and trends.

Contextualised policy process

Two major separate but interrelated policy strands constitute the ongoing dialogue on a UN development framework post-2015. One of the strands has its roots in the MDGs and focuses on human development while the other is grounded in environmental sustainability and revolves around the proposed set of Sustainable Development Goals (SDGs) to follow the MDGs. After the Millennium Declaration in 2000, the UN Secretary-General unveiled a set of eight MDGs to be achieved by 2015. With this date fast approaching, and given the lead time required to deliver a global consensus, the UN high level event on MDGs in 2010, asked the Secretary-General to initiate discussions for a successor framework by the 2013 General Assembly. World leaders met at the UN on 25 September to debate the MDGs and a new framework agreement for development. They agreed to 'scale up action against extreme poverty, hunger and disease and called for a 2015 Summit to adopt the next set of Goals to focus continued efforts after the target date for the Millennium Development Goals' (Beyond 2015, 2013c).

At the same time, one of the main outcomes of the United Nations Conference on Sustainable Development (Rio+20), held in Rio de Janeiro in June 2012, was the agreement by member states to launch a process to develop a set of SDGs (UN, 2013) following a proposal tabled by the governments of Colombia and Guatemala (Republic of Colombia, 2012). Given the different historical origins and the elaborate separate paths laid out for the two strands, they are presenting both a process as well as a convergence quagmire for proponents of a converged process both within the UN and outside.

To generate debate on a post-2015 framework, the UN Secretary-General first created a UN system wide task team that produced a report entitled 'Realizing the Future We Want for All' (UN System Task Team on the Post-2015 UN Development Agenda, 2012). At the same time, a series of thematic consultations with academia, the media, private sector, employers and trade unions, civil society and decision-makers was initiated. Additional UN processes involved setting up a High Level Panel (HLP) of Eminent Persons, a global online dialogue and national dialogues in over 100 countries. Reports from these processes fed into the 2013 Secretary-General's report to the General Assembly.

Meanwhile, in response to a Rio+20 agreement by member states to launch a process to develop a set of sustainable development goals, the Open Working Group on SDGs was created on 22 January 2013 by UN decision 67/555 (UN General Assembly, 2013). The Open Working Group on SDGs, co-chaired by Kenya and Hungary, meets monthly in New York and will report in 2014. There will probably be an intergovernmental process, but that is as yet undefined. These two UN strands inputting to the post-2015 agenda lack a defined point of convergence and clarity on whether we will have one single discussion on a single set of goals. With a lack of clarity on when and where decisions are being made, governments will most likely hold their cards close to their chest to keep their options open. They will probably await the outcomes of the various processes before backing one or determining their own approach to the new framework; at present this waiting game is generally creating inertia. There is always the possibility that, whatever the outcomes of the Secretary-General's report in September 2013, the governments might defer their decision-making for another year as they did in 2005 with the 'In Larger Freedom' report (UN, 2005), which remains the best Secretary-General report on the MDGs to date.

On the civil society front, there are six main international players engaging explicitly in this 'post-2015' agenda: The Beyond 2015 international campaign; GCAP campaign; CIVICUS, the World Alliance for Citizen Participation; the new joint BetterAid/Open Forum international Platform (CPD); and the International Forum of National Platforms of Development NGOs (IFP/FIP). These groups face stiff competition among themselves for policy influence as well as funding. They have also been criticised for letting themselves down at policy forums by raising diverse single issues resulting in wasted opportunities to agree on a way forward (Underwoods, 2012; Melamed, 2012).

One school of thought suggests that civil society groupings should create a smooth coordination mechanism with the main mandate of ensuring coherence and synergies across the different processes; mobilising resources and providing timely and transparent information (Consolo, 2012). Pollard and Haslam (2012) postulate that the diversity of perspectives raised may be an inconvenient truth but reflects a responsibility, not a failure, of civil society. Indeed, moving civil society to 'march like an army' may amount to building a structured organisation with the unintended result of suppressing a global movement building process.

The purpose of a global policy framework

With reference to the ongoing MDGs and SDGs policy discussions, this section tries to identify a vision for development post-2015. A public policy can be defined as a dynamic and value-laden process, including governments' expressed intentions and official enactments, as well as consistent patterns of activity and inactivity, through which political systems handle public problems (Fowler, 2009). A core question here then is the value of a global process in light of sovereignty of UN members and the elaborate but diverse policy tools operating at the national level. The value of a global policy framework comes in focusing on both common problems as well as shared solutions. In the case of the global framework, its role is to transform national policy regimes into a form that is consistent with the shared vision.

With globalisation, the world has become heavily interconnected resulting in many shared global problems that trickle down to the national level. Their solutions can only be found at an international level and, in this regard, the global framework helps to define a common vision and mobilise a coordinated effort towards the pursuance of the vision. If you take the policy process to be a linear one that involves defining issues, agenda setting, policy formulation, adoption, implementation and monitoring and evaluation (Fowler, 2009), the post-2015 policy development process is not the space for defining issues nor is it an agenda setting phase; it is rather a vision implementation phase. But the envisioning process is not that linear and the implementation phase involves going back to the issues and agenda both for the purpose of building clarity and common agreement on the vision and also for interrogating it further. In this process, the vision is enriched.

For the post-MDGs platform, the envisioning process has been ongoing for several years. The shared vision can be traced back to the charter that established the United Nations which identifies a four fold vision for the global family which encompasses: (i) international peace and security; (ii) friendly relations among nations; (iii) international cooperation in solving international problems of an economic, social, cultural, or humanitarian character, and in promoting and encouraging respect for human rights and for fundamental freedoms for all without distinction as to race, sex, language, or religion; and (iv) harmonising the actions of nations in the attainment of these common ends (United Nations, 2013). Over the years, this vision has been pursued through the enactment of various instruments including international treaties, conventions, guiding principles and summit declarations, the latest of which is the Millennium Declaration.

Over and above the four visions explicitly stipulated in the UN Charter, the Millennium Declaration strongly advanced a case for living within planetary boundaries (United Nations, 2000, 2001). The UN vision is quite similar to the evolving civil society vision for the post-2015 global development agenda:

> An equitable and sustainable world where every person is safe, resilient, lives well, and enjoys their human rights, and a world where political and economic systems deliver well-being for all

> people within the limits of our planet's resources. It is a world where: human rights are realized, poverty has been eradicated, the environment is safeguarded, there is social justice, and peace, safety and security are a reality for all (Beyond 2015, 2012).

There are certain key concepts that seem to consistently appear in all the dialogues concerning the MDGs and SDGs. First is the concept of a simple and actionable framework that is mentioned repeatedly, particularly in Africa. The people who participated in the Monrovia CSOs platform, for example, were clear that they do not want empty rhetoric; they want action now. In Kenya, consultations on the post-2015 framework called for policies that deliver human security, sealing the cracks through which people fall into poverty, and sustainably providing for development.

'Participation' is another vision word that is echoing loudly in the dialogue process and the call by marginalised civil society groups for participation in economic activities and decision-making has led drafters of official policy documents to coin 'inclusiveness' as an essential element of economic growth. Suspicious of the intentions of policy-makers in the growth agenda and the centrality of the private sector in this frame, CSOs and participatory researchers have added the vision of 'leave no one behind' to their contribution to the post-2015 debate; a sentiment strongly echoed in the narrative of the High Level Panel report.

In talking about living within planetary boundaries and the need for a single overarching framework, CSOs argue that concentrating on either environmental sustainability or human development will potentially deliver the unsustainable result of either a planet without its people or a people without their planet. Beyond 2015 has tried to sharpen this vision by highlighting values that should underpin the framework. The values represent elements that are integral to the vision – a world where these values are embodied – and a means by which a single overarching framework will achieve its intended purpose. Values also guide the creation of a coherent framework by framing the criteria through which we select goals, targets and indicators which are relevant, transformational, evidence-based and effective. The values also govern the process of implementation of the framework.

Learning from the strengths and weaknesses of the MDGs in articulating a post-2015 development framework

The process of framing and working toward the MDGs has provided very useful lessons that will inform the definition of a post-2015 agenda in the context of today's world that is radically different from the one that existed at the turn of the century. A contextual consideration is presented below followed by a reflection on how we can capitalise on lessons learnt.

Context

The MDGs are a set of eight goals, with 18 accompanying targets and 48 indicators. Specialised UN interest groups (secretariat, funds, programmes and several specialised agencies) created them, together with the Organisation for Economic Co-operation and Development (OECD), the International Monetary Fund (IMF) and the World Bank (Melamed, 2011a; Summer and Melamed, 2011; Vandemoortele, 2012). The goals became the authoritative development framework despite the fact that they were initially only an annex to the Secretary-General's 2001 report to the General Assembly titled, 'Road Map Towards the Implementation of the United Nations Millennium Declaration' (United Nations, 2001). In fact, the MDGs were never sanctioned as such by the General Assembly. They were, however, informally endorsed at the UN Conference on International Financing for Development at Monterrey in 2002, and it was there that funding commitments started to be made on the basis of the MDGs (Summer and Melamed, 2011).

The top-down approach in setting the MDGs was possible given the economic context at the time, demographic characteristics and the geo-political power map of the moment. It was a period of hope, unity of purpose and command; the excitement associated with the turn of a century, a booming global economy and a relative concentration of global decision-making power around a singular point, the G8 (the Group of Eight leading industrialised nations). In the so-called global South or developing world, the collapse of the Soviet Union and the resultant end of the Cold War saw a wind of democratisation sweep through hitherto autocratic countries that often derived their legitimacy from military strength rather than the ballot box. These autocratic regimes were slowly replaced by democratic governments whose legitimacy and power to rule was derived from the popular vote secured on the basis of service delivery to the electorate. Civil strive was also greatly reduced with the number of civil wars on the African continent dropping drastically (Kiruthu et al., 2011).

However, this emerging democratic leadership found it increasingly difficult to close the gap between the demand for, and supply of, development finance in the context of an accelerating population and limited national budget. At the same time, human rights were increasingly made law and this raised the cost of service delivery. It became apparent, for example, that providing education as a right meant a mandatory obligation to meet the needs of marginalised groups which brought with it higher operational costs resulting from factors such as smaller class sizes and hardship allowances for teachers in remote, sparsely populated areas. Coupled with the growing demand exerted by demographic pressures was the scarcity of public funds earmarked for social development due to the heavy indebtedness of many developing countries resulting from years of sometimes corrupt and dubious borrowing.

Furthermore, the negative effects of the twin factors of stringent aid conditionality and structural adjustment programmes forced on the global South by the Bretton Woods Institutions (the IMF and World Bank) in the 1990s, exacerbated the need for development finance. Thus, according to Melamed (2011b), an agreement between donor and recipient countries about a set of priorities for a framework involving collaboration and monitoring became quite palatable in the global South. Besides the changes in the global political landscape since 2001 when the MDGs were unveiled, the world has experienced a series of crises ranging from the global financial crisis to the sovereign debt crisis that have severely weakened some of the world's economic power houses such as the United States (US), Spain and the United Kingdom (UK) and threatened the sustainability of the Eurozone. Recovery has been weak, particularly in developed countries where increased commodity prices have harmed growth and hit the most vulnerable leaving unemployment at unacceptable levels. Tensions in the financial markets increased mostly as a result of sovereign risks in Europe and exchange rate volatility which jeopardised growth and financial stability and, worst of all, global imbalances persisted (G20, 2010).

The economic meltdown in the global North came in a period of increasing growth in emerging economies in the global South. Over the past decade the traditional division of the world into powerful 'developed' and less powerful 'developing' countries has become superseded by the emergence of a third group of countries, most notably India and China, from the global South which have large populations and experienced significant and sustained economic growth. Some of these 'rising stars' have become powerful global actors in their own right while others like Brazil, Mexico, South Korea, Indonesia, South Africa and Turkey are gaining importance in global decision-making. All of these countries will increasingly shape the world's economy and politics. Over the next few decades we may experience a seismic shift of power changing a world predominantly defined by Europe and the

US into one which is shaped much more by the largest and most dynamic countries in Asia, Latin America and, eventually, Africa (Berlin Civil Society Center and Global Call to Action against Poverty, 2011; UNDP, 2013).

A realignment of the global power map and emergence of new economic blocks has been attended by an ideological reorientation that will impact on the agenda setting for the post-2015 period. Recent reports, agenda items and communiques among G8 countries appears to indicate that human rights and democratisation are taking a back seat to the agendas and priorities of the private sector which seems to have enjoyed a raised profile too in emerging power blocks such as G20, G77 and the BRICS, an association of five major emerging economies – Brazil, Russia, India, China and South Africa (http://www.brics5.co.za/). Africa is particularly vocal in advancing an agenda of economic growth and transformation as seen in the Africa Union (AU) declarations, the post-2015 position papers published by AU agencies, and communiques and reports from African CSOs.

The process

Unlike the current MDGs, a post-2015 development framework cannot be hatched from an ivory tower. To make it much more meaningful to people, there is a general consensus that the process through which it is framed should not only be participatory and inclusive but the participation must be meaningful and reflected in the results of the process. These sentiments have been echoed by a cross section of actors including: Beyond 2015 (2013a), the Global CSO Forum on the Post-2015 Development Agenda Bali Communiqué (2013), CSOs Monrovia Outcome document (2013) and a synthesis of participatory research which indicates that, according to the very poor, participation should be built into every stage of the development process from conception, design, implementation, learning, monitoring and evaluation (Participate, 2013).

The question of participation is a sensitive one. For example, during a youth consultation on the post-2015 global framework at the University of Nairobi, one student asked, 'what are you going to do with all this data that you are collecting? Is it just going to lie in your offices and libraries or will it be acted upon?' This sentiment highlights key tensions arising from efforts to engage poor people in the post-2015 debate. It emphasises the importance of process; it should not just be an extractive and disempowering process but designed to generate useful inputs into the international process and ensure that poor people themselves are able to use the results to carry out advocacy with their own leaders to achieve better development outcomes.

A workshop held in London in 2012 that brought together different groups: those who are currently developing initiatives to engage poor people on a post-2015 framework; those who have expertise in participative engagement; and those connected to the policy-making process itself recommended innovative and empowering engagement with the poor in the post-2015 global policy dialogue (Burall, 2011). Simply engaging poor people in a consultation process leading up to 2015 is too limited – the process of engagement should be part of a broader social movement. This requires a paradigm shift from a development approach to rights-based approach in the way policy-makers perceive development and the public at large.

The development narrative that must underpin a post-2015 development framework

This section looks at the vision and purpose which a post-2015 development framework should pursue based on lessons learnt from the strengths and weaknesses of the current MDGs. Beyond 2015 has defined 'purpose' as the role that the international community ascribes to the post-2015 framework with strong in-built mechanisms for accountability (Beyond 2015, 2013b). For Beyond 2015, the *purpose* of the framework is to achieve the change needed to secure progress towards our broad vision by:

> Enabling coherence and prioritization of action – identifying what needs to be done to achieve sustainable change which benefits all, ensuring coherence between different development and environment agendas, and prioritizing those issues with the greatest potential for delivering progress towards our vision.
>
> Securing commitment to action – incentivizing and requiring coordinated, collective action by actors in all countries, at all levels (global, state, private sector, civil society) and focusing economic, natural, political and social resources to drive a process of change.
>
> Ensuring accountability for action – holding countries and other actors to account in meeting their commitments and achieving impact against the identified goals through transparent mechanisms and processes, including stakeholder participation at all levels (Beyond 2015, 2013b).

Designing a framework that can deliver this purpose with the same force that drove the MDGs will be no easy process. The delivery of the MDGs hinged upon the building of a global coordination capacity between states and other developmental actors on a single agenda; in short, the fight against poverty. This purpose is still identified by civil society as an important function for the post-MDGs agenda. The post-2015 framework should serve to incentivise action towards a shared vision by member states acting collectively as a family of the United Nations or separately as sovereign states (Beyond 2015, 2012). In this regard, it is worth noting that the agreement on the MDGs can be most likely attributed to the endorsement of the UN Conference on International Financing for Development at Monterrey in 2002, from where funding commitments started to be made on the basis of the MDGs.

Given this tie with funding, this set of goals has been credited for managing to bring together public, private and political support for global poverty reduction and provided an effective tool to stimulate the production of new poverty-related data and additional aid commitments. In some countries the MDGs became a *de facto* contract between the state and the people providing tools for civil society and other development actors to participate more effectively not only in development but also in accountability mechanisms (see Pollard et al., 2011; CAFOD, 2012). The MDGs were reminiscent of an agreement between donor and recipient countries about a set of priorities for collaboration (Melamed, 2011b; United Nations, 2000, 2001). A new framework is unlikely to spur action and commitment from members states on the basis of donor-recipient power relations.

Since 2001, when the MDGs were unveiled, the power with which overseas development assistance (ODA) could be used as an instrument of control for development policy has greatly diminished. First, following agreements reached on the principles of ownership, harmonisation, alignment, results and mutual accountability in the Paris Declaration on Aid Effectiveness (OECD, 2008), far-reaching and monitorable actions to reform the ways that the delivery and management of aid are managed have been implemented. Secondly, ODA is increasingly changing from an instrument of defining power relations to one of partnership, and its flow is under threat from the economic crisis in OECD countries. Aid to the world's poorest nations has been hit by the economic downturn across the West as industrialised countries cut back on development spending. The OECD reported that aid budgets are down by 4 percent among its members. The biggest cuts included

50 percent in Spain, 34 percent in Italy and 17 percent in Greece (*The Independent*, 4 April 2013).

Actionable framework

A global policy must serve to influence decisions and actions of member states through a definite course or method of action (Farlex, 2012; Merriam-Webster, 2012). Securing commitment to action (Beyond 2015, 2012) involves incentivising and focussing economic, natural, political and social resources to drive a process of change. Today, framing this formula and making it of equal value to the MDGs is a major challenge. The power of the MDGs to mobilise action from member states and other actors can be attributed to factors intrinsic to the framework itself. In addition to the financial factor is the structure of the framework which in the case of the MDGs took the form of an easy to communicate set of goals, time bound targets and measurable indicators many of which are expressed as ratios. The goals and targets prioritised very basic aspects of humanity that are difficult to argue against – saving the lives of mothers and infants, putting food on the table, combating sickness and getting children to school. The spirit of the millennium promise as expressed in article 11 of the Millennium Declaration inspired the framework:

> We will spare no effort to free our fellow men, women and children from the abject and dehumanizing conditions of extreme poverty, to which more than a billion of them are currently subjected. We are committed to making the right to development a reality for everyone and to freeing the entire human race from want (United Nations, 2000).

Furthermore, the goals were action oriented and motivated by a resolve to outline strategies for practically delivering on their promises. In his report that unveiled the MDGs, the Secretary-General noted:

> The international community has just emerged from an era of commitment. It must now enter an era of implementation, in which it mobilizes the will and resources needed to fulfil the promises made...what is needed...is not more technical or feasibility studies...rather, states need to demonstrate the political will to carry out commitments already given and to implement strategies already worked out (United Nations, 2001).

Nonetheless, the greatest strength of the MDGs – an actionable set of goals – has to be cited as its greatest weakness too. The MDGs undercut agreements on other goals and targets reached at the global conferences of the 1990s displacing all other processes from the global list of priorities to become the only agenda for development and not one of the many ways to eradicate global poverty; and in this regard, they did not bring a strategic advantage to the development process.

In her paper titled 'MDGs: Facing Up to the Limitations of Global Goal Setting' Fukuda-Parr (2013) postulates that, simplicity's downside is reductionism, which can lead to neglect and distortion. She acknowledges that the MDGs were too narrow in scope, and left out many priorities, such as employment, climate change and reducing inequality and discrimination, all of which are among today's challenges in virtually all countries, rich and poor. Reductionist goals can distort planning and programming of resources and development efforts, and lead to agendas that do not reflect national priorities. Furthermore, numerical targets can distort governance performance judgment and create false incentives.

The challenge then is how to build on the useful elements of the current MDGs such as simplicity and actionability and, at the same time, be ambitious and holistic in acknowledgement of the highly interdependent nature of current global challenges (UN System Task Team on the Post-2015 UN Development Agenda, 2012). Furthermore, the bigger challenge is not in framing the goals but in innovating a 'political formula' that UN member states will voluntarily and passionately pursue, working jointly as members of the global family and separately as sovereign states. In today's multipolar development arena the global geo-political map is much more complex as opposed to the turn of the century when one group of countries – the G8 – dominated the policy agenda. The challenges for the post-2015 agenda are by default going to be complex and a policy framework that builds consensus around a set of priorities could settle on the lowest common denominator to gain consensus thus becoming exclusionist and regrettably reductionist. In developing an easy to communicate framework, a question arises of how we group issues without excluding the very core specifics that perpetuate poverty.

Individuals and communities consulted by GCAP and Beyond 2015 in national civil society consultations held in over 30 countries stated that they wanted core issues to be explicitly named and addressed rather than categorised in groups of issues where they risk being forgotten or lost. Lessons from MDGs indicate that issues cannot be resolved through a silo approach; a holistic approach that removes the blockages that people face in effecting their own decisions and providing the enablers they require to unleash their potentials is needed (Mniki and Waituru, 2012). One way of doing this is to build a holistic framework while addressing specific issues and at the same time keep the framework inclusive by mentioning target populations explicitly by way of multiple cross referencing of goals and targets. A target on energy, for example, could be cross referenced with health while, at the same time, explicitly mentioning gender. Disaggregated indicators by vulnerable groups will further sharpen the focus while keeping the framework holistic.

The biggest challenge will be having an element that explicitly delivers development to hitherto marginalised and vulnerable groups. These are groups which will not benefit from an overall development framework due to the underpinning exclusionary and discriminatory nature of the societal context under which the policies are implemented. The element brings equity of outcomes for these groups. For example, the holistic framework must deliver equal educational opportunities by providing resources for hitherto resource poor children. While the holistic framework will provide for universal services, it should recognise that some vulnerable groups in society are marginalised from state services like free universal primary education.

Global policies serve to change context as well as shape the people for whom it is targeted. In this regard, the post-2015 development framework will serve to build a harmonious and standardised context in which member states postulate their development policies as well as change the welfare regimes of the member states.

Transforming welfare regimes in member states

A core question for the drafters of the post-2015 framework is how the new framework will affect policies and policy-making of member states. This question is particularly pertinent since member states have a variety of welfare state regimes that affect the way social relations are constructed. Welfare state (or state social) provisions are 'interventions by the state in civil society to alter social and market forces but one cannot a priori judge that all state interventions are aimed at, or actually produce, greater justice among citizens, access to human rights, and environmental sustainability' (Richardt, 2007).

In a just society every human being must have the opportunity to realise his or her rights in a cohesive and stable state. By contrast, in an oppressive state (Pateman, 1988) national policies – through either studied action or inaction, omission or commission – legitimise oppressive practices against some groups. Consequently, one core purpose of international instruments should be to transform the member state into a political resource for subordinate groups – from oppressive policies and practices toward social and economic rights that enhance the relative position of the marginalised (Hernes, 1987; Orloff, 1991; O'Connor, 1998). In this regard, the discourse of the post-2015 UN development agenda is about selecting a definite course or method of action that will alter the 'rules of the game' in the member states' policy frameworks.

Many struggles, processes and movements are going on at the national and local level for concrete changes and rights of the people. The question is whether there can or should be a global framework supporting this and how a global common norm can provide a reference point for local actors. Removing structural causes of poverty sometimes requires taking actions that are not politically or economically prudent. Confronting some structural causes of poverty such as discrimination and exclusion can be very unpopular for local actors given the deep-rooted historical cultural norms that societies have maintained for years and due to their effect on the way social relations are constructed. The other category of policy that is difficult to institute is structural/system change policies. Such policies require a shift of power and resources from one group to the other and consequently attract resistance from the latter (Fowler, 2009). Under these two conditions, domestic policy actors could use international legal resources to overcome welfare state resistance to reform.

For the post-2015 development agenda to deliver on this agenda it needs to enshrine people's rights within a legal framework. In this regard, for example, Amnesty International postulates that for women to enjoy living in stable and peaceful societies, what matters is not just whether they can access justice mechanisms and benefit from due process, but whether the framework challenges gender discrimination and promotes gender equality and women's empowerment (Amnesty International, 2013).

Joining the dots: The role of development education in the post MDGs development framework

Undoubtedly, MDGs introduced new thinking in development policy – a policy framework built upon a set of goals, targets and indicators.

On the basis of this success, policy actors are proposing a single overarching framework built on the same architectural design of goals, targets and indicators. By settling on improving the current architecture, policy-makers seem to be closing the doors to policy innovation which is where development education comes in. It is essential that people begin to tell their own stories about the kind of development they want to see. There is no better source of these stories than the perspectives, experiences and aspirations of ordinary citizens. When grassroots communities describe their lived realities, it becomes apparent that the development they envision is not the same as the development that the majority of the world imagines the poor want. In their own narrative, the strongest message from communities is a deep desire for the 'capability to function'. Such a capability to function is sought for the sole purpose of reclaiming 'the power to take decisions that affect their lives; access to equal opportunities; and an enabling environment to sustain livelihoods' (Mniki and Waituru, 2012).

Development education is a process rooted in the global South based on a radical pedagogy and informed by the needs of the poor. It represents an important methodology for people to express their needs in respect to a new development framework that directly tackles the priorities of marginalised communities. It can enable development education practitioners in the global North to inform their work through partnerships with civil society organisations in the global South. Development education can support the consultation process in the lead in period to the framing of the new development framework and also help to monitor the implementation of the framework by assessing its impact on priority target groups in the global South. In the global North, development education can incorporate the new development framework into their practice by communicating its purpose to learners and critically assessing its contribution to social and environmental justice.

Just as development educators critically assessed the effectiveness of the MDGs in achieving poverty eradication and as a learning tool in their practice, they can also use critical awareness to evaluate the contribution of the post-2015 framework in achieving its stated goals. The new development framework is likely to dominate development discourse over its lifespan and the role of development education in this period should be one of helping to ensure that it delivers on its promises to the poor.

References

Amnesty International (2013) *Human Rights Must Play Stronger Role in Post-2015 Development Agenda,* available: http://www.amnesty.org/en/news/human-rights-must-play-stronger-role-post-2015-development-agenda-2013-06-05 (accessed 17 June 2013).

Berlin Civil Society Center and Global Call to Action against Poverty (2011), *Global Perspectives 2011: The International CSO Leaders' Forum*, Berlin: Berlin Civil Society Center.

Bernadette, F (2012) *Post-2015 processes at UN and Beyond 2015*, available: http://cafodpolicy.files.wordpress.com/2012/11/post2015-un-and-b2015-processes.jpg?w=491&h=370 (accessed 16 June 2013).

Beyond 2015 (2011) *Who We Are*, available: http://www.beyond2015.org/who-we-are (accessed 16 April 2013).

Beyond 2015 (2012) *Vision,* available: http://www.beyond2015.org/document/vision (accessed 18 April 2013).

Beyond 2015 (2013a) *Essential Must Haves – Legitimacy*, available: http://www.beyond2015.org/essential-must-haves-legitimacy (accessed 14 April 2013).

Beyond 2015 (2013b) *Purpose,* available: http://www.beyond2015.org/document/purpose (accessed 16 June 2013).

Beyond 2015 (2013c) 'World leaders renew commitment to anti-poverty targets, agree to adopt new development goals at 2015 summit', press release, 25 September 2013, available: http://www.un.org/millenniumgoals/pdf/Press_release_Special_Event_FINAL.pdf (accessed 13 January 2014).

BRICS, the latest annual summit was held in Durban, South Africa on 26 and 27 March 2013. See http://www.brics5.co.za/

Burall, S (2011) *A Global Development Framework after 2015: Engaging Poor People in its Formulation*, London: Involve, pp. 9–10.

CAFOD (2012, October 9) *Post Millennium Development Goals,* available: http://www.cafod.org.uk/Policy-and-Research/Post-MDGs (accessed 14 April 2013).

Consolo, O (2012, October) *Urgent Call for a United and Decentralized Political Campaign for an Ambitious Post-2015 International Agenda/Framework*, Brussels: CONCORD.

CSOs Monrovia Consultation for the Post 2015 Development Agenda (2013) 'Day 3 CSO outreach with HLP members in Monrovia', available: http://www.askafricanow.org/news/day-3-cso-outreach-with-hlp-members-in-monrovia/ (accessed 16 June 2013).

Farlex (2012) *The Free Dictionary*, available: http://www.thefreedictionary.com/policy (accessed 23 July 2012).

Fowler, C F (2009) *Policy Studies for Educational Leaders* (3rd edition), New York, USA: Pearson Educational, Inc.

Fukuda-Parr, S-P (20 May 2013) *MDGs: Facing Up to the Limitations of Global Goal Setting*, available: http://www.guardian.co.uk/global-development-professionals-network/2013/may/20/millennium-development-goals-targets-global-development (accessed 16 June 2013).

G20 (2010) 'Building our common future: Renewed collective action for the benefit of all', *Cannes Summit Final Declaration*, Cannes: G20.

Hernes, H (1987) *Welfare State and Woman Power: Essays in State Feminism*, Oslo: Norwegian University Press.

Hilgartner, S and Bosk, C L (1988) 'The rise and fall of social problems: A public arenas model', *American Journal of Sociology*, No. 94, pp. 53–78.

Kerwin, C M (1994) 'Rule making' in F C Fowler, *Policy Studies for Educational Leaders*, Washington, DC: Congressional Quarterly Press.

Kiruthu, F, Kapiyo, J and Kimori, W (2011) *The Evolving World: A History and Government Course Form 4*, Nairobi, Kenya: Oxford University Press.

Melamed, C (2011a) *Creating Consensus: Political Opportunities and Barriers for a Post-2015 Agreement on Development*, available: www.odi.org.uk/resources/docs/7486.pdf (accessed 18 April 2012).

Melamed, C (2011b) *The Millennium Development Goals after 2015: No Goals Yet Please*, available: http://www.odi.org.uk/opinion/details.asp?id=5981&title=mdgs-millennium-development-goals-post-2015-goals-targets (accessed 18 April 2012).

Melamed, C (2012) *Thoughts from the post-2015 High-Level Panel Meeting in London*, available: http://www.globaldashboard.org/2012/11/05/thoughts-from-the-post-2015-high-level-panel-meeting-in-london/ (accessed 1 May 2013).

Merriam-Webster Dictionary (2012) available: http://www.merriam-webster.com/dictionary/policy (accessed 23 July 2012).

Mniki, N and Waituru, M (2012) *Joining the Dots: People's Perspective for a Post MDGs Development Framework*, available: http://post2015.org/2012/10/26/joining-the-dots-peoples-perspective-for-a-post-mdgs-development-framework/ (accessed 1 May 2013).

Moncrieffe, J (2007) 'Labelling, power and accountability: How and why "our" categories matter' in J Moncrieffe and R Eyben (eds) *The Power of Labelling: How People are Categorized and How it Matters*. London: Earthscan.

O'Connor, J S (1998) 'Gender, class, and citizenship in the comparative analysis of welfare state regimes: Theoretical and methodological issues' in J S O'Connor and G M Olsen (eds) *Power, Resources Theory and the Welfare State: A Critical Approach*, Toronto: University of Toronto Press, pp. 209–228.

OECD (2008) *The Paris Declaration on Aid Effectiveness and the Accra Agenda for Action*, available: http://www.oecd.org/dac/effectiveness/34428351.pdf (accessed 29 April 2013).

Orloff, A S (1991) 'Gender in early U.S. social policy', *Journal of Policy History*, 3(3), pp. 249–281.

Participate: Knowledge from the Margins for Post-2015 (2013) *Recommendations and Key Findings for the Post-2015 Global Development Framework*, available: http://www.participate2015.org/resources/recommendations-and-key-findings-for-the-post-2015-global-development-framework/ (accessed 16 June 2013).

Pateman, C (1988) 'The patriarchal welfare state' in A Gutmann (ed.) *Democracy and the Welfare State*, Princeton: Princeton University Press, pp. 231–261.

Pollard, A and Haslam, D (November 2012) *Consultation or Conscription? Civil Society Input on the Content of the Post-2015 Framework*, available: https://cafodpolicy.wordpress.com/2012/11/13/consultation-or-conscriptioncivil-society-input-on-the-content-of-the-post-2015-framework/#more-1927 (accessed 1 May 2013).

Pollard, A, de Mauroy, A, Polato-lopes, M and Sumner, A (March 2011) *100 Voices: Southern perspectives on what should come after the MDGs*, available:

http://www.cafod.org.uk/Media/Files/Resources/Policy/100-Voices (accessed 14 April 2013).

Ramalingam, B, Jones, H, Reba, T and Young, J (7 October 2008) *Exploring the Science of Complexity: Ideas and Implications for Development and Humanitarian Efforts*, available: http://www.odi.org.uk/resources/doc/833.pdf (accessed 11 April 2012).

Republic of Kenya (2008) *Millennium Development Goals Status Report for Kenya – 2007*, Nairobi: Ministry of State for Planning, National Development and Vision 2030.

Republic of Kenya (2010) *Millennium Development Goals Status Report for Kenya-2009*, Nairobi: Ministry of State for Planning, Nation Development and Vision 2030.

Republic of Colombia (2012) *RIO + 20: Sustainable Development Goals (SDGs) A Proposal from the Governments of Colombia and Guatemala*, available: http://www.uncsd2012.org/content/documents/colombiasdgs.pdf (accessed 16 June 2013).

Richardt, N (2007) *Transforming Europe's Welfare Regimes – Policy Innovation through European Gender Equality Laws in the United Kingdom and Germany*, North Western University, Graduate School, Evanston, Illinois: North Western University.

Summer, A and Melamed, C (2011) *A Post-2015 Global Development Agreement: Why, What, Who?* London: Overseas Development Institute.

The Global CSO Forum on the Post-2015 Development Agenda (2013) *Civil Society Communiqué*, Bali: The Global CSO Forum on the Post-2015 Development Agenda.

The Independent (4 April 2013) *European Countries Cut International Aid*, available: http://www.independent.co.uk/news/world/europe/european-countries-cut-international-aid-8559031.html (accessed 29 April 2013).

The Seed Institute (2010) *Report of the Kenya National Poverty Hearing*, Nairobi: The Seed Institute.

The Seed Institute (2011) *Towards an Enabling Socio-Economic Environment: The Seed Institute Strategic Plan 2011–2014*, Nairobi: The Seed Institute.

The World Bank (21 April 2012) *Millennium Development Goals*, available: http://data.worldbank.org/about/millennium-development-goals (accessed 23 April 2012).

Underwoods, C (3 November 2012) *London High Level Panel: Reflections*, available: http://www.chrisunderwoodsblog.com/2012/11/london-high-level-panel-reflections.html?spref=tw (accessed 1 May 2013).

United Nations (2000) *The United Nations Millennium Declaration*, New York: United Nations.

United Nations (2001) *Report of the Secretary General: Road Map towards the Implementation of the United Nations Millennium Declaration*, New York: United Nations.

United Nations (2005) *In Larger Freedom: Towards Development, Security and Human Rights for All Report of the Secretary-General*, available: http://www.un.org/largerfreedom/contents.htm (accessed 12 June 2013).

United Nations (2012) 'The Secretary-General's high level panel of eminent persons on the post-2015 development agenda', available: http://www.un.org/sg/management/hlppost2015.shtml (accessed 24 June 2013).

United Nations (2013) *Charter of the United Nations*, available: www.un.org: w.un.org/en/documents/charter/ (accessed 16 June 2013).

United Nations Department of Economic and Social Affairs (2013) *Open Working Group on Sustainable Development Goals*, available: http://sustainable development.un.org/index.php?menu=1549 (accessed 16 June 2013).

United Nations Development Programme (2013) *The 2013 Human Development Report: The Rise of the South: Human Progress in a Diverse World*, New York: UNDP.

United Nations General Assembly (January 2013), available: http://www.un.org/ga/search/view_doc.asp?symbol=A/67/L.48/Rev.1&Lang=E (accessed 16 June 2013).

United Nations System Task Team on the Post-2015 UN Development Agenda (2012) *Realizing the Future We Want for All*, New York: UN Task Team.

Vandemoortele, J (2012) *Advancing the UN Development Agenda Post-2015: Some Practical Suggestions*, Bruges: UN Task Force regarding the post-2015 framework for development.

Vives, G (2 April 2012) *UN releases Details of Its Process to Create a Post-2015 Development Framework*, available: http://www.beyond2015.org/news/un-releases-details-its-process-create-post-2015-development-framework (accessed 16 May 2012).

17

Conclusion: Whither Development Education in a Shifting Policy Landscape?

Stephen McCloskey

Introduction

Since 2008 the world has been convulsed by social and economic change with financial upheaval and social unrest becoming increasingly prevalent in the global North and South. As the latest United Nations *Human Development Report* puts it: 'Global economic and political structures are in flux at a time when the world faces recurrent financial crises, worsening climate change and growing social unrest' (UNDP, 2013: 2). It goes on to suggest that: 'Global institutions appear unable to accommodate changing power relations, ensure adequate provision of global public goods to meet global and regional challenges and respond to the growing need for greater equity and sustainability' (p. 2). The effects of the 2008 financial crisis have been particularly severe in economies most closely wedded to the neoliberal development paradigm and this chapter considers the effects of the downturn on development education policy and practice in the European Union, the largest funder in the sector, and in its member states. It begins by considering the causes and effects of the crisis in neoliberalism and the challenges this has presented to development education.

The chapter goes on to propose four possible responses by the development education sector to the financial crisis. The first is to reconnect with its natural constituency; the communities most directly impacted upon by austerity measures implemented by neoliberal economies across Europe. It is argued that the sector's practice should be informed by the needs of those on the coalface of cuts in services, welfare and unemployment. Second, it suggests that development education should challenge the dominant myths and stereotypes applied to the poor in neoliberal economies calculated to blame marginalised individuals and communities for their own poverty. Third, the sector should lead a discussion in the global North on alternative paradigms of development, drawing primarily from the increasingly resilient and more egalitarian societies in the global South. And, four, development education and the development sector as a whole should engage more directly with local decision-making processes beyond the area of overseas aid and development policy to address the causes of poverty at local as well as global levels. This is needed to add value to their own societies as well as contribute to poverty eradication in the global South.

Neoliberalism in crisis

The current global financial crisis has profoundly altered the discourse which has framed the debate on international development and development education in the period since the end of the Cold War in 1989. It has asked serious questions of the dominant neoliberal economic model that emerged triumphantly from the Cold War and was heralded as the orthodox ideology which could 'lift all ships' in a sea of prosperity. As a contagion of toxic debt created by over-extended and dangerously deregulated financial institutions created 'a fundamental crisis of legitimacy' (WDM, 2008) in the banking sector, the man who had his hand at the tiller of the financial sector in the United States (US) for 18 years, Alan Greenspan, admitted 'that he had put too much faith in the correcting power of free markets and had failed to anticipate the self-destructive power of wanton mortgage lending' (*New York Times*, 23 October 2008). Greenspan, who had been chair of the US Federal Reserve for nearly two decades told a Congressional House Committee: 'I have found a flaw (in my ideology). I don't know how significant or permanent it is. But I've been very distressed by that fact' (Ibid.).

The post-crisis period has been characterised by large injections of state financial support to banks, many of whom were on the point of failure, some of whom – like Lehman Brothers in the US – were allowed to fail. In Britain, for example, the National Audit Office (NAO, 2013) calculates that peak outlay to banks in guarantee commitments and cash in the aftermath of the crash was a staggering £1,162 billion which reveals the depth of the crisis and contrasts sharply with the UK aid budget in 2011 of £8.6 billion or 0.56 percent of Gross National Income (GNI) (DFID, 2013). Indeed, all but five countries in the global

North have failed to reach the target of allocating less than 1 percent of the Gross Domestic Product to overseas development assistance (ODA) – a commitment agreed in 1970 (*Guardian*, 20 March 2013). These statistics speak to the contorted values of neoliberal economies that have allotted bottomless amounts of financial resources to institutions that have failed society through their own recklessness, greed and moral abandon while the poor at home and overseas pay the price. As the Nobel Laureate for Literature José Saramago puts it: 'the laws of the market led to a state of chaos that brought a rescue of thousands of millions of dollars – to the culprits, not the victims. In other words, "rescue" meant "privatise the profits, nationalize the losses"' (2010: 55).

According to the neoliberal creed, state intercession on behalf of the vulnerable, limits the power of the market to generate wealth which in theory will be cascaded across society through employment and the generation of profit. In Chapter 14, Dorothy Guerrero defines neoliberalism as:

> [A] set of rules and mechanisms that encourages total freedom of movement for capital, goods and services by: eliminating barriers to encourage economic openness of international trade and investments; cutting social expenditure for social services; reducing government regulations that could diminish profits especially profits of transnational corporations; and privatisation of state-owned enterprises, goods and services to private investors.

But as the current crisis has revealed, the states in greatest difficulty since 2008 have been those most closely wedded to neoliberalism and accommodating to the needs of transnational capital. Ireland's once buoyant Celtic Tiger economy, for example, endured a spectacular collapse when forced to accept an €85 billion loan from a troika comprising the European Commission, European Central Bank and International Monetary Fund (IMF) losing its economic sovereignty in the process (*Irish Times*, 11 November 2010; IMF, December 2010). The IMF (March 2013) has committed more than $300 billion in loans to its member countries since 2007, many of whom are in the global North and have responded by introducing what the United Nations (UN) describes as 'harsh austerity measures that reduce the government's welfare role and cut back on spending and public services' (2013: 21).

Socialising the debt

The instinct of neoliberal economies in response to the financial crisis was to socialise the debt of failing financial institutions and cut government expenditure in areas of high social spending such as health, welfare and education. In Britain this resulted in 'the most swingeing programme of cuts and tax increases for 90 years' (*Guardian*, 26 February 2013) which exacerbated rather than slowed economic contraction. In early 2013, the IMF released research 'suggesting that it had significantly underestimated the damage European austerity would do to EU growth rates' (IMF, January 2013). Neoliberalism has not only failed on its own terms – markets have been negligent in their self-regulation and failed to sustain wealth and growth – but has exacerbated the financial crisis through misjudged 'slash and burn' economic solutions. Imposing market-based solutions to crises created by deregulated financial institutions operating beyond the ambit of governments has deepened the economic malaise in the global North and the misery of those on low incomes. By the end of 2012, unemployment in the Eurozone stood at 11.8 percent but was markedly higher in countries that had suffered the severest economic jolts during the crisis: for example, in Cyprus it was 14 percent, in Greece 26 percent, and Spain 26.6 percent (*Eurostat*, January 2013). Even more concerning is the unemployment rate among young people which, at the end of May 2013, had an EU average of 24.4 percent; in Portugal it was 42.5 percent and in Spain 56.4 percent (*Guardian*, 31 May 2013). Austerity programmes in most Eurozone states had the twin effects of choking off growth and increasing unemployment, thereby threatening to de-skill an entire generation of young people starved of employment.

Few countries experienced the boom and bust cycle of neoliberalism as spectacularly as Ireland which was a tyro economy from the early 1990s to 2007, enjoying high levels of growth on the back of investment from transnational corporations producing for export markets mostly in the Eurozone (McCloskey, 2011, 2012). Ireland's economic collapse in 2008 turned what David Begg, General Secretary of the Irish Congress of Trade Unions, described as the 'poster child for globalisation' into the 'poster child for austerity' (*Guardian*, 27 November 2011). The rapid unravelling of the financial sector in the United States in 2008 quickly spread to Ireland and exposed a property boom largely fuelled by a credit bubble and banks laden with toxic debt. The Irish government decided to socialise the debt, bail out the culpable banks and accept loans with conditions 'including cuts to social welfare, pensions, university grants, jobs in the public sector, among many others' (Ní Chasaide, 2012). In responding to this loss of economic sovereignty and austerity-driven pathway to 'recovery', the Debt and Development Coalition Ireland (DDCI) used a development education methodology to challenge the legitimacy of the loans and their wider impact on Irish society. By drawing upon their education and campaigning work on the debt crisis in the global South, and using their knowledge of how IMF loans had been used to shoehorn vulnerable economies into disastrous neoliberal reforms (DDCI, 2013), DDCI commissioned an audit of the Irish debt.

Using a model implemented by citizens groups in the global South, including Argentina, Ecuador and the Philippines, to examine relevant legal, political, economic, environmental and social factors resulting from the accumulation of sovereign debt, DDCI commissioned an audit to assess the legitimacy of Ireland's debt. Taken 'as a first step toward enabling people in Ireland to understand the scale and nature of Ireland's national debt' (Ni Chasaide, 2012), the audit found that:

> the Irish debt crisis was caused by the socialisation of commercial banking debt. Secondly, the audit outlined the various facets of Ireland's complex sovereign debt. Thirdly, it highlighted that while much of Ireland's debt is resulting from debt owed to private bondholders, it was not possible to identify who the bondholders are (Killian et al., 2011).

The audit represented an exemplary case study of a development organisation in the global North learning from the good practice of social movements in the global South to inform their development education work with local audiences. DDCI felt that it could not maintain 'relevance and credibility in Ireland, where people are suffering increased economic hardship, while educating people on the need for economic justice in the global South' (Ní Chasaide, 2012). The new economic context in which development education is being delivered has blurred the boundaries between the global North and South. Ireland, for example, has a government debt at 117.60 percent of Gross Domestic Product (GDP) (*Eurostat*, 22 April 2013) which has 'surpassed that of the sovereign debt levels of many Southern countries' (Ni Chasaide, 2012).

Impact of neoliberalism on education

In addition to the impact of neoliberalism on national and global economies is its marketisation of education and instilling of values promoting individualism, materialism and the precedence of the economy over the environment and society. In considering the impact of neoliberalism on education both locally and internationally, the Irish National Council for Curriculum and Assessment (NCCA) identified three key features in the external environment that impacted on its work: 'globalisation, marketisation and individualisation'. It added that '[t]he influence of the market has also been keenly felt in higher education, where individual schools and departments of universities are increasingly viewed as the components of an internal competitive market'. As a result of accelerated globalisation, education in liberal democracies is becoming increasingly commodified and a significant outcome of this process is the 'trend of individualisation' and 'the atomisation of the individual in an increasingly consumerised and consumer-led world' (NCCA 2006: 11–13).

This increasing commodification of education and other vital public services like health and utilities within a neoliberal paradigm is changing the relationship between the individual and society. As the NCCA suggests:

> In Ireland, the traditional family and the role of the family within a community are changing. The tradition of individuals volunteering to participate in initiatives for the benefit of the local community appears to be in decline, as this time is increasingly devoted to children and family and activities that directly benefit *my* family and *my* children (NCCA, 2006: 13).

This analysis of social relations in neoliberal Ireland suggests that rather than regard ourselves as stakeholders in society with shared values and attitudes open to diversity and cultural awareness, we are more inclined to consider our individual needs to the exclusion of those of the wider community and society. The question is how should the development education sector respond to the crisis in neoliberalism and its social and economic consequences?

Responding to the crisis

For development education the current crisis of legitimacy for neoliberalism represents both a valediction and an opportunity. The former lies in its refutation of a system premised on individualism, materialism and a determinism in human relations. The latter in the sense that development education can inform the debate on new paradigms of development drawing upon its roots in the global South and the opportunities to learn from contemporary processes and experiments in paradigm change, particularly in Latin America. In writing about neoliberalism at the end of last century, Paulo Freire could just as easily be commenting on the system today when he suggests:

> We need to say no to the neoliberal fatalism that we are witnessing at the end of this century, informed by the ethics of the market, an ethics in which a minority makes most profits against the lives of the majority. In other words, those who cannot compete, die. This is a perverse ethics that, in fact, lacks ethics. I insist on saying that I continue to be human...I would then remain the last educator in the world to say no: I do not accept...history as determinism. I embrace history as possibility [where] we can demystify the evil in this perverse fatalism that characterizes the neoliberal discourse in the end of this century (Freire quoted by Macedo, 2000: 27).

So, what role should development education be playing in the altered neoliberal discourse following the economic crisis of 2008? First, the sector needs to return to first principles of Freirean pedagogy by raising critical consciousness among target groups of the causes and effects of the crisis through praxis – reflective action – that facilitates debate, analysis and action outcomes. These outcomes must be agreed through dialogue with communities on the coalface of neoliberalism and most severely impacted by cuts in services and welfare, as well as suffering from high unemployment rates.

At a seminar titled 'Development Education: Responding to the Global Crisis?' held in Dublin on 17 May 2013, Cathleen O'Neill from the Kilbarrack Community Development Project in north Dublin powerfully described the effects of 'savage funding cuts' which have threatened community services in a highly marginalised area. Her address spoke of poverty, ill-health and unemployment in Kilbarrack with 1,600 people using a food bank in her community just a few days before the conference; 'soup kitchens', she said, 'are a growth industry in Ireland' (DEEEP, 2013). Communities like Kilbarrack should be the natural constituency of development education and practitioners need to inform their activities on the basis of social need delivered in partnership with local actors.

Second, development educators need to challenge dominant myths and stereotypes, often used by governments and the media, that are designed very specifically to blame the poor for their own poverty. For example, 'shirkers', 'skivers' and 'scroungers' are terms that have all too evidently and readily entered public parlance in the UK to suggest that the idle working-class are content to coast on benefits rather than do a day's work. Edwards (2013) has found a spike in the use of the word 'scrounger' by UK newspapers from just over 500 at the start of the 2008 recession to 3,500 in 2012. The press in Britain may be taking its cue from the British Chancellor, George Osborne who, in a speech to the 2012 Conservative party conference asked 'where's the fairness for the shift worker leaving home in the dark hours of the morning, who looks up at the closed blinds of the next door neighbour sleeping off a life in benefits?' (*Guardian*, 11 April 2013). Anna Coote and Sarah Lyall from the New Economics Foundation regard Osborne's contrasting of the 'strivers' as hard working, reliable and socially responsible with the jobless as unreliable and unproductive 'skivers' as 'pure fiction'. Coote and Lyall suggest that 'people hardly ever choose to be in or out of work'; it is something determined by the wider economy. They add that Osborne's comments ignore the legion of unpaid carers at home and in the community without whom 'the economy would grind to a halt' (Ibid.).

Research by the Trades Union Congress (TUC) published in January 2013 'found widespread ignorance about spending on welfare, the reality of unemployment, the generosity of benefits and the level of fraud'. This research suggests that dominant myths are influencing public attitudes to the poor and being used by government to 'conduct policy' and generate support for cuts in welfare to 'some of the most vulnerable people in society' (TUC, 2013). Development education's critical consciousness represents a vital platform for the demystification of social relations and causes of inequality. As Paulo Freire suggests: 'Manipulation, sloganizing, "depositing", regimentation and prescription cannot be components of revolutionary praxis, precisely because they are components of the praxis of domination' (1970: 107). Neoliberalism has engendered a sense of fatalism into the operations of the markets whereby they are described in terms approximating the ethereal and treated accordingly with god-like reverence demanding financial sacrifice, as never fully satiated. Development education needs to make clear that a human hand controls how we create and use capital and human needs should drive how we expend capital.

This leads us into a third possible response from development education to the financial crisis which is to nurture a debate on alternative paradigms of development. Chapters 11–14 have considered the lessons that the sector can learn and share from countries in the global South which the *Human Development Report 2013* suggests 'have shown greater resilience in the face of the current global economic crisis' (p. 22). Titled 'The Rise of the South', the report argues that African and Latin American countries have been more pragmatic in their response to the global crisis, 'taking countercyclical measures and postponing debt reduction for more appropriate times'. Moreover, 'after transitory setbacks following the 2008 crisis, African and Latin American countries have resumed their upward trajectories of human development and growth' (Ibid.). The development education sector is well positioned to share the lessons of development that are emerging from the global South with communities in the global North. The level of public discontent with neoliberalism evidenced in the global North and South through the Occupy movement (Hayes and McNally, 2012), the *Indignado* movement in Spain (Delclós and Viejo, 2012), the Arab Spring (Khosrokhavar, 2013) and popular mobilisations around the world (*The Observer*, 22 June 2013), suggest that development education has a prime opportunity to initiate debate on economic alternatives rooted in equality and social justice. In today's globalised society, discussions on new development paradigms need to be framed in both local and global realities, and development education's local and global axis makes it ideally placed to meet this need.

A fourth response to the financial crisis requires that development education and wider international development sectors get more engaged with local decision-making processes beyond the area of overseas aid and development policy. This means adopting a more critical perspective on government policies that impact on the poor at home as well as overseas. A research report from the Irish development agency Trócaire has suggested that:

> Many INGOs now rely heavily on official funding from donors with the risk of compromising their independent voice. It is unclear whether they consider themselves as extensions of government, or something different. INGOs first need to clarify their own understanding of the politics underpinning these respective roles (Trócaire, 2011: 63).

For example, to disconnect the debate on the budget for overseas aid from the wider management of the local and global economy is to limit the possibilities for analysis and social change. As Trócaire suggests, INGOs 'need to look honestly at the drivers of change and how change should be substantive, structural and sustainable' (p. 62). This means engaging in domestic as well as international policy arenas 'to add value within their own societies and their own political systems "as part of a global movement for justice, development and peace"' (p. 66).

While development education reassesses its role in the midst of an entrenched economic recession in the global North, the next section takes stock of the sector's capacity to weather the storm.

The shifting policy landscape of development education

Development education's funding base at a national level is largely intertwined with overseas development assistance through which it is supported in most European states. This has left the sector vulnerable to reduced aid flows to the global South (OECD, 2012) and greater scrutiny from funders in terms of impact and value for money. A recent working document published by the European Commission on Development Education and Awareness Raising (DEAR) stated that:

> In many EU Member States, the current economic crisis has once again underlined the need for a sound justification of DEAR programmes. Budgets allocated to DEAR have often been drastically reduced in recent years. In many Member States, an ever stronger emphasis is being put on impact evaluation and 'value for money' (European Commission, 2012: 8).

Funding from the EU itself has held up well to date with €63 million allocated in 2011 and 2012 combined with 72 non-state actors and 11 local authorities averaging €760,000 per grant (Ibid.: 12). This represents a considerable investment by the EU which argues that: 'A strong and informed engagement of EU citizens in development issues is considered essential for an ambitious EU development policy' (p. 2). On 5 July 2012, the European Parliament approved a declaration on development education and active global citizenship which called on the European Commission and the Council of Europe 'to develop a long term, cross-sectoral European strategy for development education, awareness-raising and active global citizenship' (European Parliament,

5 July 2012). It also called on 'EU Member States and the European Commission [to] strengthen their strategies for Development Education and Awareness Raising' (Ibid.).

The main European Union institutions therefore clearly regard DEAR as an integral element of the EU's development assistance programme but this commitment has not yet been framed by a dedicated strategy for development education. The adoption of such a strategy will clearly inform the work of the DARE (Development Awareness Raising and Education) Forum which comprises representatives of the national development platforms and networks across the EU. As a working group of Concord (the European Confederation of Development and Relief NGOs), the DARE Forum 'establishes common strategies to strengthen Development Education in Europe' (CONCORD/DEEEP, 2011). DEEEP (Developing Europeans' Engagement for the Eradication of Global Poverty) is a project initiated by the DARE Forum, now in its fourth funding cycle, which 'aims at strengthening the capacities of NGDOs to raise awareness, educate and mobilise the European public for worldwide poverty eradication and social inclusion' (DEEEP, 2013). With funding for DEEEP assured to 2015, this project will play an important advocacy role in pushing for a strategy for development education in the European Commission that will strengthen the policy profile of the sector and its long-term security. CONCORD, DEEEP and the DARE Forum will also need to mobilise NGOs and political allies across Europe to resist the possibility of cuts to the EU's overseas aid and development education budgets. As the European Parliament's resolution on development education warned, in a period of 'austerity, crises and the rise of nationalist and populist movements, it is particularly important to support active global citizenship' (July 2012).

Policy and practice at national levels

At a national level, a major survey of development education activity across 27 EU member states in 2010 found that approximately €220 million was committed by governments to Development Education and Awareness Raising activities (Davis et al., 2010: 10). The survey found that this funding was often supported by national strategies for development education that mostly emanated from the ministries for development cooperation, foreign affairs or overseas aid. While this strategic intervention by government bodies at policy and practice levels provided state recognition for development education activities, some member states 'do not have any specific programmes and provide only minimal, if any, funding for DEAR-related activities' (European Commission, 2012: 6). There is therefore a mixed picture of development education policy and practice across the EU with the DEAR sector often under-supported in accession/new member states that lack the capacity found in countries such as Ireland and the UK. More positively, the EU's main funding instrument for development education started supporting actions aimed at enhancing DEAR activities in new member states and acceding countries (European Commission, 2011–12: 7). This approach included building partnerships between non-state actors and local authorities in countries with more established DEAR sectors and those in new member/accession states with less well supported sectors.

In terms of development education practice in the EU, the Commission has found evidence of greater integration of development education in formal and non-formal learning in member states often 'through state funded teacher training, curriculum institutions and civil society organisations' (Ibid.: 6). Moreover, at third level a 'greater number of universities devote explicit attention to research and teaching on Development Education and Awareness Raising, including in the Czech Republic, Finland, Germany, Spain, the United Kingdom and many other EU Member States' (Ibid.). Other examples of good practice include: greater numbers of global North-South learning partnerships based on equality and shared learning; the development of effective methodologies based on values such as respect, diversity, self-esteem and social justice; more attention paid to sustainability through long-term partnerships with target groups; and coherent advocacy strategies seeking concrete change at structural/institutional levels (Davis et al., 2010: 11).

While development education is clearly broadening and deepening its reach across EU member states and within national ministries responsible for development cooperation and education policy, there are weaknesses that remain to be addressed in strategic planning, policy and practice. These include: the lack of strategic objectives and related policy documents at an EU level; the absence of coordination between EU activities and those of national bodies in EU member states responsible for DEAR; inadequate frameworks and opportunities for sharing learning from DEAR projects and initiatives supported by the EU and its member states; and an 'insufficiently transparent' grant system that tends to favour large NGOs better positioned to cope with a demanding application process (Ibid.: 12–13). There is also a concern that DEAR activities led by development cooperation ministries rather than education ministries weaken the permeation of DEAR issues, values and methodologies into national education structures and curricula. It also leaves the sector vulnerable to shifts in policy in member states that favour DEAR activities designed to promote development cooperation 'rather than on enhancing critical citizen engagement with global issues that are relevant to development' (p. 14).

Conclusion

The aftermath of the global financial crisis has created new challenges for development education, like many other sectors in civil society, that have included national policy changes, funding cuts and enhanced scrutiny in demonstrating value for money and impact on target groups. The sector's largest funder, the European Union, has maintained its commitment:

> To develop citizens' awareness and critical understanding of the interdependent world, of their role and responsibility in relation to a globalised society; and to support their active engagement with global attempts to eradicate poverty and promote justice, human rights and a sustainable social-economic development in partner countries (European Commission, 2012: 20).

It is important that this objective is translated into a long-term strategic policy for the sector that builds on the recent European Parliament resolution. While huge strides have been made at national levels across the EU to embed DEAR in formal and non-formal education programmes and curricula, competition for EU funding streams is likely to increase in the future as national budgets become squeezed by austerity programmes. To address these inconsistencies, Rilli Lappalainen of CONCORD has called for an EU 'common framework' and a 'legally binding document for European nations' to ensure good practice in development education across the sector in all member states (2010: 83).

While the crisis in neoliberalism has added to financial pressures on the development education sector, it has also created new opportunities to reconnect with the Freirean principles that underpin DEAR practice. The sector can take the lead in debating alternatives to the failed neoliberal paradigm that has driven development since the end of the Cold War. The need for critical consciousness, problem-posing education and open-ended action outcomes informed by praxis has never been greater. Whatever the vagaries of national and international policy-making in development education, the sector needs to reconnect with, and have its work informed by, the communities that should be its natural constituency – those most directly impacted by the austerity measures adopted by most governments in the global North. The sector needs to learn from the resilience to neoliberalism that has taken root in the global South which is increasingly exploring alternative paradigms of development imbued with the values of interdependence, social justice and equality that are central to development education practice.

References

CONCORD/DEEEP (2011) 'Development needs citizens', May 2011, available: http://www.deeep.org/images/stories/DARE/PositionPaper2011/development%20needs%20citizens%20flyer.pdf (accessed 26 June 2013).

Coote, A and Lyall, S (2013) 'Strivers versus skivers: Real life's not like that at all', *Guardian*, 11 April 2013, available: http://www.guardian.co.uk/commentisfree/2013/apr/11/strivers-v-skivers-divisive-notion (accessed 10 May 2013).

Davis, P, Fricke, H-J, Krause, J, Surian, A and Rajacic, A (2010) 'DEAR in Europe: Recommendations for Future Action by the European Commission: Final Report of the "Study on the Experience and Actions of the Main European Actors Active in the Field of Development Education and Awareness Raising"', SOGES SPA: November 2010, available: https://webgate.ec.europa.eu/fpfis/mwikis/aidco/images/d/d4/Final_Report_DEAR_Study.pdf (accessed 25 June 2013).

Debt and Development Coalition Ireland (DDCI) (2013) 'World Bank – IMF Watch 2013', Dublin: DDCI.

Developing Europeans' Engagement for the Eradication of Global Poverty (DEEEP) (2013) 'What is DEEEP', available http://www.deeep.org/ (accessed 27 June 2013).

Delclós, C and Viejo, R (2012) 'Beyond the indignation: Spain's indignado's and the political agenda', *Policy & Practice: A Development Education Review*, Vol. 15, Autumn 2012, pp. 92–100.

DFID (2013) 'Statistics at DFID', available: https://www.gov.uk/government/uploads/system/uploads/attachment_data/file/142459/SID-2012-Key-Statistics.pdf (accessed 6 June 2013).

Edwards, G (1 May 2013), available: https://twitter.com/GavinEdwards77/status/329203347208949760/photo/1 (accessed 10 May 2013). The survey of UK newspapers excluded *The Times* and *Financial Times*.

European Commission, 'Raising public awareness of development issues and promoting development education in the European Union: Guidelines for grant applicants', 2011–12, Reference: EuropeAid/131141/C/ACT/Multi.

European Commission, 'Commission staff working document on Development Education and Awareness Raising (DEAR) in Europe', 20 December 2012, available: http://ec.europa.eu/europeaid/how/finance/dci/documents/swd_2012_457_dear_en.pdf (accessed 23 June 2013).

European Parliament (5 July 2012) 'Declaration of the European Parliament of 5 July 2012 on development education and active global citizenship', available: http://www.europarl.europa.eu/sides/getDoc.do?type=TA&language=EN&reference=P7-TA-2012-302 (accessed 25 June 2013).

Eurostat (8 January 2013) 'Euro area unemployment rate at 11.8%', available: http://epp.eurostat.ec.europa.eu/cache/ITY_PUBLIC/3-08012013-BP/EN/3-08012013-BP-EN.PDF (accessed 26 June 2013).

Eurostat (22 April 2013), available: http://epp.eurostat.ec.europa.eu/cache/ITY_PUBLIC/2-22042013-AP/EN/2-22042013-AP-EN.PDF (accessed 25 June 2013).

Freire, P (1970) *Pedagogy of the Oppressed*, London: Penguin Books.

Guardian, 'Ireland becomes poster child for implementing austerity programmes', 27 November 2011.

Guardian, 'George Osborne hasn't just failed – this is an economic disaster', 26 February 2013, available: http://www.guardian.co.uk/commentisfree/2013/feb/26/george-osborne-has-not-just-failed (accessed 10 May 2013).

Guardian, 'Eurozone unemployment hits new high with quarter of under-25s jobless', available: http://www.guardian.co.uk/business/2013/may/31/eurozone-unemployment-new-high-quarter-under-25s (accessed 25 June 2013).

Guardian, 'George Osborne declares "historic moment" on UK aid target', 20 March 2013, available: http://www.guardian.co.uk/global-development/2013/mar/20/george-osborne-historic-moment-aid?INTCMP=SRCH (accessed 6 June 2013).

Hayes, A and McNally, E (2012) 'Occupy development education', *Policy & Practice: A Development Education Review*, Vol. 14, Spring 2012, pp. 100–109.

International Monetary Fund (IMF), 'IMF approves €22.5 billion loan for Ireland', 16 December 2010, available: http://www.imf.org/external/pubs/ft/survey/so/2010/car121610a.htm (accessed 25 June 2013).

International Monetary Fund (IMF), 'International Monetary Fund admits it severely underestimated cost of austerity', 3 January 2013, available: http://thinkprogress.org/economy/2013/01/03/1395321/international-monetary-fund-admits-it-severely-underestimated-cost-of-austerity/?mobile=nc (accessed 10 May 2013).

International Monetary Fund (IMF), 'IMF's response to the global economic crisis', 29 March 2013, available: http://www.imf.org/external/np/exr/facts/changing.htm (accessed 11 June 2013).

Irish Times, 'Ireland to receive €85 billion bailout at 5.8% interest rate', 11 November 2010.

Khosrokhavar, F (2013) *The New Arab Revolutions that Shook the World*, London: Pluto Press.

Killian, S, Garvey, J and Shaw, F (2011) *An Audit of Irish Debt*, University of Limerick, available at: http://www.debtireland.org/download/pdf/audit_of_irish_debt6.pdf (accessed 20 March 2012).

Lappalainen, R (2010) 'The European consensus on development education: From scratch to implementation and monitoring', *Policy & Practice: A Development Education Review*, Vol. 11, Autumn 2010, pp. 77–83, available: http://www.developmenteducationreview.com/issue11-perspectives2

Macedo, D (2000), 'Introduction to the anniversary edition' in P Freire, *Pedagogy of the Oppressed*, 30th anniversary special edition, London and New York: Continuum Publishing Group.

McCloskey, S (2011) 'Rising to the challenge: Development education, NGOs and the urgent need for social change', *Policy & Practice: A Development Education Review*, Vol. 12, Spring, pp. 32–46.

McCloskey, S (2012) 'Creating new economic paradigms: The role of development education', *Policy & Practice: A Development Education Review*, Vol. 14, Spring 2012, pp. 1–18.

National Audit Office (NAO) (2013) 'Taxpayer support for UK Banks', available: http://www.nao.org.uk/highlights/taxpayer-support-for-uk-banks-faqs/ (accessed 6 June 2013).

National Council for Curriculum and Assessment (NCCA) (2006) Strategic plan 2006–08, available: http://www.ncca.ie/uploadedfiles/publications/strat%20plan%20EN%2006-08.pdf (accessed 26 June 2013).

New York Times, 23 October 2008.

Ní Chasaide, N (2012) 'From debt audits to debt justice: Drawing lessons from the global south in development education in Ireland', *Policy & Practice: A Development Education Review*, Vol. 14, Spring 2012, pp. 33–44.

Organisation for Economic Co-operation and Development (OECD) 'Development: Aid to developing countries falls because of global recession', 4 May 2012, available: http://www.oecd.org/newsroom/developmentaidtodevelopingcountriesfallsbecauseofglobalrecession.htm (accessed 25 June 2013).

Saramago, J (2010) *The Notebook*, London: Verso.

The Observer, 'Global protest grows as citizens lose faith in politics and the state', 22 June 2013, available: http://www.guardian.co.uk/world/2013/jun/22/urban-protest-changing-global-social-network?INTCMP=SRCH (accessed 26 June 2013).

Trades Union Congress, 'Support for benefit cuts dependent on ignorance, TUC-commissioned poll finds', available: http://www.tuc.org.uk/social/tuc-21796-f0.cfm (accessed 10 May 2013).

Trócaire (2011) *Leading Edge 20:20: Critical Thinking on the Future of International Development*, Maynooth, Ireland: Trócaire, available: http://www.trocaire.org/sites/trocaire/files/pdfs/policy/LeadingEdge2020websizedfinal.pdf (accessed 26 June 2013).

UK Aid contribution in 2010–11, 'The total spend was £7.7 billion in 2012 and this graphic shows how it was spent', available: http://www.guardian.co.uk/global-development/interactive/2011/oct/05/dfid-future-aid-plans-interactive (accessed 11 June 2013).

United Nations Development Programme (UNDP) (2013) *Human Development Report 2013*, available: http://hdr.undp.org/en/media/HDR_2013_EN_complete.pdf (accessed 11 June 2013).

World Development Movement (WDM), 'Responding to the crisis: Five ideas for a new world order', November 2008, available: http://www.dochas.ie/pages/resources/documents/wdms_five_point_plan_for_kidtronic.pdf (accessed 12 June 2013).

Index

Printed and bound in the United States of America